AF633072

REGIONAL ECONOMIC TRENDS AND SOUTH ASIAN SECURITY

REGIONAL CENTRE FOR STRATEGIC STUDIES

The Regional Centre for Strategic Studies (RCSS) is an independent, non-profit and non-governmental organization for collaborative research, networking and interaction on strategic and international issues pertaining to South Asia. Themes related to regional security, conflict and cooperation constitute the principal focus of work.

The work of RCSS is planned, designed and implemented under the supervision of an International Research Committee, drawn from South Asian countries and outside the region. The RCSS serves its South Asia and international constituency by: (a) networking programmes that promote interaction, communication and exchange between institutions and individuals within and outside the region engaged in South Asian strategic studies; (b) organizing regional workshops and seminars; and sponsoring and coordinating collaborative research; and (c) disseminating output of the research through publications which include books, monographs and a quarterly newsletter. The RCSS facilitates scholars and other professionals of South Asia to address, mutually and collectively, problems and issues of topical interest for all countries of the region.

The RCSS is a South Asian forum for studies, training and multi-track dialogue and deliberation on issues of regional interest. All activities of RCSS are designed with a South Asia focus and are usually participated in by experts from all South Asian countries. The Centre is envisaged as a forum for advancing the cause of cooperation, security, conflict resolution, confidence building, peace and development in the countries of the South Asian region.

Inquiries may be addressed to:

Executive Director, Regional Centre for Strategic Studies
4-101BMICH, Bauddhaloka Mawatha, Colombo 7, SRI LANKA.
Tel: (94-1) 688601; Fax: 688602; e-mail: rcss@sri.lanka.net
http://www.lanka.net/rcss

Regional Economic Trends and South Asian Security

Edited by

IFTEKHARUZZAMAN

REGIONAL CENTRE FOR STRATEGIC STUDIES
COLOMBO

MANOHAR
1997

First published 1997

© Regional Centre for Strategic Studies, Colombo, Sri Lanka, 1997

All rights reserved. No part of this publication may
be reproduced or transmitted, in any form or by any
means, without prior permission of
the author and the publisher

ISBN 81-7304-205-5

Published by
Ajay Kumar Jain for
Manohar Publishers & Distributors
2/6 Ansari Road, Daryaganj
New Delhi 110002

Printed at
Replika Press Pvt. Ltd.
Plot No. A229, DSIDC Narela Indl. Park
Delhi-110 040.

Contents

Introduction

IFTEKHARUZZAMAN

THE END OF the Cold War has induced fresh thinking on approaches to security. The focus is on non-conventional aspects, particularly economic strength, interest and interdependence of nations. As distinct from the notion of security mainly focused on military power, the idea is to consider a more expanded agenda. The lexicon of economics, particularly trade and investment, is increasingly fused with that of politics and security.

The post-Cold War era, to be sure, continues to be in flux. While work on drawing a conceptual map of the so-called 'new world order' continues,[1] it is possible to identify some relevant features. In terms of political ideas, for instance, democracy is on ascendancy compared to communism and any form of totalitarianism. This is not to suggest that in practice democracy and its institutions stand on a sound footing, particularly in the vast majority of developing countries as well as East Europe and post-Soviet States. The process of democratic transformation in these States continues to suffer from significant setbacks, often traumatic. What is important to note, nevertheless, is that the universal acceptance of democracy as the cherished goal has widened considerably. Economically, liberalization and free-market system are the order of the day. Economic and financial strength and performance today appear more important than ever in defining the comparative position of nations and regions around the world. As a corollary, there is also a renewed stampede of regionalism as an instrument for achieving greater economic cooperation and political harmony.

Viewed in this context, the critique of the conventional wisdom on national security assumes increasing importance. Recent literature on the subject provides strong support to the thesis that security cannot be properly understood, nor can the issues related to it be effectively addressed without due focus on such other factors as societal, political and economic.[2] Some of the noted works on the security of developing

States have found poverty and socio-economic underdevelopment an important source of threats to security and conversely, social and economic uplift has been identified as almost a universal prerequisite for achieving 'real security'.[3] This socio-economic approach to security cannot be taken to undermine the other dimensions, particularly issues related to the protection of national independence, sovereignty and territorial integrity. The point is that if viewed only in the traditional military sense, security 'cannot have enduring appeal for hungry masses', and while poverty constitutes a major source of insecurity of the vast majority of the developing States, security cannot be ensured without effectively challenging the menace of poverty and underdevelopment.[4] Security, in the end, is freedom from threat to one's survival, and should, therefore, include concerns that are much more than the conventional issues of political independence, national defence and territorial integrity.

During the Cold War period, conceptually as well as operationally, security was viewed in terms of ideological and military confrontation between the two superpowers and their respective blocs. This confrontation was transfused to the rest of the world by the superpowers' policy of expanding their zones of influence for which they used a variety of instruments, including direct or indirect involvement in hostilities and conflicts, some of which already existed while others were fuelled by superpower confrontation. In the post-Cold War era, the security agenda is much less dominated by ideological and military confrontation, and instead political, socio-economic and environmental issues are receiving greater priority.

As observed by an analyst,

> economic and political assurances responsive to social demands, now expressed with pervasive force throughout the international system (albeit with varying weight, intensity and salience), must also be fashioned to ensure stable and legitimate security systems.[5]

Examining the collapse of the Soviet State, he writes:

> disillusionment of the Soviet elite and enlarging segments of Soviet people with the abject failure of a centralized economy to meet the nation's welfare needs eroded political support for Soviet security institutions, viewed increasingly as a brake on economic growth and development.[6]

It is clear that the security of the Soviet State, in the end, was mortally affected by its obsession with military might, both conventional and nuclear. The importance of relative economic performance was grossly overlooked and the emphasis was more on building up huge military-industrial complexes and weapons of mass destruction and not on the dynamism of economic institutions. The over-extended nature of the Soviet State also worked behind the collapse of the system as a culmination of decades of tremendous social frustration and pressures for change.

One other area of the debate is the place of the people as the referent unit in security. As underlined by the UNDP,

> the concept of security has for too long been interpreted narrowly: as security of territory from external aggression, or as protection of national interests in foreign policy or as global security from the threat of nuclear holocaust. It has been related more to nation-States than to people. . . . Forgotten were the legitimate concerns of ordinary people who sought security in their daily lives. For many of them, security symbolized protection from the threat of disease, hunger, unemployment, crime, social conflict, political repression and environmental hazards.[7]

The ideological and institutional decay that the modern State has been suffering from have also been reinforced as a result of the recent wave of global transition. As observed by a noted scholar, 'it may be that the crisis of the multi-ethnic State, not the disappearance of communism, will be the most profound political event of our generation'.[8] He identifies five factors that may be considered to be eating away the power of the State—the entity that has been the building block of international politics. These are:

(a) the loss of State monopoly over information in the context of galloping technological revolution, particularly in the electronic media;
(b) the failure of the State in protecting its citizens in wartime in view of the massive build-up of similar weapons of other States;
(c) the failure of the State in ensuring economic prosperity;
(d) the loss of the State's monopoly over justice in view of the growing role of international organizations, lending institutions, foreign governments, human-rights groups and self-appointed spokesmen for democracy; and
(e) the threat to the States from within, particularly in case of multi-ethnic States.[9]

The other source of challenge against the authority of the State is the growing economic globalization of national economies through the sweeping wave of the free-market system, freer trade, interpenetration of industries and investment, increasing network and influence of multinationals, and non-governmental organizations, both national and international.

Despite such strains on the State, the role of the State in economic and infrastructural development, social welfare, external policy direction and national security remains vital. The experience of East Asian and South-East Asian newly industrialized economies is particularly relevant where the concept of the shrunken State as a panacea has been effectively challenged.[10] In the context of developing societies like South Asia, where not only the safety net, but also sustainable participatory development for vulnerable groups takes primacy, the imperative of reposing responsibility on the State is clear. And

> despite the erosion of their boundaries and capacities in recent decades, States continue to be central actors on the global stage. To stress that they are no longer the only actors of consequence is neither to dismiss their relevance nor to imply that the advent of other central players has forced States into secondary roles removed from the core of world politics.[11]

This also brings into focus the growing importance of non-State actors and factors in influencing security and strategic matters in the contemporary world. This is consistent with the global ascendancy of democracy and economic liberalism which provide greater legitimacy to the activities and perspectives of political parties, national and international non-governmental organizations, media, various social and ethnic groups, women and youth groups, business and other professional groups and activists. Conceptions and approaches to security are, therefore, bound to remain partial if the traditional approach of treating the State or regime as the only actor is not changed in favour of a more broad-based outlook in which participation of these proliferating non-State 'track two' actors is ensured.

In this context, emerging strategic trends in South Asia may be understood by referring to Immanuel Kant who wrote that for perpetual peace progress is needed in three main areas: (a) institutionalization of war-preventive and peace-facilitating instruments; (b) greater sharing of common economic interests through developing economic interdependence; and (c) promotion of democratization of States as democratic accountability works against the tendency to resort to conflict and war with each other.[12] A review of recent developments in South Asia would reveal encouraging indications that the region has made some progress in these directions. An institutional set-up within the

South Asian Association for Regional Cooperation (SAARC), despite all its limitations, is in place; countries of the region have made considerable progress in their respective processes of democratization, not free from setbacks though; and all of them have taken bold and positive measures for economic liberalization followed by some notable steps towards promoting economic interdependence. At the beginning of the 1990s new democratically elected governments emerged in Bangladesh, Pakistan and Nepal while elections took place also in India and Sri Lanka. Another round of general elections was held in 1996 in Bangladesh followed by one in India. The dismissal of the elected government of Pakistan on charges of corruption and inefficiency in the same year was a setback for the democratic process. But an authoritarian backlash in the form of one other round of military rule was hardly anticipated, as demonstrated by the subsequent transfer of power to the democratically elected government at the beginning of 1997. By all objective assessment, the countries of the region have a long way to go before democratic institution-building process can take lasting roots. But there is no doubt that notwithstanding continuing setbacks in the respective processes the recent trends are of a refreshing nature.

Indicators of policy changes on the economic front have also been stronger than ever before throughout South Asia. Nearly every country of the region embarked in a rather big way on the process of privatization and promotion of free-enterprise economic system to keep pace with the winds of change worldwide. Basic reforms have been introduced to make currencies convertible, easing restrictions on foreign investment and eliminating import controls. Efforts are on to deepen and broaden the reforms aimed at achieving self-reliance through greater internal resource mobilization, reducing public expenditures and subsidies, and promoting public sector efficiency. Reforms have also been introduced to attract greater foreign investment and to strengthen interface with the rapidly changing, increasingly competitive international economic order.

Despite all this, prospects of stability, security and peace remain far from being firmly rooted in South Asia. Indeed, the positive picture remains clouded by the continued trends of instabilities within the countries as well as between them. The region has the unenviable record of suffering from at least three rounds of major inter-State wars in less than five decades of post-independence history and a ceaseless process of intra-State conflict, most often with cross-border ramifications. South Asia is a region where a paradox of sustained conflicts and instabilities has long been an invariable feature. Sources of conflict in South Asia are of structural nature and have their roots in its history, geo-politics, economics and ecology. The same features and values of historical, ethnic, linguistic, cultural, and religious nature that bind the nations together also contribute to the mutual mistrusts, perennial tensions and occasional hostilities.

Whether or not South Asia has reasons to look forward to better times is not known. The kind of political institutions and processes that are going to evolve will be important. Similarly, much would depend on the success and impact—national as well as regional—of the economic liberalization process. Against this backdrop, the Regional Centre for Strategic Studies mobilized a group of experts of established reputation for a seminar on 'Regional Economic Trends and South Asian Security in South Asia'. The present volume contains the papers presented at the seminar. Central to the focus of analysis are the political and economic trends in the region at a time of sweeping transformations in global politics, economics and security, and the linkage of regional economic trends with South Asian security.

The first paper in the collection by Jayadeva Uyangoda departs from the traditional approach to security studies in South Asia which has essentially focused attention on the nation-state within a global or regional State system as the central domain of inquiry. In a historical phase where the very social-structural foundations of the pre-existing State system are in rapid transition, the question of security runs much deeper, reaching to the processes of State transformation in a new historical space characterized by fundamental changes in property relations, economic role of the State, the dissolution of social alliances of power and, in short, the entire political economy of South Asian political formations. What is at stake today in South Asia is not just the security of the States, but the very continuity of a master model of the State, conceived in a historical period of State-centric capitalist development which has already reached its end.

It is the State which will in any case be called upon to deal with the challenge. Uyangoda's concern, therefore, is not with the State *per se*, but its capacity to deal with the challenge, the most likely ways in which the State will respond to it and the consequences on democracy, human rights, conflict management and further social transformation. The author casts doubts over the capacity of the South Asian State to be a peaceful agency of historical change in the period ahead. The absence of an effective agency to facilitate transition in the age of globalization will in effect sum up the post-colonial predicament of South Asia. The most troubling implication of this is that the South Asian State is very likely to exercise a monopoly in charting South Asia's historical future, implying greater violence than has been witnessed in the recent past against domestic social classes.

Dipak Gyawali proposes that the conventional growth model of economic development adopted in South Asia so far has not been successful in bringing economic security to the immense mass of the poor. The poor have not acquired the organizational strength that would make a difference, and the institutional 'bargaining tool' has been denied to them in the past by the very forces that have so corruptly benefited from this State of affairs in the past. The existing State delivery mechanism in South Asia is rife with corruption and cannot be expected to deliver economic security to the most vulnerable without massive reforms. Gyawali's paper looks at economic development from the perspective of the informal world, and critiques the formal development interventions that oftentimes have increased the insecurity of those subsisting in this manner.

Gyawali argues against a nation-State expanding its control over nitty-gritty resource management functions. The State has a role to play, as have other units in the social system as a whole. South Asia is already home to a rich plurality of social institutions which have survived major catastrophes, historical or natural, through the centuries. The State should confine its role to that of a facilitator promoting the development of these intermediary institutions, such as the family, the village clan as well as cooperative arrangement between village and villagers. The pursuit of this objective demands the political vision and will for real decentralization, or rather devolution of power, to bodies outside of the regular chain of command rather than mere 'decongestion' of the centralized chain of command.

Prem Shankar Jha visualizes seeds of future conflict mainly in competition for economic and trading opportunities and advantages. He argues that security strategies for South Asia need to be formulated at not one but two levels simultaneously. The first is the promotion of regional peace through economic integration. The second is the adoption of political and economic strategies that strengthen the region's bargaining power in its relations with the industrialized countries. Needless to say, success in the first will make the second palpably easier to achieve.

The most important step that South Asia must take, therefore, is to open its economies to transnational investment by large global companies. The prescription to open up the economy and to 'go global' is not new. It is being followed with varying degrees of enthusiasm by all the South Asian countries. But the rationale given for it has so far been purely economic. Jha's contention is that the political rationale is as strong as the economic. South Asian countries can simultaneously increase their attractiveness to foreign investors and their bargaining power with them, if they also open up their own markets to each other. The recent formation of the SAARC Preferential Trading Arrangement (SAPTA) is a welcome step in this direction, but only a small one. The lead in further unification of markets should be taken by India, which can afford by virtue of its size and industrial depth, to extend non-reciprocal tariff concessions to its neighbours, for a mutually agreed period of transition.

Taking a closer focus, Abdur Rob Khan examines the political economy of trade liberalization in South Asia in view of the experience of India-Bangladesh trade relations. The analytical context is the incipient globalization of the world economy characterized by integration of the economies and lowering of the national borders parallel with intense economic nationalism and regional trading blocs behind protectionist barriers. Khan argues that contradictory tools of liberalization and protectionism are simultaneously used to gain access and market share for final product on the one hand, and to protect and expand the domestic production base on the other. The contradictory tools and policy goals have their political resonance because not only some degree of political sovereignty is involved in these policy options, but also different interest groups within and across the political boundaries are affected differently. The dialectics of these economic and political processes with varying degrees of security implications constitute the political economy of trade liberalization.

The issues of Bangladesh-India relations are outlined from the varying perspectives of the two countries. Bangladesh's main concern is the sky-rocketing trade imbalance which should be reduced by twofold policy measures by New Delhi: importing more commodities from Bangladesh, and reducing tariff restrictions on Bangladeshi products. Infant industry argument, informal trade or smuggling across borders, and lack of market access contribute to the colossal trade imbalance that has political resonance and, therefore, has to be dealt with in all seriousness. The Indian position is analysed keeping in view the Indian demand for the use of Chittagong port facilities for Indian commerce using a transit route through Bangladesh. The author offers threefold suggestions aimed at balancing Indo-Bangladesh trade relations: reciprocity and control of smuggling in the short run, joint venture with buy-back arrangement in the medium term, and promotion of SAPTA, in the long run.

Shahnaz Karim looks at the background and technical aspects of transit for economic cooperation at the sub-regional and regional level. Her paper examines the existing land transport networks between the two, what hurdles need to be overcome in order to facilitate trans-border movement of traffic, how existing facilities can be upgraded and what benefits India, Bangladesh and other sub-regional neighbours stand to gain if transit facilities are improved. It also analyses the security implication of this economic venture, specially highlighting Bangladesh's apprehension in this regard.

Considered purely on its own, and delinked from other issues, mutual granting of transit facilities is solely an economic matter. But not even a purely economic aspect of Indo-Bangladesh relations is free from political undertones. The most important factor conditioning the attitude of Bangladesh towards cooperation with India is the apprehension of being dominated. Fears of economic domination are compounded by political and security considerations. Bangladesh is haunted by the fear that the growth of the transportation network may ultimately result in the establishment of Indian hegemony in Bangladesh. The context is changing, however. It is being increasingly recognized that long years of non-cooperation have not served the interest of either party. The time has come for both India and Bangladesh to leave behind the legacy of distrust and conflict, and strengthen bilateral and regional cooperation conducive to development, peace and security in each other's country. Shared stakes in the sub-regional economic integration can become a vital instrument for ensuring security in the contemporary world.

Mohamed Jaleel and Ahmed Shaheed argue in their paper that security is related to economic performance. The paper analyses the various predominant trends in the South Asian region, and examines their relevance to the Maldives especially with respect to national security. Maldives enjoys a comparatively comfortable security scenario, specially with respect to internal socio-political and economic dimensions. Other kinds of threats that it faces, namely military vulnerability with respect to looming threat of mercenaries and sea-level rise, are not related to the economic trends in the region. The country has experienced sustained economic growth, the socio-economic benefits of which have been distributed with reasonable degree of equity. However, looking into the future with an economic perspective, the country needs to address certain issues to sustain its current positive socio-economic status. These are sustainable development, both in terms of resource exploitation and human development, public finance and private investment, and the development of organic linkages across different sectors of the economy.

Lok Raj Baral argues that security is meaningless without taking development in its totality into consideration. The linkage between economy and security in the context of South Asia can be conceptualized as well as operationalized within the framework of intra-SAARC economic cooperation. The underlying proposition is to promote 'security through regional cooperation'. Internationally, strengthening of intra-regional interdependent relationship will also contribute to the region's cooperation with other regions.

The negative implications of the lingering political divergence and disputes cannot, however, be underestimated. Cooperation in even some of the non-controversial areas like poverty alleviation, regional development fund, and food security reserve, remain bogged down due to the lack of confidence between the SAARC members. Political considerations and endemic mistrust among the member States, especially India and Pakistan, have stultified regionalism. Even if the countries of the region have moved towards liberalization either collectively or by integrating domestic economy with regional and global economic regimes, the South Asian challenge looks to be as formidable as ever. The role of government, the State and the market have to be properly defined and practised to ensure that the adopted policies yield public welfare.

Pervaiz Iqbal Cheema examines Pakistan's security challenges and perceptions from a 'comprehensive' outlook. He argues in favour of a balanced approach in emphasizing non-military factors in national security as against the military ones. Cheema argues that the possibility of reducing expenditure on the purchase of modern sophisticated weapons and equipment appears somewhat unrealistic in Pakistan. The threat from India is viewed as real in Pakistan, and hence, contemplating reduction of defence spending amounts to endangering national survival. The question persistently being asked revolves around whether or not it is possible to reduce defence budget without compromising the security needs of the country. The defence allocation is measured in terms of magnitude of threat confronting Pakistan, mainly from India.

The major dispute haunting both countries is the Kashmir dispute which is the product of the Cold War days. Since both countries are still caught in the cobweb of Cold War imperatives, the emerging economic imperatives of the post-Cold War era have not been able to obviate the imperatives governing the deeply entrenched attitudes.

Amera Saeed reviews the background in which SAARC was launched, and the first decade of its existence in which the process of cooperation under SAARC has continued despite all predicaments. There is a growing recognition in the region that the potential for regional cooperation could be realized even if in small ways. The Association has survived recurrent setbacks because of continued political differences between member States including postponement of high-level meetings on more than one occasion. Core areas of economic concern like trade and food security are being increasingly included in the cooperation agenda. On the other hand, the Association has played an important role, although indirectly, in defusing some of the regional tensions.

The author looks at the SAARC process in the context of the rising trend of regional organizations in various parts of the world as witnessed in the post-Cold War era. She argues that in the new realties of the post-Cold War global order, regional cooperation in South Asia under the aegis of SAARC has multidimensional opportunities and possibilities before it. The emergence of Indian Ocean Rim Initiative (IORI) and International Forum for the Indian Ocean Region (IFIOR) is also viewed in the same context. An incremental approach, rather than ambitious agenda might develop confidence among the member States of the region. The existing regional cooperation mechanisms should be considered building blocks. Whether it is SAARC or the Indian Ocean region as a whole, cooperation in core economic areas like trade, investment and commerce should receive top priority, which happens to be the global trend.

Christian Wagner examines the relevance of the experience of the European Union (EU) to the South Asian situation. He argues that the institutional network established in the context of bipolar confrontation also helped initiate a process of permanent exchange and consultations both between the member countries and between the antagonistic blocs. Thus, the experiences of West European and other successful regional organizations bring into focus the close connection between political, economic and security issues. The importance of political stability in order to achieve socio-economic development is quite obvious.

South Asia faces a difficult task so long as there are neither common political interests nor strong economic incentives to enter into closer collaboration. The low level of economic interaction makes it necessary to strengthen political understanding and confidence-building measures. These will create a favourable climate which will pave the way for closer economic collaboration. Politically, SAARC is the only forum in the region where confidence-building measures can take place at the highest political level. Transnational interaction between societal and professional groups must be expanded and strengthened in order to promote people-to-people contacts. In the near future, the major challenge for SAARC will be to take regional cooperation from the national bureaucracies and research institutions to the markets and the peoples of South Asia.

P.R. Chari analyses the possibilities and limitations of regional cooperation in South Asia to address the national security concerns in the region. The future of regional cooperation in South Asia is inextricably linked with the politics of the subcontinent. The extent to which SAARC can succeed will depend on the willingness of the South Asian countries to subordinate their mutual animosities for achieving the larger extra-territorial objective of regional cooperation. Unfortunately these mutual animosities derive from elite perceptions of their national interests. Chari suggests that a relaxation of Indo-Pak trade barriers would let market forces transcend political borders and reverse the steady criminalization of politics in India and Pakistan, which is among the root causes of their crisis of governance. These dangers need to be articulated more forcefully by opinion-makers in the region. Enlargement of people-to-people contacts offers the most fruitful means to erode the mistrust and suspicions pervading the region.

Chari suggests a series of confidence-building measures, especially belonging to the non-military genre, that can be catalytic to transformation in South Asia. His stress is on 'track-two' initiatives and the role of the private sector in fostering confidence-building measures. Non-governmental agencies also have a potential role to play, especially in areas that the State machinery fails to deliver.

In planning and approaching the project, RCSS had in consideration the far-reaching political and economic changes that have over the past several years dominated the discourse and practice in international relations in and outside South Asia. Issues related to the theme were approached from the perspective of both space and time. The seminar looked at the contemporary South Asian space in which economic and security decisions are made. Considerations were given to sub-national, national, regional, international and transnational levels. South Asia's history and geo-politics, and the wide range of perceptual issues at the State and official levels came up for discussion. But, looking beyond that, the discussion focused on the needs and priorities from the point of view of the people and civil society as increasingly important referent units in economic and security concerns.

The time canvas in which South Asia acts and reacts in relation to economics and security was the other area of consideration. The on-going changes in the international system following the end of the Cold War, specially their impact on approaches to security, were discussed. Issues related to continued arms race and other conventional factors in defence and security came up for discussion. But the stress was mainly on non-military dimensions, particularly growing national, regional and international imperatives for economic transformation.

Political understanding was considered essential for the success of economic cooperation which cannot, however, be allowed to remain hostage to political discord. Wider and deeper interaction in trade, investment and other economic sectors were viewed as a stabilizing factor in terms of political and security relations which would in turn be conducive to economic transformation, both nationally and regionally. Economic interdependence can promote shared stakes in maintaining political stability at both national and regional levels. In relation to perceptual issues, stress was given to the importance of 'track-two' initiatives through greater people-to-people interaction, specially of representatives of the media, private and non-governmental organizations, business and various other professional groups. Recent initiatives in this direction are notable, and need to be further sustained. The publication of this volume is a part of RCSS initiatives to promote and sustain further debate and deliberation on the theme that the Centre considers crucial to the understanding of emerging trends in security thinking in the South Asian region.

The book owes a great deal to Prof. Robert O'Neill, Chairman of the Council of International Institute for Strategic Studies, London, and member of the International Research Committee of RCSS. The Centre is grateful to him for ideas and inspiration behind this project. This volume would not have been possible without the support of the Ford Foundation which provided bulk of the fund for the seminar as a part of its overall cooperation with the Centre. I also thank the Asia Foundation for sharing the cost of the programme and the Friedrich Ebert Stiftung for facilitating the participation of German experts in the seminar.

This volume is produced by the RCSS, and while the individual authors are responsible for the views expressed in the chapters, these may not necessarily be attributed to the RCSS.

NOTES

1. Other expressions used to describe the post-Cold War era include 'a world transformed', 'turbulence in world politics', 'end of history', 'end of geography', 'back to the future', 'clash of civilizations', and so on. See for details, articles on the theme 'World Transformed' by R. Tucker, S. Hoffman, K. Keller and W. McNeill, *Foreign Affairs* 69(4), 1990; James Rosenau, *Turbulence in World Politics*, Princeton, 1990; Francis Fukuyama, 'The End of History', *The National Interest*, 16, Summer 1989; Takashi Inoguchi, 'Dialectics of World Order: A View from Pacific Asia', in Hans-Henrik Holm and Georg Sorensen, *Whose World Order? Uneven Globalization and the End of the Cold War*, Westview Press, Boulder, 1995; John Mearsheimer, 'Back to the Future: Instability in Europe after the Cold War', *International Security* 15(1, 2 and 3), 1990; and Samuel P. Huntington, 'The Clash of Civilizations', *Foreign Affairs*, Summer 1993 and September/October 1993.
2. See for example, Barry Buzan, *People, States and Fear: An Agenda for International Security Studies in the Post-Cold War Era* (2nd edn), Lynne Reinner, Boulder, 1991; Robert McNamara, *The Essence of Security*, Harper and Row, New York, 1986; Theodore C. Sorensen, 'Rethinking National Security Studies', *International Studies Quarterly*, June 1991; Stephen D. Krasner, 'National Security and Economics', in Thomas Trout and James Harf (eds), *National Security Affairs*, Transaction Books, New Brunswick, 1983; and Muthiah Alagappa, 'The National Security of Developing States: Lessons from Thailand', ISIS, Malaysia, 1987. For studies highlighting the comprehensive approach to security, published from Bangladesh, see M. Abdul Hafiz and A. Rob Khan (eds), *Security of Small States*, UPL, Dhaka, 1987; Iftekharuzzaman, 'The India Doctrine: Relevance for Bangladesh', in Shaukat Hassan and M.G. Kabir (eds), *Issues and Challenges Facing Bangladesh Foreign Policy*, Bangladesh Society of International Studies, 1989; and Iftekharuzzaman (ed.), *South Asia's Security: Primacy of the Internal Dimension*, Academic Publishers, Dhaka, 1994.
3. Yezid Sayigh provides an interesting insight into the subject in his 'Confronting the 1990s: Security of the Developing Countries', *Adelphi Papers* no. 251, IISS, London, 1990.
4. Ibid.
5. Edward A. Kolodziej, 'What is Security and Security Studies? Lessons from the Cold War', *Arms Control* 13(1), April 1992, p. 29.
6. Ibid., p. 4.
7. UNDP, *Human Development Report 1994*, New York, 1994, p. 22.
8. Stephen P. Cohen, 'US Security in a Separatist Season', in Glenn Hastedt and Kay Knickrehm (eds), *Toward the Twenty-first Century, A Reader in World Politics*, Prentice-Hall, Englewood Cliffs, 1994, p. 432.
9. Ibid., pp. 432-5.

10. See for details, Iftekharuzzaman, 'Bangladesh in the Post-Cold War Era: Relevance of the Experiences of the East Asian NIEs', *BIISS Journal* 15(1), 1994.
11. James N. Rosenau, 'New Dimensions of Security: The Interaction of Globalizing and Localizing Dynamic', *Security Dialogue* 25(3), 1994, p. 258.
12. Immanuel Kant, *For Perpetual Peace*, reproduced in Howard Williams, Moorhead Wright and Tom Evans (eds), *A Reader in International Relations Theory and Practical Theory*, Open University Press, Buckingham, 1993, quoted in Takashi Inoguchi, 'Japan and the United Nations', *Japan Close-up, Views from Kansai*, March 1995.

Emerging Issues in South Asia's Insecurity

JAYADEVA UYANGODA

TRADITIONAL STUDIES on security in South Asia have essentially focused attention on the nation-state within a global or regional State system as the central domain of inquiry. Dimensions of State security in that framework were conceived in terms of inter-State relations where tensions (associated with war-preparedness, war, deterrence, strategic balance, arms race, etc.) as well as cooperation (in the form of security pacts, military cooperation, arms sales, etc.) between States to constitute the security problematic. This focus underwent some change in recent years when internal civil strife and ethnic separatist movements began, along with their trans-territorial implications, impacting on the 'unity and sovereignty' of States.[1] Here the concern became twofold: (i) the threat posed by internal armed rebellions to the stability of the State, and (ii) extra-national spill-over effects of internal rebellions of one country on another, usually a neighbouring country, often bringing the countries thus affected into conflict. For instance, India-Sri Lanka and India-Pakistan relations at one time or another have been characterized by this particular 'national security' concern.

The purpose of this essay is to shift the focus of security inquiry to a somewhat different terrain and to do it in a slightly unconventional manner. Its starting point is that the emerging macro-economic processes in South Asia, as elsewhere, clearly defy the inter-nation-State-centric parameters of security studies, as they were traditionally conceived. In a historical phase where the very social-structural foundations of the pre-existing State system are in rapid transition, the question of security runs much deeper, reaching to the processes of State transformation in a new historical space characterized by fundamental changes in property relations, economic role of the State, the dissolution of social alliances of power and in short the entire political economy of South Asian political formations. If one takes the security problematic seriously, one could argue that what is at stake today in South Asia is not just the security of the States, but the very continuity of a master model of the State, conceived in a historical period of State-centric capitalist development which has already reached its end. A radical questioning of the old reasoning of South Asia's nation-state narrative—its modular categories of sovereignty, national interest, nation-based economic progress, social justice through direct State intervention in economic engineering and the political domestication of subordinate social classes through the distribution of the social surplus—has begun under the intellectual leadership of the international capital. This incidentally has coincided with another process, the seeming inability of almost all South Asian societies to decide whether the existing forms of nation-state in the region have any legitimacy or meaning, to continue as political entities.

In the contemporary historical context, it is also necessary to note that the issues of security in South Asia derive a significantly new meaning in the current process of market-centric economic development and globalization of national economies. During the entire post-colonial period of South Asia, national economies functioned within a general framework of relative isolation from the world capitalist economy; that regime of political economy also shaped to a great extent South Asia's social transformation. Political alliances that presided over the post-colonial change in South Asia and of course a variety of power blocs that were constructed within different regime formations were primarily facilitated by the State-centric economic processes. The rapid breaking up of this pre-existing political economy regime and its possible consequences in the current period of globalization are seldom talked about in South Asia. This essay is an attempt to steer the academic concern in that direction.

AN ANECDOTAL ENTRY TO THE PROBLEMATIC IN THE MAKING

To highlight the central focus of my paper, let me begin by citing some anecdotes. In October 1995, I visited Japan and my itinerary included meetings with members of the Japanese business community, government officials and of course academics. In Nagoya, I was welcomed by some senior officials of the Noritake company, which has its largest industrial operation in Sri Lanka. Noritake's ceramics production in Sri Lanka began in 1972. After a guided tour in the Noritake head office and factory, the officials and I sat down to a talk about Noritake's business operations in Sri Lanka. Responding to my queries about their concerns, they turned to the question of labour unrest. Noritake in Matale in Sri Lanka had just recovered from a bitter labour dispute which originated in December 1994, soon after the People's Alliance won the presidential election. Noritake officials in Nagoya appeared quite apprehensive about expansion of their operations in Sri Lanka, not knowing the trends on the labour front. They asked many questions about Sri Lanka's political stability, the prospects for the new Constitution and the devolution package, and the implications of the Workers' Charter that the Sri Lankan government announced in September 1995.[2] The unmistakable impression this conversation created in my mind was that if labour strikes, even outside their own factory, continued to spread in Sri Lanka, Noritake was very likely to review their investment expansion programmes in the country. 'Security' was one of their major concerns, and that notion of security had nothing to do with the military-strategic balance in South Asia.

The encounter that leads us to the second anecdote occurred the same evening in Kyoto. I was meeting a group of Japanese academics and students, and a few Sri Lankans living there. Invariably our conversation turned to the theme of Japanese investments in Sri Lanka. 'How safe is Sri Lanka for Japanese businessmen to invest there?' was the question posed by a Sri Lankan who had been for many years promoting Sri Lanka in Japan. I said, 'Safety is a relative concept. Colombo is a safe place as much as Tokyo can be a safe place amidst the threats of gas attacks and earthquakes.' We all agreed that the Japanese people were hyper-conscious of their safety and security, yet for investors there was hardly any threat from any quarters. No sooner had we ended our consultation, than the Japanese television carried pictures of Colombo in flames. The attack on fuel storage facilities in Colombo and the resultant fire, as seen on television, quite nicely demystified the relative safety theory we had constructed just a few moments ago. 'Obviously, they are now attacking economic targets. What goes up in flames in Colombo is also investor confidence in safety and stability there', commented my host, a Professor of Economics at a university in Kyoto.

Back in Tokyo, I met some Japanese Foreign Ministry officials. They were reporting to me a seminar held in the previous week in Tokyo where prospective Japanese investors were briefed by a delegation from Colombo's Board of Investments. They told me that there was a fairly positive response from the business community, but there were also many questions raised by them about the war in the north. 'It is difficult to convince our businessmen that Sri Lanka is more secure and stable than Myanmar, Cambodia or Vietnam. Look what they see in the newspapers.' One official showed me a Japanese-language daily which carried a photograph of Kolonnawa burning. 'If the war ends quickly and a settlement is reached, Sri Lanka can attract many Japanese investors', said the official. While listening to my hosts, I was thinking of the implications of the same observation formulated in a negative form.

Two conclusions, directly relevant to the theme of this paper, can be drawn from the above anecdotal experiences. First, South Asia now has a new community of 'outsider' entrepreneurs which is structurally embedded to the current macro-economic transformation and is acutely concerned about the political stability and the internal security of these countries. That concern emanates essentially from an anxiety for the security of international capital. Secondly, this community's perceptions and expectations of security come into direct conflict with the minimal guarantees which the embattled South Asian States can ensure for external capital in a period of multiple social dislocations characterized by a state of generalized political anomie.

INTERNAL RESISTANCE TO THREATS TO 'PEOPLE'S SECURITY': WHOSE SECURITY, THEN?

The construction of 'security' as a felt experience is not the prerogative of the State alone. Social groups active in the production as well as consumption of economic surplus may engender their own, specific conceptualizations of security and insecurity in an historical period of rapid change and uncertainty. Such varying constructions of security can very well be mutually antagonistic and even in conflict with the State-centric security concerns. A newspaper report originating from India, which I happened to see while writing this paper, illustrates this point. Headlined 'Indian activists vow to drive out multinationals', an AFP report from Bangalore begins: 'An Indian farmers' association which had targeted Pepsi, Coke and Kentucky Fried Chicken, vowed Wednesday to drive multinationals out of India, saying the firms were plundering its resources.'[3] According to this report, tens of thousands of activists of the Karnataka Farmers' Association held a protest meeting in Bangalore and were planning to extend the campaign to the rest of

India. The report also related some events that occurred recently. The Kentucky Fried Chicken restaurant in Bangalore, the first in India, was closed on this day of protest as a 'precautionary measure'. Opened in June 1995, this outlet had been earlier forced to close briefly 'after it was accused of serving unhealthy food'. This Farmers' Association had quite a history of activism. To quote the AFP report again: 'The Association, which twice ransacked the Bangalore office of the US firm Cargill Seeds three years ago, said it would seek the help of other activists in its anti-MNC campaign.'

What is the central argument in this anti-MNC campaign? If we once again turn to the report which we just quoted, we find the following answer coming from a leader of the movement. Medha Patkar, who came to prominence a few years ago in a massive anti-dam environmentalist campaign in Gujarat, says: 'We have no place for multinationals. The people's movement will not allow them to set foot in our country. They bring big machines and destroy the forest and sea wealth. They are here to loot the country.'

Here we can see two competing perspectives of 'security' in conflict. They clash, because one view of security cannot be reconciled with the other. What the Indian agrarian activists understand as security is irrevocably threatened by the operations of the Western companies that are euphemistically called MNCs. Here lies a basic contradiction located at the core of the change in South Asia: a strong current of both economic nationalism and populist isolationism among middle-class interventionist groups in direct opposition to the arrival of global economic forces—international capital, big business, new machinery, globalized consumer habits, etc. Interestingly, what the recent political trends in India and the rest of the subcontinent appear to suggest is that the ideology of militant antipathy to international capital may primarily emanate from domestic elite who articulate agrarian as well as 'national-industrial' interests. More significantly, their mobilizational intervention may even map out a path for future class action—more disorganized, sporadic and unconventional—among the working-class masses.

Curiously though, it so happens that economic globalization coincides with the demise of the traditional working-class movements in South Asia, thus leaving social space for non-working-class agents to occupy the centre-stage of resistance to international capital. The radical anti-imperialists of the urban, middle-class intelligentsia and the weaker sections of the domestic bourgeoisie have already begun to form the ideological and social core of the emerging alliance for resistance. It is perhaps not a coincidence that the new economic nationalism and ethno-nationalism have appeared in South Asia almost simultaneously. This new form of economic nationalism, curiously, has little resemblance to the economic nationalism of the early phase of State capitalism in the sense of the confluence of extremely xenophobic social and ideological forces that spearhead the contemporary resistance. In this backdrop, it is also hardly necessary to emphasize that the evolving tendency towards reconstituting social alliances of resistance is assuming a qualitatively different character from the alliances that governed movements of resistance in the period of post-colonial State capitalism.

LOCATING THE INSECURITY OF THE STATE

Rajni Kothari in a recent essay identifies some key contours of what he calls a 'drastically changed global context in which old "balances", "deterrence", and multilateral and pluralistic engagements are no longer working'.[4] Quite rightly, he notes the deep erosion of the building blocks of the pre-existing system—the nation-state—while giving rise to 'a new style of nationalism' the precise directions of which remain 'unclear'. According to Kothari's reading of present trends, uncontrolled violence, undeclared wars and civil wars seem to be the order of the day. He also notes 'the upsurge and spread of a new and different political consciousness at grass roots level, and located outside the nation-state' as constituting the new context, although the precise directions of this consciousness also remain 'unclear'.

Kothari's prognosis is in a way illustrative of the predicament of the new radical intelligentsia in South Asia, who juxtapose civil society against the nation-state as the most adequate form of political association capable of confronting the horrors of modernity. I wish to problematize Kothari's prognosis through a different reading of the emerging history in South Asia. One contemporary historical trend points to the multiplication of States in South Asia as agencies of the very modernity that has already created much havoc, rather than as a new form of the State in which the democratic civil society acts as an effective and durable domain for voluntaristic political associations. One key political characteristic of ethnic separatist movements in India, Sri Lanka, Pakistan and Bangladesh is the inherently anti-democratic potential of the mini-States that are being imagined by all national-self-determinists. As veritable caricatures of post-modernity—in the sense that the separatist imagination mirrors the selfsame nation-statist modernity against which it has already sent to death thousands of men and women—they have not yet demonstrated any capacity to engender a single narrative of democratic emancipation.[5] Seldom does the populist wing of the civil-societist school of thought recognize this dilemma of *contra* nation-state political practice in South Asia. Hence Kothari's apology for the absence of 'the precise direction' of the new styles of nationalism as well as of the 'political consciousness at grass roots level'.

To further illustrate the point I am making, let us examine the political characteristics of South Asia which are likely to result in an extreme, and—as many see it—implausible, conjuncture of events—the break up of the South Asian nation-states. Let me, at least in passing, express my own nagging suspicion that it may not be the case that all South Asian biographies of ethnic nationalism should end in suicide.[6] The main trend towards that reckoning which the South Asian nation-statists refuse so obstinately to acknowledge emanates logically from their vigorous and emphatic rejection of the historical need for updating, reconstituting and redefining the political relations of the majoritarian nation-state which has enshrined centrifugal modernity in South Asian post-colonial societies. By enforcing national unity on pulverized ethnic communities through military and administrative means, particularly during the past decade, the nation-statists have been doing the greatest disservice to their own project of nation-building. In case the existing 'nations' break up, the setting up of a number of mini-States in the region would be inevitable. Theoretically, there is no historical guarantee to rule out such a proliferation of mini-States, because the process of State formation is a continuing one—there is no material reason for the State to remain static—and the present nation-state cannot by any means be viewed as the modular end of State-making in South Asia. An alert student of South Asian politics even during the past few years would not fail to observe how historical forces have been converging towards reconstituting the political geography in the region.

The issue that should concern us most is not the formation of multiple States in South Asia, but its immediate consequences. These would largely be shaped and conditioned by the process in which new ethnic sovereignties are most likely to take territorial forms. The mini-States to emerge in the conjuncture outlined above would be the outcome of mutually hostile, highly militarized and irreconcilably destructive ethno-nationalist politics. Once such States are established, the inter-State relations can legitimately exist primarily in highly militarized and belligerent forms where the concerns for security of the States may take pathological dimensions. Currently, there is hardly any move in South Asia to minimize, let alone arrest, such catastrophic consequences of a grave crystallization of probable historical forces.

Even a less extreme scenario would not provide much solace to South Asian States. In this scenario, the majoritarian State may succeed in defending national unity by militarily defeating ethnic separatist movements and introducing some measure of political reforms. Nevertheless, the way in which secessionist ethnic communities have been responded to by the State through exceedingly repressive, military means has already established a lasting divide between the centres of these States and ethnic peripheries. Multi-ethnic nations, reunified through military means, will take a new political form, involuntary political associations of ethnic communities with no firm historical bases, established and sustained in the present period of crisis, for collective and shared sovereignty. This may quite ironically place the State in a new, uncomfortable role—that of a quasi-imperial authority occupying, controlling and administering territories in the periphery of the State. Edward Said's insightful observation on imperialism comes to mind: 'At some very basic level, imperialism means thinking about, settling on, controlling land that you do not possess, that is distant, that is lived on and owned by others. For all kinds of reasons it attracts some people and often involves untold misery for others.'[7] Punjab, Kashmir and Jaffna under the occupation of the centre's armed forces and bureaucracies can hardly be voluntary regional units of a pluralistic and federal State. Unless ethnic communities decide to totally erase their recent collective memories of war and violence in favour of national unity imposed on them from above, by forces with which they cannot identify in subjective terms—an enormous historical burden, by any standard—the relationship between triumphant majoritarian centres and conquered ethnic peripheries may run the definite risk of being transformed into one of the occupier and the occupied. Not even in pre-colonial historical formations did the relationship between the occupier and the occupied function smoothly.

COMPETING EXTERNAL PRESSURES

Meanwhile, the States in South Asia are under pressure from two external macro-spaces, that are ironically not complementary. The focus of this pressure is on the nature of the political reforms that the States are supposed to implement. The first source of pressure is West-centric and the other East-centric.

The West-centric pressure emanates from South Asia's traditional economic and political allies in Europe and North America.[8] Closely linked with the 'traditional', or pre-existing, world economic order, the concern in this instance is to replicate in South Asia the political structures, institutions and practices of Western liberal democracy. Democratic political reforms that should accompany macro-economic reforms have become the new orthodoxy of Western industrial capitalism's relations with the developing world. Codified in the economic as well as political discourse of Western development assistance in the 1990s, this argument favours a less interventionist and, therefore, a minimalist State, a stronger civil society, retreat of the State from the economic sphere, enshrining of civil and political rights of individuals in the constitutional as well as administrative practices, and of course, total democratization of the body politic.[9]

There is a combination of political, economic and civil society agencies located in the West that have been constantly articulating this West-centric argument for democratic political reforms—Western governments, World Bank and its allied economic institutions and human rights organizations. The annual aid consortia meetings held in Paris have been in recent years the primary site where these three global interest groups have been performing their politico-economic rites in relation to each aid-dependent developing country. Recent additions to the political vocabulary of development assistance of such notions as good governance, accountability and transparency are essentially manifestations of this globalization of a political model, shaped along the liberal democratic State of the West.[10]

With world-wide implementation of structural adjustment programmes intended for greater marketization of the world economy, the new ideology of the global capital recognizes the need for political stability, to be achieved through means other than ones associated with the authoritarian developmentalist State model. One of the major points against the latter model, developed by the so-called 'reformist' elements of the World Bank is that authoritarian capitalism lacks public legitimacy as well as stability. In the 'new thinking' of 'democratic developmentalism', the notion of political conditionality, demanding democratic internal reforms, began to be annexed to development aid in the late 1980s. The *World Development Report* of 1991 sets out the broad political-economic parameters of the new policy regime towards the developing world. The Report postulates that 'democracies . . . could make [economic] reform more feasible in several ways: political checks and balances, a free press, an open debate on the costs and benefits of government policy can give a wider public stake in reform'. Democracy, according to this reasoning 'could help, rather than hinder, economic change: it increases governments' incentives to perform well and keeps predatory behavior [of the State] in check'.[11]

Institutional reform, meaning in effect downsizing the State, is a major credo in the revisionist agenda of the Bank. Its economic justification of institutional reform is presented in the most unambiguous language. Arguing for redefining existing property relations, the Report recommends the 'establishment of a well-functioning legal system and judiciary, and of secure property rights' as an essential complement to economic reforms. Liberalization of property relations developed during the State-centric post-colonial capitalism requires the reconstitution of the State itself. Stripping of the State of its traditional instruments of economic control and social domestication is a necessary step in this reform enterprise. To quote the Report:

> Reform of the public sector is a priority in many countries. That includes civil service reform, rationalizing public expenditure, reforming State-owned enterprises, and privatization. Related economic reforms include better delivery of public goods, supervision of banks, and legislation for financial development. Strengthening these institutions will increase the quality of governance and the capacity of the State to implement development policy and enable society to establish checks and balances.[12]

Actually, the *World Development Report* sounds like a charter for political-economic reforms in the developing world. What is also interesting in it is the ideological assumption that the Western liberal democratic State should be the master image, guiding reforms in all spheres of politics and economics in the developing world. Let us, once again, see how the Bank ideologues articulate the problematic:

> Political instability is a fact of life in many countries. The past forty years have seen scores of racial, tribal, communal and guerrilla wars. . . . And there is more to political stability than mere avoiding coups. . . . Repressive governments can create a semblance of stability even when they entirely lack political support. . . . Social consensus, [on the contrary] helps governments to establish legitimate authority to govern. Without this authority, even the most basic functions such as taxation and allocation of public spending can become problematic. . . . In many developing countries, political and economic instability have put the social consensus under strain.[13]

The Report goes on to offer a remedy, arguing against the traditionalist authoritarian imagination. In an utterly revisionist spirit, it says that political stability should be firmly anchored in democracy and the capacity building of democratic institutions. Free economies and free politics—such are the outer boundaries of the re-imaging of the developmentalist State which is supposed to embody all the liberal philosophical virtues attributed to the classical bourgeois State of industrial Europe.

The Bank's 'charter' for political reforms, quoted at length above and the enormity of which is obscured by its plain, common-sense and straightforward formulations, signifies an extremely disquieting political outcome for any South Asian society, if it chooses to implement it. Those who are familiar with South Asian politics will have some doubt about the capacity and commitment of the political elite to liberalize the State in the West European or North American modular fashion, as envisaged in the above citations. The Western political demands for State reforms should not, however, be brushed aside, because some key aspects of them are already under implementation, undermining the 'traditional' social consensus that ensured the South Asian regime of States some degree of continuity, albeit with recurrent internal convulsions. Retreat of the State from its traditional obligations—generating employment on a mass scale, facilitating upward social mobility of varied social classes, protecting clientist social groups, distributing public resources almost untrammelled by procedural norms to maintain social bases of power, etc.—is a key dimension of what has been conceptualized by the donor community as transparency, political accountability and good governance.

The problem here is that little does the neo-liberalist idealism of the Western donor community take cognizance of the possibility that making the South Asian State a mere manager of market-centric economic transition would irreparably damage the existing forms of social consensus that have characterized State-society relations for many years. To identify the tension that has already been created in business, political and bureaucratic strata in the subcontinent as a result of the good governance and transparency project, one has to only take note of how the anti-corruption drive has already resulted in discouraging new investments and slowing down the economic decision-making process in Sri Lanka, India and Pakistan. While transparency—rationalization of public decision-making process in a Weberian ideal-typical model—may not guarantee the best mechanism for capital accumulation and investment enhancement, it has already endangered social and political relations of economic power.

ASIAN PRESSURE: FREE MARKETS AND UNFREE POLITICS?

The political demands from East Asia, meanwhile, have entirely different dimensions. They come indirectly, in the form of political prerequisites for private investments to be made in the region by East Asian, primarily Japanese and South Korean, companies. It is perhaps too early to say anything definitely about the nature of the political baggage that will accompany East Asian economic relations with South Asia. It is important to note, however, that in the coming period of the world economy, South Asia's economic relations will primarily centre on the South-East and East Asian economies. A likely outcome is that South Asian States may be compelled to refashion their internal politics in order to respond to this important change in their external economic relations.[14]

A few initial observations could be made regarding the politics of this emerging trend in South Asia's external economic relations. First, South Asia and East Asian industrialized countries represent two different political histories and experiences concerning the relative place in the polity for the government, capital and labour. Secondly, the South-East Asian as well as East Asian countries are not guided by an overarching political ideology as are the Western industrial democracies. Their attitude to South Asia will not be informed by any particular colonial sentimentalism or a sense of political evangelism. Thirdly, their interest in South Asia will essentially be guided by economic pragmatism. The need for relocating their manufacturing industries in relatively low-labour-cost economies is the main reason for these economies to look towards the South Asian region.[15] Fourthly, economic pragmatism may preclude any intervention in democratic political reforms in investment-recipient countries. Rather, it could even be in the opposite direction.

It is in this context that East Asian capital will look at the question of stability and security in South Asia largely in terms of the security of their investments. One can observe in the main pattern of East Asian investments the concentration of short-term, labour-intensive capital. Mainly driven by cyclical fluctuations of domestic economies, East Asian capital is unlikely to invest in long-term ventures, as it has been the historical case of European capital invested in South Asia. The point, then, is that South Asia's expanding economic ties with East Asia in future are unlikely to have the same 'reformist' political agenda which is currently associated with the West.

Here, another contrast may be made between the Western and Eastern political agendas in South Asia as well as elsewhere. East Asian societies are entities without strongly mobilized civil societies, and the recent upsurge of these economies and their historical process of capital accumulation have taken place in the absence of a strong and autonomous civil society. Suppression and subjugation of civil society has been a major aspect of the politics of development in East Asia whereas Western capitalism has historically evolved itself with a variety of ideologies for civil society. The political conditionality of development aid, as laid down by the multilateral economic agencies as well as donor countries in this period of globalization, emanates from that civil society tradition which Europe and the United States had earlier found not particularly urgent to the needs of the developing world during the Cold War era.

It would, therefore, be interesting to see the nature of 'East Asian political conditionality' in South Asia, if the region is closely incorporated into Asian capitalism which would perhaps create conditions for a fair degree of autonomy for South Asia *vis-à-vis* the West. The point is that unlike Europe, the industrially developed Asian countries have not had any tradition of democratic civil society being tolerated for their own social classes. A pointer to the future, though somewhat disturbing, is the preference of China, Myanmar, Thailand, Malaysia and Vietnam to South Asia—the 'messy region' in Asia—already shown by East Asian investors.[16]

GOVERNING TRANSITION: SOUTH ASIA'S HISTORICAL CHALLENGE IN A WORST CASE SCENARIO

It is in a way amazing that the extent and gravity of the transformation that South Asia has already witnessed under economic globalization and structural reforms has not been acknowledged among academic or policy-making communities. Without being alarmist, or narrowly historicist, one may still identify the transformation of pre-capitalist economies and social formations under the aegis of British colonial capital in the nineteenth century as the closest historical parallel of what takes place in South Asia today. This parallel should be seen not in a sense of summoning theories of colonialism to account for it, but essentially in terms of social-structural, class and political transformations and dislocations that are very likely to crystallize in the years ahead. Economic globalization and its macro-economic reform components will certainly alter, within a relatively brief time span, the pre-existing forms of post-colonial mode of production, the class structures anchored in that mode and social relations of political power embedded to it.

In this backdrop of possibilities, one may note that the resistance to the dismantling of the public sector of South Asian economies and to private foreign capital is also symptomatic of how social forces, who benefited from the old regimes of political economy, deeply feel about externally induced changes. Any South Asia-watcher would have noticed how in India, Nepal, Bangladesh and Sri Lanka, the politics of resistance to globalization has taken the rather popular form of protesting against privatization of State economic ventures. On surface, this represents a growing economic nationalism fighting a losing battle against an irresistible global trend. But on reflection, one may find how it represents deeper social anxieties—anxieties in an age of globalization—easily experienced by people across a variety of social classes. It, therefore, is too simplistic to say that globalization, paradoxically, germinates localist, nationalist resistance or forces of its own negation. The point, rather, is that economic globalization and its working in national economies is predicated on radically altering a set of relations that had constituted the pre-globalization South Asia. It has already begun to dismantle a form of social structure that has historically been embedded into a specific kind of colonial capitalism and post-colonial State capitalism, rested on social classes who emerged and grew up within it and maintained a great stake in it.

If South Asian economies are rapidly de-staticized, as mandated by international capital, one major implication of such a scenario will be the dissolution of a particular social-economic and political structure at the apex of which has been the post-colonial State. This has been a historically specific edifice held together and articulated by the State with all its utterly repressive, interventionist, regulatory, paternalistic, welfarist, social redistributionist and Bonapartist characteristics. Seldom does the theoretical literature on post-colonial social formations acknowledge or account for this very vital historical role undertaken by the post-colonial State.[17] With a long list of tragic failures of this supreme agent of modernity, it has held together a set of social formations by means of historically specific social relations. It is the pain of the dissolution of these social relations—to make way for a new process of class formation—that is likely to be felt by left-oriented labour unions as well as by many social strata including the privileged as well as the under-privileged. Not a social revolution, but prolonged social violence—uncoordinated, scattered, unorthodox and from unexpected quarters—is very likely to characterize the next phase of history in South Asia.[18]

The challenge for South Asia in the period ahead is then a historical one, to govern the rapid transformation of entire social formations—with decisive alterations in the mode of production, social relations and economic and political structures—without leaving room for major dislocations.

FACING THE CHALLENGE

Who will undertake this challenge? The State? We have to ask this question with all its seriousness, because rightly or wrongly, it is the State which will in any case be called upon to deal with it. But our concern should not be about the State *per se*, but its capacity to deal with the challenge, the most likely ways in which the State will respond to it and the consequences on democracy, human rights, conflict management and further social transformation.

The problematic of State capacity in the period ahead may take two dimensions. First, in a literal sense, its capacity to preside over the macro-economic transition, in response to the imperatives of economic globalization. As long as the South Asian States are assisted in this enterprise by multilateral economic and financial institutions, capacity for policy formulation is not likely to be a major difficulty. The real issue would, however, involve the management of the following crisis tasks: (a) the dissolution of the pre-existing class structures, (b) the re-constitution of social relations of political power without leaving political space for dispossessed social strata to form alliances of resistance, and (c) the forging of new power blocs that can mediate, within the framework of representative democracy, the consequences of social and political dislocations.

The nature of political transformation in South Asia in the entire period ahead will largely be decided by the way in which the South Asian regimes will deal with this triple task.

In all probability, the kernel of South Asia's problem of security and insecurity would be the managing of a historical transition peacefully and democratically. Two historical lessons can be seen at the outset as mitigating the capacity of the South Asian State to facilitate such a colossal process peacefully. First, when pre-capitalist modes of production and social formations were transformed by the colonial State, that enterprise was pushed through unlimited exercise of violence, running through a time span exceeding a century. There were no compulsions on the colonial State at all to account for its violent and repressive behaviour, except for occasional inquiries held by the House of Commons on gross excesses that violated the norms of the imperial mission. Second, the post-colonial State in South Asia has presided over the working of the post-colonial modes of production and social formations with a similar deployment of generalized violence. The norms of accountability concerning State behaviour are still not very strong in arresting the arbitrary practices of the State, although they are exceedingly important in the civil society discourse. The South Asian State is already addicted to violence, just as an alcoholic to liquor.

CONCLUSION

South Asia's security problematic is being reconstituted by a variety of competing discourses. Each discourse is powerful in its own domain and in its ability to place demands on the State; and these discourses emanate from a multiplicity of anxieties, specific to the era of globalization. The mediation among these conflicting discourses of security by the State is enormously complicated by the rapidity of the transformation that is taking place in South Asian social formations, the post-colonial modes of production and social relations of political power.

All the reasoning of this essay casts doubts over the capacity of the South Asian State to be a peaceful agency of historical change in the period ahead. The absence of an effective agency to facilitate transition in the age of globalization will in effect sum up the post-colonial predicament of South Asia. The absence of an agency to chart the desirable paths of historical transformation is one of the fundamental questions of our times. The bourgeoisie, the working classes, the middle-class intelligentsia, the new civil society formations—all these potential agencies of change are, at least in South Asia, forces characterized by the lack of long-term historical vision. The most troubling implication of this comment is that the South Asian State—already weakened within, yet assisted by the post-Cold War imperial system—is very likely to exercise a monopoly in charting South Asia's historical future, necessitating the exercise of greater violence than has been witnessed in the recent past against domestic social classes.[19]

NOTES

1. Some examples of this genre of literature are Mohammed Ayoob, *The Third World Security Predicament: State Making, Regional Conflict and the International System*, Lynne Reinner, Boulder, 1995; Kanti Bajpai and Stephen Cohen (eds), *South Asia after the Cold War: International Perspectives*, Westview Press, Boulder, 1993; K. Subrahmanyam, *India's Security Perspectives*, ABC Publishing House, New Delhi, 1982; Stephen Cohen (ed.), *The Security of South Asia, American and Asian Perspectives,* University of Illinois Press, Chicago, 1987; P.V.J. Jayasekere (ed.), *Security Dilemmas of a Small State: Sri Lanka in the South Asian Context*, South Asia Publishers, New Delhi, 1992.
2. 'Devolution package' is the euphemism for the set of constitutional proposals which the People's Alliance (PA) government of Sri Lanka put forward in August 1995, as the basis for a political settlement to the island's Tamil ethnic grievances. It envisaged a semi-federal form of political autonomy to Tamil regions. The Workers Charter, meanwhile, was introduced by the PA government to fulfil one of its election pledges made in 1994. The local and international business community in Colombo became highly suspicious of the Charter, because it promised to legally guarantee the labour's right to unionization.
3. *Daily News* (Colombo), 3 November 1995.
4. Rajni Kothari, 'Globalization and "New World Order": What Future for the United Nations?', *Economic and Political Weekly*, 7 October 1995.
5. Partha Chatterjee's observation, made in another context, is quite appropriate to encapsulate the point here:

   [A]utonomous forms of imagination of the community are overwhelmed and swamped by the history of the post-colonial State. Here lies the root of our post-colonial misery. It is not in our ability to think out new forms of the modern community, but in our surrender to the old forms of the modern State.

   See Partha Chatterjee, 'Whose Imagined Community?', *Millennium* 20(3), 1991, p. 524.
6. For an extended discussion on this theme, see Jayadeva Uyangoda, 'Ethnicity, Nation and State Formation: Antinomies of Nation-Building in South Asia', *Pravada* (Colombo) 3(4), June/July 1994, pp. 10-17.
7. Edward Said, *Culture and Imperialism*, Vintage Books, New York, 1994, p. 7.
8. The political project contained in the World Bank's *World Development Report 1991* is so utopian that only a new form of political colonialism can implement it on a global scale. Nevertheless, it is a strong ideological restatement of the new global mission of advanced industrial capitalism.
9. In the developing world, there is considerable resistance to this wave of political pressure and that resistance emanates both from the governments and civil society organizations. Prime Minister Mahathir Mohammed of Malaysia is spearheading a

campaign defending the argument that imperatives of rapid economic growth should not coincide with the arbitrary implantation of Western-style liberal democracies in the developing world. Meanwhile, the bitter debate at the UN Conference on Human Rights in Vienna sharply divided the human-rights communities in the developing world, when an influential section of 'non-Western rights advocates' argued that the concept of the universality of human rights is an attempt by the Western governments to impose their value system on the non-Western world. Chandra Muzaffar, Malaysian scholar and activist, represents one of the most articulate voices for the cultural relativism argument of democracy and human rights. See Chandra Muzaffar, *Human Rights and the New World Order*, Just World Trust, Penang, 1993.

10. The ideology of international capital is interestingly conceptualized in the Western industrial democracies. Their political conditionalities attached to development assistance reflect a kind of vision, along with a maximalist political programme, for the State in ex-socialist countries and the 'third world' to be the embodiment of the liberal philosophical reasoning concerning the State, the government and the citizen. For someone looking for historical ironies, it is amazingly simple to contrast this with the illiberal political projects implemented by international capital in the colonial and post-colonial worlds, from say the late nineteenth century to the early 1980s. History has gone through a full circle.
11. World Bank, *World Development Report 1991: The Challenge of Development*, Washington, 1993, p. 133.
12. Ibid.
13. Ibid., pp. 128-9.
14. India's recent interest in expanding economic ties with South-East and East Asia is seen by some observers as necessitated by strategic calculations as well. According to this view, India is seeking closer economic ties with all South-East Asian countries in order to establish a strategic balance when China appears to be the power that would emerge dominant in the Asia-Pacific region in the early decades of the twenty-first century. See Michael Richardson, 'ASEAN Nations and India Warm Up: Closer Ties Could Create an Important New Regional Axis', *International Herald Tribune*, 29 January 1994.
15. In Japan, an interesting policy debate is taking place about the need to relocate branches of the manufacturing industries. Since Japan is a very-high-labour-cost economy, it is being argued that the labour-intensive manufacturing industries should be relocated in Indochina, South Asia and Burma. This particular period of the Japanese economy is called the 'hollowing out phase'.
16. Many reasons are currently adduced by observers to explain the reluctance of Japanese or Korean companies to invest in South Asia. A less recognized and compelling reason for such reluctance is perhaps a combination of cultural and political factors. No South Asian country so far appears to have produced social forces in its society that would be seen by East Asian corporate communities as their cultural or social allies. South Asian business and bureaucratic elite are still culturally and politically distant from their East Asian counterparts. The emerging ethno-nationalist elite *à la* BJP in India, with their avowedly authoritarian political goals, may perhaps fill this gap.
17. In a recent essay, Mustapha Kamal Pasha writes:

The post-colonial State, however, has also grown to become more heterodox—to become more than simply modernity's reckless agent against hapless nativism. The

State is also seen as an expression of greater capacities against want, hunger, and injustice; as an escape from the arbitrariness of communities established on narrower rules of inclusion/exclusion; as identity removed from capricious attachments.

Mustapha Kamal Pasha, 'Security as Hegemony', *Alternatives*, no. 21, 1996, pp. 292-3.

18. Two very significant alarm signals have recently come from Sri Lanka and India. In the late spring-summer 1996, Sri Lanka experienced a grave hydro-electricity power crisis, due to a long drought in hydro-catchment areas. Totally dependent on hydro power, Sri Lanka could cope with the problem only by restricting the power supply to only a few hours a day, beginning in June 1996. At a time when the power crisis was at its height—resulting in enormous suffering for rich and poor alike—the unions of the State Electricity Board, which had the monopoly in the power sector, decided to launch a continuous strike to protest against the planned privatization of the Board. With no electric power at all, the life of an entire population became a nightmare for four days. Patients died in hospitals, masses of children suffered without food or water in urban areas and life stood still—indeed, a rare experience of mass trauma. In the venerable traditions of trade union politics, this was an unthinkable move by the organized labour who would in the past have first of all been concerned with the human cost of their industrial action. An action closer to barbarism, yet symptomatic of sectarian social anxiety in an age of globalization. The signal from India is a seemingly stupid, yet profoundly troubling one in its implications—the protest against holding the Miss World beauty contest in India. Although dismissed by Ashis Nandy as a typically southern Indian phenomenon of political theatricality, the nature of the protest—with threats by some women activists to swallow cyanide capsules in defence of 'Indian womanhood'—tells us something different. A raw nerve has been touched somewhere by someone, germinating social hysteria for symbolic purity about a manifestly forgettable event of glamour, money and middle-class entertainment in a culture where the modernity of woman is imaged in the cinematic public culture of everyday life in an utterly erotic fashion.
19. It must be said, appropriately in a footnote, that a new form of transformatory politics, formulated in the democratic civil society, could perhaps make an effort to arrest this process predicated on present conditions. That will, one must admit, require an absolutely daring form of political imagination.

Economic Security in a Predominantly Informal World: South Asian Realities and Global Elation with Liberalization

DIPAK GYAWALI

JUDGING FROM standard development reports which take the nation-state as the basic unit of discourse, all of South Asia would rank among the economically most deprived regions of the world. Out of its billion-plus people, a staggering 40 per cent would be below the poverty line even by official count based on conventional measures such as access to adequate nutrition. Studies based on other measures place the incidence of poverty in specific regions and countries even higher, with over two-thirds of the population being below the defined poverty line.[1] There is, however, growing realization that the vulnerability that these poor have to grapple with in their everyday living is much worse than the statistics quoted above would lead us to believe. Consider the following:

> South Asian thinking on poverty should move away from the delusion that production *per se* guarantees availability or affordability of food for the poor. The hungry millions are proof that it has not happened in any substantial fashion despite the phenomenal achievements in agricultural production in certain countries within SAARC. South Asia should concentrate on increased, decentralized food production, emphasizing research into and application of technologies relevant to deprived geographical areas . . . while at the same time conveying through a leakage-proof and corruption-free delivery system, the fruits of the agricultural revolution that has materialized already. Organizations of the poor are an essential prerequisite to complete this system. These organizations would not only ensure that the delivery system is leakage proof and corruption free but would also permit the poor to assert their right to food, promote higher levels of health, employment and wages.[2]

There are significant lessons in this quote from important SAARC personages that are relevant in discussing the economic security of

The author is grateful to the discussants and other participants in the RCSS seminar as well as Bikash Joshi and Betty Wilkinson of IRIS in Nepal for their comments on the earlier version of the paper.

South Asia. The first is that the conventional growth model of economic development adopted so far has not been very successful in bringing economic security to this immense mass of the poor. The second is an admission that the poor have not acquired the organizational strength that would make a difference, the corollary being that this institutional 'bargaining tool' has been denied to them in the past by the very forces that have so corruptly benefited from this state of affairs in the past. The third is that the existing State delivery mechanism in South Asia is rife with corruption and cannot be expected to deliver economic security to the most vulnerable without massive reforms. In other words, economic insecurity in South Asia for that vast majority is as much (or more) due to internal reasons as external ones. All this, of course, goes without saying anything about the employed lower class or the smaller productive professional (or lower middle) class of South Asia and their vulnerability.

Currently the general debate in the South on economic security does not begin with this basic and endemic reality. Thinking is often seen not as a result of the social anomalies in our midst but as some kind of a visibly unpleasant surface disease which the antiseptic balm of foreign aid and well-meaning government projects can easily take care of. Very little exposition is heard in the mainstream corridors of media and power about the structural imperatives that have kept, and will continue to keep, millions of South Asians in abject poverty. This is currently true of the intellectual debate regarding liberalization and privatization which fails to see the role the State has played in those very countries which are clamouring for liberalization, whether in Europe, USA or East Asia. This essay looks at economic development from the perspective of the informal world; questions formal development interventions that oftentimes have increased the insecurity of those subsisting in this manner; and asks what factors legitimize (as opposed to legalize) formal interventions and thus makes them more effective.

DEFINING THE INFORMAL

The informal economy, which is the socio-political response of the poor to their economic vulnerability, predominates South Asia. Its size is the subject of an unresolved debate. This is all the more so when there are increasingly frequent questions being asked about the size and nature even of the formal economy.[3] Some speculate that the informal sector is much larger than the formal economy, may be even as high as 90 per cent of the total economic activity in a predominantly rural country like Nepal. But it all depends upon how and what one counts. Even in a more measurable sector such as finance and informal credit, indigenous bankers account for one-twelfth to one-half of all credit to different categories of industrial units.[4]

Jagannathan uses the concept of informal property rights to describe the informal economic processes.[5] His basic distinction is between property rights protected by the formal legal system, and informal property rights protected by self-policed contracts which are used to appropriate income from either existing assets and tangible resources or intangible property rights and social assets. He estimates that this sector would cover economic transactions anywhere between 30 per cent and 70 per cent of a country's gross national product. It covers the bridge between most rural markets and the rapidly growing chaotic urban transactions from those of slum dwellers to family firms where perceived economic opportunities are seized upon by the poor to earn their livelihood. These opportunities are utilized through voluntary agreements that are remarkably stable and serve as effective substitutes for many institutional deficiencies in the formal sector.

Smith defines the informal sector as one that produces goods and services, some of which are marketed, but which for various reasons escape enumeration, regulation, or other type of public monitoring or auditing.[6] It covers all activities in which people engage to augment deficiencies in income or consumption opportunities in the formal sector, from underpaid civil servants moonlighting or soliciting 'grease money' to rural migrants to the city who must attempt to market what skills they have and find jobs where they can, whether they are legal or not. It also includes pastoralists suddenly finding their transhumant movements impossible because of new international or administrative borders. This last example is significant in Nepal's case (and perhaps for Pakistan and India as well): with the advent of Chinese control over Tibet in 1950, the transhumants of northern Nepal suddenly found that, in Smith's general phrasing also applicable to Nepal, 'a traditional move from summer to winter pasturage became an illegal border crossing, gifts and other exchange item became contraband'. Such pastoralists from Manang in the north, finding their subsistence survival at stake, were the first to exploit any economic opening they could discern: instead of bringing in salt on yak backs from Tibet, in the 1970s they were able to bring consumer items from Hong Kong on Boeings to cater to the large demand in Nepal, and eventually, India.

Thomas sees several types of informal economic activities all of which have the common characteristic that none of them is fully recorded in the national economic account, but differ in whether they involve market transactions and whether their output as well as distribution are legal or illegal.[7] The household sector activities are legal but involve market transaction and are excluded from national accounting. The informal sector production (involving small scale, often self-employed, producers in commerce, transport and cottage industry) also do not break any laws but the output enters market transaction. The irregular sector activities have outputs that are legal (such as redecorating a house through an informal builder), but the production and distribution of these goods and services involve some illegality (such as tax evasion). There is finally the criminal sector where significant market transactions take place but both the product (e.g. drugs) and production and distribution are illegal.

What these definitions do is to reconstitute the boundary of our understanding of economic activities to include the vast reality of coping with everyday living that the majority of the population in South Asia indulges in, but which have yet to see academic insights, policy foresight or legal hindsight. There is a tendency in managers of the formal national economies to classify these extensive sets of activities as illegal or heavily dutiable; but even they are so classified that it is nearly impossible to do anything about them. In the example of the Manangi Hong Kong traders mentioned above, all attempts to control the import of luxury items in personal baggage only ended up increasing the rent-seeking value of a customs posting at Tribhuvan International Airport without making a dent on the volume of items imported. That reduction occurred only when India began liberalizing under the tutelage of Narasimha Rao and Manmohan Singh, making large-volume imports for subsequent disbursement in India unfeasible.

In resource management, perhaps the best example of the formal forgetting the informal reality to the detriment of both is the irrigation sector. Of the total Nepal area of 14.75 million hectares (ha.), 55 per cent is occupied by forest and grazing land, 19 per cent is rock, ice, urban areas, etc., and only 26 per cent is under any form of cultivation. Of this cultivated area, 52 per cent is non-irrigable. Of the approximately 2 million hectares which remain irrigable, 16 per cent lie in the hills and 84 per cent in the Tarai. In the hills, half the irrigable area is already under some form of irrigation of which 94 per cent has been developed by farmers through the ages, and only 6 per cent has resulted from three decades of government intervention. The former is generally referred to as 'farmer managed irrigation systems (FMIS)' and the latter 'agency managed schemes' through central government intervention. In the Tarai, only a fifth of the potentially irrigable land has some form of irrigation; and of this 71 per cent is farmer-developed and only 29 per cent agency-developed.[8] These FMIS are basically in the informal system, despite attempts by the State to bring them under classification and registration.

One difficulty in estimating how much irrigation there is in Nepal lies with the very definition of irrigation.[9] There has been a tendency to count as irrigation only that which has been under some form of formal agency intervention. The small FIMS irrigation systems often employ simple but effective 'brush wood' dams on small streams which are economic enough to build and within the farmer's capacity to rebuild after they are washed away by floods, while the State-constructed massive concrete structures are not, given the extreme and violent nature of Himalayan hydro-geology. Such irrigation systems have not been properly inventoried and the State is only dimly aware of their existence. This transfer of risk resilience capacity from village to State has been the hallmark of much of State-led development intervention in the field of irrigation.

Estimates of the area of land under irrigation could, in principle, be arrived at from land taxation records; but in reality this is not easy. In the past, there did exist a classification system that differentiated land by its productive potential. For taxation purpose, the State classified land as *abal*, *doyem*, *sim* and *chahar*. *Abal*, the highest quality land, was land that could comfortably grow two crops of rice and hence was in all probability well irrigated. This classification is still valid for the revenue agencies but has not been internalized by the irrigation department whether in its engineering or financial planning. Even within revenue agencies, there has not been a systematic effort to monitor and refine land classification, especially land that is falsely classified as of lower category to cheat on taxes. A joint effort by the revenue, the irrigation and the agriculture departments might have succeeded in finding out how much land is under farmer-managed irrigation system and of these how much needs civil engineering upgrading, if at all; but these agencies do not talk to each other as there exists no underlying political imperative to do so.

The failure to consider taxation as an institutional tool which, besides raising revenue, assures that assets are maintained at optimal productivity to successfully offset the tax burden and thus leads to better returns has been the bane of land management in Nepal. Land tax is negligible:

although agriculture is said to contribute 60 per cent to the GDP, it provides only 2 per cent to the State's revenue. The inability to integrate State-level irrigation intervention with attempts to reclassify irrigated or irrigable land through a sensible tax frame is one more indicator of the divorce of State irrigation activities from farming and their sequestering into a pure civil engineering effort. In the process, the real farmers were slowly edged out of the formal into the informal economy, may of them pushed into informal tenancy.

Estimates of how much irrigation there is in Nepal under the farmers' primitive but effective systems are only recently being made and the results have been surprising. It was conventionally estimated that there are some 17,000 farmer-managed systems in Nepal.[10] A detailed study of water use in central Nepal's Dhading district, one out of the country's seventy-five, revealed, however, that there were 2,961 farmer-managed systems in the district using river, stream and spring sources which covered 15,919 ha. of the district's agriculture area.[11] If Dhading were taken as a typical hill district of Nepal, and this figure were extrapolated over the area of the country's hills, one would see that the number of farmer-managed schemes in the country would be perhaps four or five times more. This is to be expected because of the plethora of the country's micro-watersheds and the many hamlets formed on caste and kinship basis which influence land ownership or at least its stewardship. These are what Jagannathan, quoted above, would call voluntary behavioural contracts of the informal economy that are stable and honoured over a reasonable period of time, even though they may not be recognized by the formal mechanisms of the State.

PITFALLS OF THE FORMAL

Irrigation is a good example of the real becoming the informal, or almost unreal to national accounts. This transmogrification of irrigation activities in Nepal—from something done by farmers into an exercise by bureaucrats to meet the socio-anthropological requirements of funding agencies, with farmers forming a dismal backdrop—has been remarkably rapid. The advent of modernization after the revolution of 1951, which overthrew a feudocratic dynasty of the hereditary Rana prime ministers, and the concurrence of the global phenomenon called foreign aid, contributed significantly to this transmogrification. The end result has been not only an alienation of the farmers from State-initiated irrigation exercises but also an estrangement of irrigation from its ideals of increasing food production. The consequence is that food production in Nepal has been declining and irrigation efforts, unable to initiate a fruitful dialogue with farmers, are withdrawing into a protective shell of civil engineering brotherhood. A similar situation has occurred with community-managed forests in Nepal when forests were nationalized in the 1950s, leading to entire villages and communities becoming alienated from their traditional resource base and their day-to-day activities of survival and subsistence suddenly acquiring an illegal tinge.

To a modern Nepali, writing about farmer-managed systems is both exhilarating and depressing—the former because new insights about natural resource management cannot but fail to excite and the latter because such discoveries (akin to Columbus 'discovering' America) only highlight the alienation of the modernizers from the existing reality of grass-roots farmers at large. One way of looking at the situation is by considering the entry point. Farmers enter the picture as a social group which has been tied to the land and has been struggling to coax it to yield the wherewithal for subsistence and survival. If a nearby spring or stream was perceived to help in this endeavour, collective effort was marshalled to tap the resource. Modernizers such as irrigation engineers, on the other hand, enter the picture as agents of the State once the State has decided to intervene in irrigation efforts. The market for civil engineers in irrigation has not been created by a demand from farmer-managed irrigation system but by the State and its partner foreign aid.

State involvement in irrigation is a modern phenomenon which began in earnest only in the late 1950s. Traditionally, the State had remained aloof from direct intervention in agricultural land management, confining itself to taxing land according to its productive capacity. Such was the practice under the Rana rulers till 1951. Indeed, even during Rana rule, State intervention was limited. The first record of direct State intervention was in 1920 when the British sought the permission of Rana Chandra Sumshere to construct a barrage on the Mahakali river which forms the border of Nepal with India in the west. That the Ranas were least interested in irrigation is highlighted by the fact that one of the main items of trade-off was not a 50 per cent sharing of irrigation waters of a border river but tracts of forests from which the Ranas hoped to derive profit by selling timber and subsequently from resettled farming. Further development on this river by India in the 1980s in the form of the Tanakpur project continues to sour Indo-Nepal relations.

That there was profit in indulging in 'development works' began to dawn on the feudal Ranas only a decade and a half before their downfall.

During the reign of Rana Juddha Sumshere (1932-45), retired Indian irrigation engineers were hired by the then public works department to work under the military district governors. The three irrigation projects undertaken were the Chandra Canal in the Trijuga valley north of Biratnagar, Manusmara east of Birganj in the central Tarai and Banganga near Taulihawa in the midwest. Interestingly, and not surprisingly, most of the land to benefit from this bounty belonged to large feudals with linkages to the Rana hierarchy. It was only after the overthrow of the Ranas that the State began to play an increasingly large-scale interventionist role in irrigation. Two guiding motives have been identified:[12]

— A State that had made the transition from the feudal family dictatorship of the Ranas to a modern State based on the idea of mass welfare felt that improving the productivity of land was its paramount concern, for which harnessing the country's irrigation development was essential; and

— Indian effort at improving its irrigation works as well as providing flood protection for the U.P. and Bihar plains, based on structural measures undertaken on Nepali soil (Mahakali in the 1920s and Kosi in the early 1950s), put pressure on the State to undertake similar irrigation development activities.

The 1950s and the 1960s were also the period when a Cold War was raging between the First and the Second Worlds, with the First World creating the instrument of foreign aid to prevent the Third World from becoming a part of the Second World. This phenomenon of foreign aid becoming an increasingly important (and eventually an overwhelming senior) partner in Nepali irrigation development matches a global imperative with a national one. The first important foreign entrants were the Indian Cooperative Mission which initiated a 'Small Irrigation Programme' in the early 1960s, and USAID which entered with its Point-IV programme. The efforts of these bilaterals were subsequently dwarfed by those of the multilaterals such as the World Bank and the Asian Development Bank whose aid accounts for virtually all government-initiated irrigation efforts. This logical culmination of an institutional mode of behaviour began with an important milestone. The Development Board Act 2013 (in 1957), under which almost all foreign-aided irrigation efforts are institutionalized, has an important provision included in the laws of Nepal: Article 5.1 (Kha) for the first time in the country's history allowed the Nepal government to accept foreign sovereign loans.

The nexus between the State that needed to justify its legitimacy by doling out projects and a foreign aid market that needed projects to pour funds into, created the phenomenon of an internally 'expanding nation-state' which grew to usurp the resource management functions of its relatively autonomous villages.[13] A Department of Irrigation was eventually created out of the Rana Public Works Department, and at present efforts are underway to expand its presence in every district as a full-fledged administrative unit handling the project within them. This phenomenon itself cannot be seen as alarming unless it is seen in conjunction with the 100,000-plus informal farmer-managed systems with which it has little contact and which it is trying to subsume under its control, marginalizing them in the process.

The expansion of the irrigation bureaucracy has not been because of an expressed demand from the farmers: rather it is an attempt to streamline a structure that allows the infusion of more foreign aid. Judgment to this effect can be passed by examining 'Irrigation Regulations 2045' of the Ministry of Water Resources. The pressure from donor agencies to allow development aid to be channelled closer to the farmers rather than the higher echelons of the bureaucracy has resulted in this piece of legislation that ultimately strives to salvage some of the powers of the bureaucracy that would otherwise have been lost because of the imperatives of decentralization inherent in creating users' groups.

The most important thing this new regulation *does not do* is that it does not recognize the existence of farmer-managed irrigation systems. The position of the district irrigation engineer is made stronger by making him chief of not only agency-initiated schemes but also the final adjudicator of water withdrawals by non-agency bodies. Nevertheless, in a tacit recognition of the existing reality of farmer-managed irrigation schemes in Nepal, the law provides the caveat that the need to apply for permission to withdraw water will only apply to those areas (or basins) prescribed by a notification in the gazette, and that individuals withdrawing water as well as informal bodies need not await permission from the district irrigation engineer. To date, no such areas have been prescribed.

Such provisions in effect mark the regulation as something applicable only to large agency-initiated schemes where the problems of repair, operation and maintenance are becoming severe and the distinct phenomenon of donor fatigue is beginning to be noticed. Farmer participation in large schemes is envisaged in three tiers—at the primary turnout, at the branch canal level and at the overall project level which may span several districts. They are expected to cooperate and assist the district irrigation office in fee collection, repair and maintenance. While they are entrusted with responsibility, they enjoy little or no authority to set rates or spend the money they have collected (which must be deposited with the irrigation office and of which 25 per cent will be refunded to them, if the district engineer is pleased with their cooperation, to be spent only on repair and maintenance). In each tier, a representative of the Department of Irrigation is envisaged, a fact which, when extrapolated over all of Nepal, requires the Department to embark on an employee hiring spree. These provisions, when seen against the backdrop of simply not recognizing existing farmer-managed schemes, indicate an internally expanding nation-state bloating its bureaucracy rather than catering to the needs of its farmer.[14]

A recent event highlights how insensitive the bureaucracy can be towards the reality on the ground. In the mid-1980s an idea was born that Nepal, which had only recently completed a hydro-electric project of 73 million cubic metre storage called Kulekhani I, should use the regulated tailwater discharged into the East Rapti river to irrigation parts of the Chitwan valley. The idea was picked up and expanded into a full-scale project to irrigate 9,536 ha. Unfortunately the project would also divert all the water of the East Rapti from the Royal Chitwan National Park. A hue and cry from environmentalists precipitated an environmental impact assessment. This study discovered that, of the 9,536 ha. proposed to be irrigated by the project, 1,786 ha. were already under full irrigation and 2,525 ha. had supplemental irrigation, i.e. 68 per cent of the area was already under some form of irrigation, some of it with 180 per cent cropping intensity, and that there were 86 farmer-managed systems within the area.[15] That the farmers had also never been consulted about the project serves to highlight the 'by the bureaucracy for the aid agency' nature of this project, typical of so many others.

The ideal sequence of events that lead to a project selection should be—farmers express a felt need; the scale of physical intervention is beyond the capacity of farmer to finance; the State is requested to be a partner; the State finds out who owns the land and makes an *a priori* agreement with the farmers regarding what tithe to take from the farmers in the form of water cess/tax; the State then initiates construction with as much participation from the farmers as possible. The sequence of events that actually occurs, however, is the following: there is money to be spent for the consecrated cause of increasing food production or rural development or whatever, either with the national government or with aid agencies; a search is on for a possible site; a design of a massive irrigation schema ensues; the floating of tenders; interminable irrigation works; if they ever reach near completion, then the problem of operating and maintaining them becomes insurmountable; even so there is no record of who owns the land.

The gossamer link between State-led irrigation activities and the proper husbanding of land for increased food production has contributed significantly to the existing predicament of agriculture in Nepal. Even the Basic Needs Programme promulgated with much fanfare some six years ago expected the food production to increase solely based on an increase in irrigation facilities, ignoring all the other inputs needed such as credit, fertilizer, market, tenancy rights, etc.

Among all the factors that have an impact on agriculture production, one that stands out sharply—and is at the very base of the informal economy—is the question of land tenure. It is indeed amazing that after years of construction work on irrigation canals or damsites, there exists no official list of people who actually own the land to be benefited from the irrigation works. This fact has prevented the intervening agency from coming to an *a priori* agreement with the landowner, absentee or otherwise, of the need to pay for the construction costs through increased earnings. Cost recovery is such a difficult task today (and it need not have been if irrigation had been approached in a more business-like way) that there is no attempt to recover capital cost. Only operation and maintenance costs are deemed redeemable.[16]

The inability to identify the actual beneficiaries of irrigation intervention efforts has been a major cause behind the poor operation and maintenance of irrigation schemes. In many cases, tenants have not been able to exploit the potential to increase production because the insecurity of their tenure militates against any permanent investment. It has been found that those who own the land, or those who are sure of their tenancy, are more prone to marking productive investment of their labour and savings in agricultural improvements than those who are not similarly placed.[17] Since State-led irrigation initiatives are not the result of a felt need at the bottom but that of an imperative from above, a simple business detail such as identifying and concluding an agreement with one's partners is missing as in the obvious investment principle of being able to account for every unit of investment by a certain amount of increased production.

A question is often asked: why should the informal ('primitive' to some of the modernists) not be brought under the formal as quickly as possible? Is not allowing the informal to remain that way a romanticizing of the 'noble savage' and against the very ethos of modernization and development? The answer is simple: given the imperatives and stress of change no structure, formal or informal, will 'remain that way'. The real question is: how is the change to be effected, by whom, how fast, with what proportion of winners and losers, and with what degree of participation by those whose lives are being changed, sometimes so violently? When phrased this way, the history of marginalization of the poor is seen in sharp context, with ethnically or geographically vulnerable groups being the first to pay the price of losing their social and physical assets.[18] And the real answer is to be found in the process by which this change occurs. As highlighted in the quote at the beginning from an eminent SAARC personage, the rent-seeking nature of the State structures in South Asia is obvious. In its procedures for subsuming the informal under it, the process of marginalization of the poor moves forward at an accelerated pace, as the example of irrigation regulations in Nepal shows.

To borrow another example from across the world, an experiment was conducted by Hernando de Soto and his Institute for Liberty and Democracy in Lima, Peru which showed that officially registering a small business, whose workshop consisted of nothing more than two sewing machines, took 289 working days, the equivalent of 32 months' income at the minimal wage.[19] Experience indicates that, if grass-roots NGOs repeated this experiment in South Asia, they would arrive at similar result. This is another common instance of a rent-seeking State creating very high transaction costs of operating in the formal sector, the very costs that are at the roof of a dynamics of marginalization and vulnerability of the poor.

SECURITY FOR WHOM?

In a predominantly rural South Asia, the concept of economic security is tied to the issue of political economy of land and water management. The debilitating condition of marginality can be simply defined as finding oneself within a structure that has, and promotes, a condition of severe lack of options. Being landless may not frighten a West European youngster entering the job market because of the availability of other options to generate income where the remotest connection with land may be at the super market. It does frighten the vast majority of the rural poor in South Asia for whom there are very few other options: and arguing that growth would provide opportunities for non-agriculture jobs has now proved too simplistic. Indeed, the jobs created in the booming urban housing and other sectors demand skills of the kind that the marginalized rural poor simply do not have at present and thus are filled by in-migrants from elsewhere. This phenomenon has led to its own kind of economic insecurity and tension in South Asia.

In trying to understand these fears, and provide explanations for the reactions they induce, it is important to begin the analysis from the various perspectives that arise from within the mooring of various institutional environments. Institutions are patterns of behaviour that sustain themselves over time. Using a framework devised by Cultural Theory[20] allows the spotlight to shift from an excessive preoccupation with the nation-state in social sciences to some of the broader social realities in our midst. It is the thesis of this paper that such a shift in lateral thinking may help us find a way to bring the informal economy within the ken of South Asian intellectual discourse rather than further marginalizing it.

Cultural Theory would say that an excessive focus on governments and what they should do—a bane of South Asian thinking—is how a rigid hierarchy would respond, but that is only 20 per cent of social reality, since there are four other possible responses—those of the individualists, the communards, the conscripted and the hermits. These five possible social environments emerge from boundaries prescribed by two parameters—grid and group—and the dynamics wrought by a third—manipulation. The group defines the choice of interpersonal contacts (group control, where loyalties to one's grouping and sense of identity are generated) and the grid defines behavioural options within personal interactions (grid ascription, where preservation of the overall structure is as important as maintaining the group). These two parameters remain fairly static under a given level of change. Manipulation, on the other hand, represents the use of power in society (exercise of coercion) and imparts an element of dynamics to changing social environment.[21]

These mutually exclusive social environments can be visualized in three-dimensional imagery if the group is considered the X-axis, grid the Y-axis and manipulation the vertical Z-axis (see figure). At any horizontal cross-section with a fixed level of coercion, the XY plane results in four environments which can be described using the animal images colourfully provided by another Cultural Theorist, Mars:[22] the worlds of the hierarchist wolves at the north-east corner (NE) who are represented by secretaries of governments, ministers, generals, *mullahs, rimpoches*, Sankaracharyas and the like; of the communard/egalitarian vultures at the SE such as environmentalists, underground groups,

SOCIAL ENVIRONMENTS

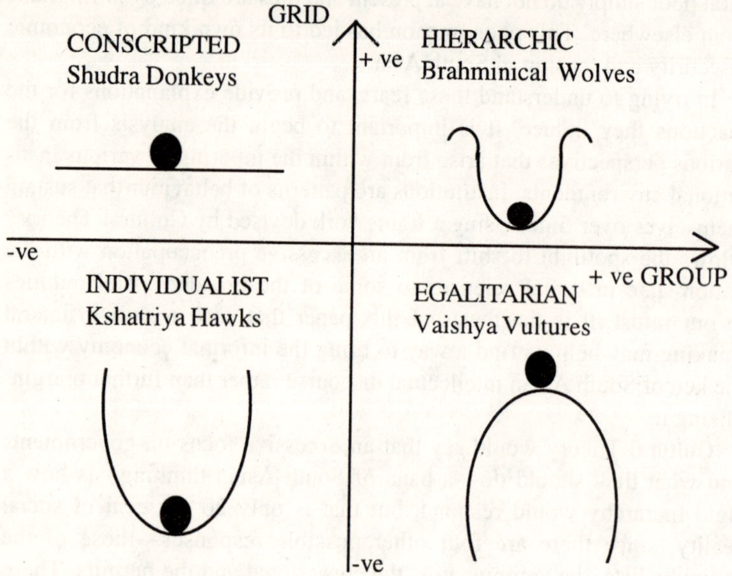

Source: M. Thompson *et al.* (1992)
M. Douglas ed. (1982)
G. Mars (1982).

brotherhood and the like; and finally of the conscripted donkeys representing the fatalist masses at the NW corners of the map. At the centre of the vertical axis where the four environments meet, one finds the autonomous hermit who can manipulate but does not and who could be manipulated but will not allow others the opportunity because he has voluntarily reduced his involvement in social interaction.

The result of strong, pecking-order group control and high grid ascription is the world of the hierarchist wolves. It is a world that prizes security and preservation of order. A government bureaucracy, a public utility department such as irrigation, water supply, telephones, roads or electricity are ideally such an environment. It is a pyramidal structure of defined authority as well as privilege allocation set according to constitutions, rules, procedures and by-laws. Under static conditions, many things operate mechanically like clockwork. If a problem arises, it is channelled to the unit with the right authority and competence to be dealt with. The profits, perks and privileges flow downward to each according to his status and seniority. There is 'order under the heavens' and life moves on as it should. This social environment is at perpetual tension with the others and has a strong sense of self-preservation.

But when external circumstances change, hierarchies come under stress in both their dimensions. They find it stressful to justify what to them is the self-defined divine legitimacy of their structure and to keep their group loyalty intact. Depending upon the nature of the stress, they may or may not succeed in preserving the structure and loyalty towards it. The study of the problems of modernization and change in South Asia must begin at the point where hierarchies are placed under stress both in their internal order of things and in the changing external circumstances.

Advertising of the 'good modern life', for one, is a powerful coercive force which defines new needs in a manner ubiquitous and sparing no one in the hierarchy. All developing countries are subject to mind-bending exercises of colossal energy in the form of constant bombardment of advertising messages. Both the overt and subliminal messages do leave powerful imprints in society—from the cogs of a bureaucratic machinery to the fatalistic masses. Inflation is another powerful coercive force of a different kind from advertising. It systematically, persistently and insidiously undercuts the established reward allocation mechanism set by hierarchies by creating new wants requiring higher salaries to fulfil. While advertising is an overt means of changing individual behaviour, inflation is a covert one leading the masses to a sense of fatalism that no matter how much they strive, they can never improve their lot. This is as true in the First World as in the Third.[23]

To cope with a constant artificial enhancement of the basic human need for material acquisition, whether actively by advertising or covertly by inflation, hierarchies in the form of governments and companies strive to increase their profits and give their employees hikes in salaries, bonuses and other perks, thus keeping relative privileges and hence group commitment as well as commitment to the structure still intact. Hierarchies in Third World countries, however, especially government departments, soon find out that no matter how much they keep revising salary scales and increasing bonuses, group commitment cannot be maintained by the attractiveness of the perks. When the level of stress wrought by advertising and inflation increases beyond what the hierarchy's privilege allocation mechanism can cope with, it finds it difficult to maintain group allegiance.

Most Third World societies, and South Asia more than anywhere else, are a collage of overlapping loyalties. Besides loyalty to the country, there are loyalties to linguistic, ethnic, religious, regional and clan groupings. When governments are at best unable to deliver the goods fast enough, and at worst perceived by certain groupings as exorbitantly rent-seeking or downright corrupt, loyalty to the State begins to recede to other social groupings, much of it in what is defined as informal sector. Governments then have the chance to mend their ways and devise more creative means of meeting the aspirations of their people, or opt for coercion.

Such moments of stress are the ripe time for the flowering of individualist hawks who maintain neither loyalty to the group nor uphold the order of a structure and communard vultures who thrive amidst shrill alarm and signs of the impending death of the old order. A hawk's is a very pragmatic world where only the very smartest survives. He operates alone, living by his wits, his ability to move faster and earlier than others and skills in pulling the wool over everyone else's eyes. He knows that if he is caught no one will come to his aid, and does not expect anyone to. He has neither group affiliation nor a need to preserve any ordered structure. A vulture, on the other hand, thrives only because the wolf's world is dying. If government departments and State delivery mechanism performed properly, the vulture world have little to cry about.

The fourth social environment—that of the conscripted donkeys—is found mostly within the bottom rungs of the hierarchy or next to it and controlled by it. The poor farmer at the tail of a distribution canal, the day labourer working at maintenance or the peon and the typist in the irrigation office are wholly dependent upon the mercies of the supervising overseer or engineer. This category of fatalist masses are bombarded by the same advertising and squeezed by the same inflation. They too desire the good life; but these untouchable Shudras cannot be independently audacious like the Kshatriya hawks. Neither can they systematically coalesce like the Vaishya vultures, nor are they accepted into political and management decision-making by the brahminical wolves. They are, however, the raw material of reaction. Quiet and in their place, they preserve the order under the heavens. Frustrated, they are the vote-bank dough in the hands of the brotherhood of vultures which fills it with revolutionary yeast.

The stress of advertising and/or inflation is among the manipulative forces that impart a dynamics to the boundaries between the four possible social environments. There could be stresses of other types such as perceived injustice, wars and revolutions that change the context within which everyday life functions, and many other, the like which place a severe strain on the collage of loyalties. The privileges allocated by the State can then be seen in relative terms which makes the privilege pie shrink or increase in the eyes of the beholder. Under the stress of rapid change, people can find themselves being attracted to a different social environment from the one they belong to. As discussed above, a hierarchist wolf may find his cosmology under stress and himself wishing he were a hawk or vulture. Because these four different social environments are mutually exclusive (you cannot be a free-ranging hawk and hunt with the pack), transitions have to be discontinuous, and often painful.

The purpose of this long excursion into Cultural Theory is to highlight the importance of enlarging South Asian discourse on economic security from an econometrician's narrow focus on GDP and the like to the broader context of social dynamics where perceptions of security are made and unmade in a collage of loyalties that are under stress. The power of the vulture-and-hawk world to successfully challenge the order sought to be imposed by the wolves has increased significantly with the availability in South Asia of decentralized technologies such as fax, e-mail, desktop computers and the like. Access to information is no longer the privilege of the few brahminical wolves. Networks of NGOs can share their concerns across administrative, national and international borders with remarkable success for their cause.

The recent experience of successful opposition to the 200 MW $1.1 billion Arun-3 project in Nepal by a network of Nepali and international NGOs is an example of individualist-hawk-and-communard-vulture opposition to the designs of hierarchical wolves in the form of the World Bank and the Ministry of Water Resources in Nepal. In this battle, the concept of economic security depended upon which social quadrant of Cultural Theory the protagonists came from. To the hierarchists, Arun-3 represented the continuation of the only order they were familiar with and were prepared to uphold. They would feel secure if this mega-project came through. To the communards advocating an alternative development paradigm, this project—which would soak up all financial resources for the next decade—represented a big threat of loss of small-scale local capacity to build small hydro projects, a capacity that was established over a twenty-five-year period. Arun-3 is an example only of the many economic security issues in South Asia, especially at the interface between the formal and the informal worlds, which acquire salience once the State-centric bias is removed in one's thinking.

A WAY OUT

The arguments against a nation-state expanding its control over nitty-gritty resource management functions, encroaching and overtaking resource management functions done by autonomous villages in the informal world, is not an advocacy of some form of anarchy, as water or forest bureaucracies are wont to retort. The State has a role to play, as have other social units in the socio-system as a whole. South Asia is already home to a rich plurality of social institutions which have survived major catastrophes, historical or natural, through the centuries. The State should confine its role to that of a facilitator promoting the development of these intermediary institutions, such as the family, the village clan as well as cooperative arrangement between village and villagers. The pursuit of this objective demands the political vision and will for real decentralization, or rather devolution of power, to bodies outside of the regular chain of command rather than mere 'decongestion' of the centralized chain of command. In the case of irrigation, real decentralization would mean transferring power not from the superintending engineer to the district engineer but to farmer-managed irrigation systems outside the departmental chain of command. In the case of forestry, these are the *gaons* of South Asia and not an expanding network of forest ministry offices.

The failure of the Panchayat regime of the past in Nepal to officially even recognize the existence of farmer-managed irrigation systems matched its inability to recognize 'banned' political parties. It was essentially a State that hijacked local resource management functions and marginalized local institutions. But ground realities have a way of asserting themselves; and no attempt at increasing food production in the country can succeed without promoting healthy intermediary institutions, many of them currently informal. To restore the State as an institutional resource, which in the current adversarial mode has been lost to these marginalized groupings, perhaps a beginning can be made by trimming the bureaucracy. For example, in Nepal's case, amalgamating the four ministries of agriculture, forestry, land reform and water resources into one ministry of land management with separate departments for land, water and forests may provide for better integration and co-ordination of government activities, while at the same time providing some window for local management groups to assume some of the local resource management functions.

A trimmed bureaucracy would have to find partners outside of itself for development and make the informal a part of the solution rather than a part of the problem. In return, the autonomous villages—autonomous in the sense of having relatively more local control over the management of local resources—could begin to see the State as an institutional resource rather than adversary. The role of the State then would be to nudge local systems towards more scientific as well as more equitable production possibilities.

Such a shift would then probably induce new institutional modalities of economic interactions and security for a wider variety of social groupings within. Capitalism, after all, grew and succeeded at the western end of the Eurasian peninsula because of the historical factors which prevented the rise of a monolithic State. After the collapse of the Roman Empire, all attempts at an imperial resurgence were checked by successive destructions wrought by waves of nomadic *Volkerwanderung*. Unlike the monolithic structures of Sinic or Indic civilizations, which were scientifically more advanced at the time, Western civilization thus found a historical niche to develop competing institutions—feudalism in the realm of politics, papacy in the realm of Church-State relations and manorialism in the realm of economics. These competing institutions prevented the State from becoming excessively rent-seeking and allowed a technologically precocious merchant class to emerge and define what is today's global order.[24]

As with other civilizations, South Asia missed such a historical opportunity. In its cultural make-up it is still in deep fascination with the patrimonial State. Toynbee was critical of the Indic civilization which was content to import rulers and have them maintain the status quo. Civilizations grow when they face challenge—they disintegrate when they cannot meet the stimulus of challenge whether internal or external. The greatest internal challenge in South Asia is the inability of the dominant minority to continue becoming a creative minority.

> A creative minority degenerates into a dominant which attempts to retain by force a position that it has ceased to merit. This change in the character of the ruling element provokes, on the other side, the secession of a proletariat which no longer admires and imitates its rulers and revolts against its servitude.[25]

Furthermore:

One of the most conspicuous marks of disintegration [of civilizations] is a phenomenon in the last stage but one of the decline and fall, when a disintegrating civilization has its universal State in the Mughal Empire and its successor, the British Raj.[26]

Creative ecumenism is still missing in the States of South Asia with the most reliable and stable social unit still being the family. Even in the most advanced (in terms of adoption and creation of the instruments of capitalism) South Asian country in this regard—India—businesses are still family enterprises. Its powerful and impersonal joint-stock companies are still family manipulated affairs with family shares of as low as 10 per cent controlling even the investment of State-owned financial institutions. The informal world of South Asia has not been able to find confidence in the ecumenism of this powerful tool of capitalism and hence the centripetal force moving away from the State (and often in conflict with it) are stronger than the centrifugal forces binding South Asians and its marginalized poor closer together into a large joint family of SAARC. This is true even as unofficial South Asian collaboration—whether at the formal academic business level or even more at the informal level of 'free marketeer' hawks who recognize no borders—is moving forward with increased vigour.

At this point, one needs to step back and ask how Jagannathan and Toynbee come together in this paper. It would be presumptuous to present that a ready-made *sutra* is available; but one can discern the vague outlines. When an informal economy is as large and vibrant as we have in South Asia, it is a sign that the dominant minority which controls the State apparatus ('hijacked the State') is not as powerful as it is made out to be, and that the internal proletariat is also not as docile as may appear on the surface. Many of the societal forces that maintain stagnation are not narrowly economic but what may be generically called 'cultural', including religious hierarchies of almost all hues. In Cultural Theory terms, the former brahminical wolves are desperately trying to hold on to an old order that is coming apart at the seams while the latter Kshatriya hawks and Vaishya vultures are exploring new possibilities. Perhaps, out of this vibrancy a new creative minority is ready to be born, only waiting for its own Dara Sukoh to lead it to a new synthesis of a more just social order, a more legitimate ecumenism that excludes none, of which economic security is but a part.[27]

NOTES

1. The World Bank's *World Development Report 1995* places all countries of South Asia, except the Maldives, in the low income category defined as having a 1993 GNP per capita of less than US$695. Maldives barely makes it to the lower middle income group. In the UNDP's *Human Development Report 1995*, things are slightly better with Sri Lanka and Maldives in the medium HDI rank and the rest in the low category.
2. Report of the Independent South Asian Commission on Poverty Alleviation (ISACPA), *Meeting the Challenge*, SAARC Secretariat, Kathmandu, November 1992.
3. Recent years in Nepal are an example of this uncertainty. His Majesty's Government of Nepal under the United Marxist-Leninists said before Parliament that the GNP had been growing at over 40 per cent in the previous year. When that government fell and the coalition opposition came to power it said that the growth rate was only 2.5 per cent. What is unknown is the methodology used to calculate GNP and other such indices of the formal sector as neither party has let that be known.
4. Banking Commission of the Government of India, quoted in Anand G. Chandavarker, *The Informal Financial Sector in Developing Countries—Analysis, Evidence and Policy Implications*, Occasional Papers no. 2, Research and Training Centre, The South East Asian Central Banks (SEACEN), August 1987.
5. N. Vijaya Jagannathan, *Informal Markets in Developing Countries*, Oxford University Press, Oxford, 1987.
6. M. Estellie Smith, 'The Informal Economy', in Stuart Platner (ed.), *Economic Anthropology*, Stanford University Press, California, 1989.
7. J.J. Thomas, *Informal Economic Activity*, London School of Economics Handbook, Harvester/Wheatsheaf, London, 1992.
8. From Dipak Gyawali, *Water in Nepal: An Interdisciplinary Look at Resource Uncertainties, Evolving Problems and Future Prospects*, Occasional Papers no. 8, Environment and Policy Institute, East-West Center, Hawaii 1989, Figure 9, p. 82. Subsequently, a much more resource-intensive master planning exercise by the Department of Irrigation downgraded potentially irrigable area in the hills by 19 per cent and in the Tarai by 23 per cent. See, Master Plan for Irrigation Development in Nepal (Cycle 2). Main Report, Annex vols. 1A, 2B, 2C, 3D, 4E, 4F, prepared by the Canadian International Water and Energy Consultants (CIWEC) in association with EAST Consult, Nepal, for Department of Irrigation, Ministry of Water Resources, HMG, with the assistance of the UNDP and the World Bank, 1990.
9. Ministry of Water Resources, *Irrigation Sector Review*, Report no. 3/2/190981/1/1, His Majesty's Government of Nepal, Kathmandu, 1981.
10. Prachanda Pradhan, *Patterns of Irrigation Organization in Nepal: A comparative Study of 21 Farmer-Managed Irrigation Systems*. Country Paper (Nepal) no. 1, International Irrigation Management Institute (IIMI), Colombo, Sri Lanka 1989. Also, idem, *Increasing Agriculture Production in Nepal: Role of Low Cost Irrigation Development through Farmer Participation*, Country Paper (Nepal) no. 2, IIMI, Colombo, Sri Lanka, 1989.
11. *Report on Water Resource Utilization Inventory and Potential Study of Dhading District*, Study conducted for Dhading District Development Project (DDDP), SILT Consultants, Kathmandu, August 1990.
12. Taken from CIWEC & EAST.

13. Dipak Gyawali, *Water in Nepal*. Many social scientists have had problems with the use of the term 'autonomous villages' and the Maldives seminar was no exception. Absolute autonomy is never there in any village and it is not intended to give that impression. The question is of relative autonomy in being able to decide locally issues of local resource management. Currently, agency-managed systems and the State bureaucracy that operates them have resisted any inclination for partnership with local communities. The term is also not meant to imply that there is utopic equity in locally managed irrigation schemes. Schemes can be found where local landlords operate as hydraulic 'oriental despots' quite as effectively as in Babylonia! The question really is: should central agencies try and usurp the position of the local hydraulic despots or should they try and set up something more equitable? The nature of the State and its legitimizing mission are the issue.
14. Details in CIWEC & EAST 1990, Annex E2.
15. SILT, *Environmental Impact Assessment of East Rapti Irrigation Project*, Study Conducted for Nippon Koei (Japan) and Asian Development Bank, Kathmandu, 1990.
16. *Implementation of Cost Recovery for Government Irrigation Schemes: An Interim Report to His Majesty's Government of Nepal and the Asian Development Bank*, by Robert R. Nathan Associates, Inc. (USA) and East Consult (Nepal), Kathmandu, 4 November 1988.
17. *Land Tenure System in Nepal*, a study conducted for the World Bank by Integrated Development System (IDS), Kathmandu, 1986.
18. Dipak Gyawali, 'Challenge of Mountain Economy: Marginality or Risk Resilience?' in Kurt Luger and Karin Inmann (eds), *Verreiste Berge: Kultur und Tourismus in Hochgebrige*, Osterreichischer Studienverlag, Innsbruck, Austria, 1995.
19. Quoted in M. Estellie Smith.
20. The exposition of this theory of social environments is found in Mary Douglas, *Risk and Blame*, Routledge, London, 1992; and Michael Thompson *et al.*, *Cultural Theory*, Westview Press, Boulder, 1990.
21. The two dimensions of grid and group are described in the Introduction in M. Douglas (ed.), *Essays in the Sociology of Perception*, Routledge and Kegan Paul, London, 1982. The third dimension of power manipulation comes from the contribution of M. Thompson, 'The Problems of the Center: An Autonomous Cosmology' in ibid.
22. Gerald Mars, *Cheats at Work: An Anthropology of Workplace Crime*, Unwin Paperbacks, London, 1982.
23. See R. Nisbet, *Prejudices: A Philosophical Dictionary*, Harvard University Press, 1982, where the author argues how, because of inflation, 'Bryce's fatalism of the multitude is indeed a reality today' in America.
24. L.S. Stavrianos, *Global Rift: The Third World Comes of Age*, William Morrow, New York, 1981.
25. Arnold Toynbee, *A Study of History* (abridgement by D.C. Somervell), Oxford University Press, London, 1960, p. 246.
26. Ibid., p. 144.
27. Dara Sukoh was the eldest son of the Mughal emperor Shahjahan. He was a Sufi mystic who at least personally in the spiritual but not temporal sense succeeded in 'commingling two oceans'—Hinduism and Islam, a venture in which Kabir and other Sikh gurus achieved greater temporal success. It is this kind of a societal break with the past and a forging of a new future that needs to be probed before a stagnant order would give way.

The Seeds of Future Conflict: A Security Strategy for South Asia

PREM SHANKAR JHA

DISCUSSIONS ON South Asian regional security have nearly always been held within a particular framework of assumptions. These are, first, that the end of the Cold War has eliminated the potential for major global conflicts, of the kind that led to the two world wars, and the Cold War itself. Second, that the main sources of tension in future years will be sectarian and ethnic violence born out of the resurgence of such sentiments. Third, that since such conflicts tend to be localized, their resolution is essentially a local matter, preferably pursued bilaterally or at the regional level. And fourth, that since the older industrialized countries of the West are not embroiled in these conflicts, they are qualified to act as referees, and suggest, or even decree solutions.

Within this framework, there are often sharp differences, for instance on whether economic cooperation can pave the way for the resolution of political conflict, or whether a resolution of political differences must come first. The main purpose of this paper is to suggest that this framework of assumptions is flawed. In particular, it questions the first assumption, that the end of the Cold War has ended the potential for global conflict, and the corollary, that the industrialized nations which were front-line States in the Cold War have, by virtue of their detachment, the right to determine the international regulatory framework of the future. It is argued in this paper that far from having been erased, new seeds of future global conflict have been planted. Neither the form nor the intensity of the conflict can be predicted at this stage. Nor can it be specified whether conflict will be primarily economic, or will spill over into a military confrontation. What can safely be said, however, is that it will not be initiated by the ethnic-violence-prone nations of the Third World, or the flock of transitional, unstable regimes that have been hatched by the collapse of the Soviet Union, but by the industrialized nations of the West.

It is further argued that as a result of the current attempts to build a new, hierarchical international order, by drawing a clear and permanent line between the nuclear-weapon States and those without such weapons, and sanctioning the use of a variety of coercive economic and political instruments against countries that do not accept this division; restricting the dissemination of dual-use technology, and redefining the role of the UN, the WTO and the IMF and the World Bank, take on a very different hue, for they appear less as attempts to build a world free from conflict and more as the creation of a quasi-legal superstructure designed to legitimize and give moral sanction to actions by the industrialized nations that are designed to maintain their superiority and nip incipient economic and political challenges in the bud. It is, therefore, argued that a relevant security doctrine for the South Asian region must be shaped within this altered framework of assumptions.

This view is, admittedly, completely at odds with the prevailing belief in the industrialized world that the new international political and economic order now being built will greatly increase the well-being of all nations. In seeking to create it, therefore, the industrialized nations are acting, if not altruistically, then out of a rare convergence of their own with the larger interests of the world community. It is this assumption of a convergence of interests that is questioned below.

The threat of global, as distinct from regional or local conflicts, is imbedded in a truism: for any international order to be stable, it must be underpinned by power. In earlier eras, power usually meant military power alone, but today, with the growing economic integration of the world, military power is hollow if it is not founded on economic power. The unspoken premise beneath the present efforts by the West to construct a new international order is that the present distribution of economic power, which is skewed heavily in its favour, is stable. As is shown below, this assumption is questionable and will become more so with the passage of time. The potential for conflict lies in the fact that the West, and particularly the United States, enjoys an unquestionable military supremacy, whereas its economic power is in relative, if not absolute decline.

Economic power has been shifting to East and South-East Asia, first to Japan and now to the other countries of the region. If the present trend continues, it is inevitable that the dominance of the West will be challenged. The institutionalization of the West's dominance which is now under way, will impart a rigidity to the international order that will make the resolution of the conflict through an adjustment of political power to economic reality more, and not less difficult. This will further heighten the chances of global conflict.

THE ECONOMIC ROOTS OF CONFLICT

Ironically, the seeds of future global conflict lie buried in precisely that very development that led to the emergence of a global marketplace, the collapse of the Soviet Union and end of the Cold War. This was the emergence, not long after World War II, of technology as the driving force behind social and economic change. Technology has unified markets, through revolutions in information gathering and dissemination, brought transport costs down to a fraction of what they were in the 1950s, and thereby created a global market. Technology has also given countries the means to exploit that market. But since technology only thrives under conditions of fierce competition, it has also rung the death-knell of economies that chose to shun competition. These were, notably, the centrally planned economies of the socialist countries.

Just as competition has promoted the growth of technology, technology has fostered the growth of competition. Today barriers to the movement of goods and services have all but disappeared. For the average company in an industrialized country, there are now literally no safe heavens, no protected markets. To survive and prosper, it can harness newer and newer cost-cutting technologies. Alternatively it can develop new products that meet consumer needs a shade better than the existing ones, and enjoy a temporary monopoly of their sales. But the third and easiest option is to exploit the huge and ever widening differences in real wage rates, between the industrialized and the developing countries. These differences exist and are growing larger because international labour market, in sharp contrast to the market for goods and services, and for capital, remains virtually frozen in the age of mercantilism. Not only is its movement severely constrained by consular prohibitions against immigration backed by deeply rooted cultural sanctions, but these barriers are being raised higher and higher all the time. The decline of the West, and now the levelling off of growth in Japan, can be traced to this sole remaining anomaly. It cannot be reversed if this anomaly is not removed.

To harness cheap labour, capital is moving to the countries where this cheap labour is located.[1] When it does so, jobs are created in the country where the capital and enterprise originated. When the export of capital involves the transfer of entire production lines to the low-wage country, jobs are actually lost, which have to be regained in other sectors of the economy. This pits a large section of the population of the capital-generating country against the people of the capital-receiving country.

The highly industrialized countries are losing their competitive edge not because the rate of technological change has slowed down, but for three other reasons: First, global companies already very well established in the newly industrialized countries are deploying new technology in them almost as quickly as in the industrialized countries. Secondly, throughout the 1970s and 1980s, the USA, which is the main generator of new technology, devoted a disproportionately high proportion to military applications, while its competitors busied themselves in applying the same technology to commercial production. Last and perhaps most important, while the NICs have been experiencing quantum jumps in productivity in manufacturing industry, the United States and to a lesser extent Western Europe and Japan have been experiencing their largest growth in productivity in the service industries such as banking, insurance, telecommunications, finance and secretarial services. These advances in productivity are far harder to turn into export earnings than productivity increases in the manufacturing sector.

There is abundant evidence to support the above hypothesis: For fifteen years the OECD countries have been happy to achieve growth rates of 2 to 3 per cent in good years and to avoid declines in GDP in bad ones. By contrast, the growth rates of East and South-East Asia have ranged from over 3 to 4 per cent in Japan to between 7 and 10 per cent in Singapore, Hong Kong, South Korea, Taiwan, Indonesia, Malaysia, China and, most recently, Vietnam. With India about to set sail on a sustained 6 per cent-plus growth rate, most of South Asia too is likely to enjoy about 6 per cent growth rate. That will mean that more than three out of the world's five billion people will soon be enjoying a growth rate that is between two and three times that of the OECD countries.

A comparison of unemployment rates between the East Asian NICs and the older members of the OECD tells its own story. It was 1.9 per cent in Hong Kong in 1994,[2] and 2 per cent in South Korea in the first quarter of 1995. By contrast it was over 12 per cent for France, almost 8 per cent for Germany, and overall around 9 per cent for other OECD countries. The average unemployment rate for the European members of the OECD is well over 10 per cent, and has been at a similar high level throughout most of the 1980s and 1990s.

The engine that is driving the furious growth in Asia is the vast and still widening differentials in wage rates between the highly industrialized and the newly industrialized countries. In 1992, the German worker earned $24 an hour, the American about $19, and the British, around $14. By contrast the Vietnamese skilled worker today earns just over $100 a month, the Indian about $150. It is hardly surprising that the 1990s, in particular, have seen a disproportionate rise in private capital flows to developing countries, at a time when the overall investment by private foreign companies in developed and developing countries has risen only slowly, and declined in 1991 and 1992.[3]

A close look at the figures for foreign direct investment in developing countries also reveals a strong correlation between recession in the industrialized countries and higher capital inflows into the developing ones. Thus between 1980 and 1985, when the world went through a sharp recession (1979-84) 26 per cent of the capital flows went to the developing countries. Between 1985 and 1990, when there was mild prosperity in the developed nations, their share went down to 17 per cent. In 1991 when recession returned, it shot up to 24 per cent, in 1992 to 32 per cent and in 1993 to 41 per cent.[4] In all these years, FDI inflows into the developed countries fell in absolute terms. With the exceptions of South Korea and India, which have developed their own entrepreneurial classes, the catalytic role in the frenetic East Asian growth has been, and continues to be, played by foreign capital from the very countries that are now in relative economic decline.

In sharp contrast, the way in which an overvalued exchange rate has bled jobs away to the newly industrialized countries is revealed by the statistics for the size of the labour force in manufacturing industry. In Britain this fell from 7.5 million in 1971 to 4.5 million in 1991. The fall is equally sharp in the midwestern and eastern states of the USA. None of this is the 'fault' of the West. Nor is it ascribable to the laziness of its working class or the superior discipline and diligence of the East Asians (or any of the other reasons as are often given in popular literature). On the contrary, what is clearly visible is a kind of parabolic prosperity curve, in which earlier developments lay the groundwork, inexorably for those that follow. Every industrialized country is at some point on this curve, and the so-called East Asian Tigers are no exception.

The curve goes somewhat as follows: in their initial stages of the application of new technology to production, there are quantum leaps in productivity and an immense growth in GDP exports, and foreign exchange reserves. This leads to rapid increases in the real wage rate, especially of industrial workers. As technological progress slows down, inter-firm and inter-country competition forces capital to start looking for cheap labour bases of production to keep down costs. This is found in countries that are at an earlier stage of industrialization, and the outflow of capital and the diversion of job creation to other countries begins. The way to check this is to bring down labour costs, but this has in practice proved impossible because trade unions will not even consider it. The only other way—bringing down the rate of exchange—is impeded by the attractiveness of the currency and the country's high foreign exchange reserves, which are themselves hangovers from the earlier epoch of prosperity.

Since the UK was the first industrialized country, it went through this cycle first. But after World War II, the United States was the first to experience this, followed by Western Europe and Japan. This pattern is reflected in the changing pattern, over time, of the origins of transnational investment. In 1968-9 almost 60 per cent of the 7,000 transnational corporations (TNCs) from fourteen developed countries came from the UK and USA. In 1990-1, the UK had slipped to seventh place, and other than the USA, the three other countries that accounted for 49 per cent of the 24,000 companies were Germany, Japan and Switzerland.[5] In Western Europe, Germany remained on the upward part of the cycle the longest, and only began to slide down and export jobs in a serious way in the last four or five years. The end of the 1980s saw a sharp rise in Japanese foreign investment in search of competitive advantage. Initially much of this went to Europe and the USA. Today a much larger portion of a smaller total volume of foreign investment is going to developing countries, mostly in East and South-East Asia. Even South Korean capital has begun to look for cheap labour abroad. With the steady rise of investment by larger Korean companies in Vietnam, and more recently in India and other countries of South Asia, there is a brisk debate going on in the country over the advisability of letting in more guest workers to rein in galloping wage rates. The problem, however, is most acute in Europe and the USA, because the loss of industrial jobs to the NICs is coinciding with the loss of millions of service sector jobs to computers and other advancements in technology.

Unlike the past, the present phase of unemployment does not seem to be cyclical but stable. It has affected only certain types of people—mainly those who do not have a high degree of technical ability or education and who, in the past, found a secure niche in agriculture and unskilled or semi-skilled industrial labour. It is also putting a premium on having a young work force, for the young are able to adapt more easily to the integration of computers into the production process than the older generation of factory and office workers. As a result, a large segment of society now feels that it has become a victim of changes over which it had no control, and which government and the ruling class did nothing to protect it from.

This is generating new social tensions in the industrialized countries, and a search for scapegoats among those hurt by the change. Racism, religious antagonism, and a new belligerent nationalism are all raising their heads. The immediate, knee-jerk response to the growing unemployment by the governments concerned has been to tighten immigration laws, to modify laws like those that govern the grant of asylum, and to curb illegal immigration by making it more difficult for people from Third World countries to get visas. These laws have so far had only a limited effect on the flow of migrants, but even if they were to succeed they would only worsen the disease. For their purpose is to prop up the real wage rate, and this can only accelerate the outflow of capital.

THE EVIDENCE

Had this decline been temporary it would not have caused political repercussions. But because it is structural and has been unfolding over a decade and a half, more and more people have begun to perceive that there is no light at the end of the tunnel and are resorting to political action to change their lot in life. The result is a recrudescence of the far right. The French experience is a good barometer of this phenomenon. In the 1970s, Le Pen, the leader of the National Front, obtained less than one per cent of the vote in a presidential election. In the 1991 elections to the National Assembly, his party gained 11 per cent of the vote. In the first round of the 1995 presidential election Le Pen got 15 per cent of the vote. Various surveys in western Germany in the early 1990s confirmed that 13 to 14 per cent of the population would vote for a party to the right of the Christian Democratic Party. Italy's elections in 1994 showed a similar far right vote. The rise of the so-called Christian Right, which swept the Republicans to power in the US Congress and Senate in November 1994, is fully in line with this vast transnational political shift. It is significant that both in the US elections in 1994, and the French in 1995 the unemployed tended to vote for the far right.

The political and economic demands of the new right are not only frightening in themselves but doubly so because they will worsen the disease they are supposed to cure. Domestically, the far right would like to terminate all health, housing, special education and other affirmative action programmes that were designed in the 1960s, during the era of the productivity surge, to help disadvantaged minorities join the mainstream and add to the supply of skilled labour and management. Since it considers itself to be severely disadvantaged, its hatred of others who are receiving special favours while it is being driven to the wall, is understandable. That these very minorities are the first to have lost their jobs because of the forces that now threaten the lower reaches of the national core seems to have escaped notice. Since these disadvantaged minorities are identified, more often than not, in ethnic terms, this defensive anger has spilled over into overt racism. The attacks on Rumanians, Turks, and gypsies in Germany and Austria; on Algerian and other Arabs in France, on illegal Mexican immigrants who have on occasion been hunted down and killed by vigilantes in the USA, are all outliers of what could become a storm of racial hatred.

Closely allied to this trend is the reduction of quotas for immigration, the adoption of more elaborate methods of scrutiny to detect and foil illegal immigrants, and the simplification of procedures for their deportation. It can now take an East European, or an Arab up to twenty-one days to be granted (or refused) a visa for the EEC countries, and the Republican Congress has introduced a bill in the House that is likely to go through without any opposition which will cut immigration into the USA by a third.

All these measures are self-defeating because their ultimate effect can only be to restrict the supply of labour and reduce the pressure for the dismantling of the high-wage economy. So long as this does not happen, the drain of capital to low-wage, newly industrialized countries with skilled and disciplined work forces will continue, and the deindustrialization of the West will not be halted.

The international counterpart of these policies is a relentless strengthening of protectionist pressures in the weakening industrial States, and a gradual rise in economic confrontation. Protectionism has taken the form of an ever-widening variety of non-tariff barriers, such as widening distributors' margins; ever more stringent quality and safety standards for imports, and the demand for environmentally safe packaging. Well-intentioned campaigns such as those against child labour and for dolphin-free tuna have been hijacked to serve a false god. Most recently, a demand has been raised for the levy of penal duties against the products of 'dirty' factories and labour forces that do not receive enough pay to enjoy a minimum quality of life.

The other side of protectionism is increasingly strident demands that this country or that should open up its domestic market to exports from this or that country. The stand-offs between the United States and Japan on automobile parts and food items are only a few examples of the increased resort to strong-arm methods. These were preceded by the widespread use of Super and Special 301 against so-called delinquent States by the United States. The Uruguay Round of GATT legitimized the use of such strong-arm methods against specific countries even within the multilateral trading system by allowing the principle of cross retaliation.

The irrational has not yet surfaced in international relations, but the day when it might begin to do so does not appear to be far away. The demonization of Islam, the growing tendency to treat China as the next colossus whose wings should be clipped now before it becomes a real threat to Western dominance, and the so-called clash of civilizations in which the Confucian and Islamic worlds are destined to join forces against the European, have progressed far beyond the realm of scholarly debate, and are beginning to permeate fiction on the one hand, and policy debate on the other. The European Union envisages absorbing the Baltic States, Poland, Hungary and the Czech Republic, but intends to leave out Turkey, a member of NATO. The US administration has already allowed itself to be pushed by popular demand into sowing the seeds of a two-China policy that could lead to Taiwan's independence, or to a war between it and mainland China. Either would suitthe purpose of the rising irrationality in the West equally well.

The gut-deep awareness of a loss of power is not affecting popular sentiments and reactions alone. It is equally apparent in the carefully planned moves of the governments of the highly industrialized countries to create a post-Cold War world order that will buttress their dominance and legitimize the use of coercion to perpetuate it. This may not be the avowed aim. But it would be the inevitable and not unwelcome result.

One has only to look at the way in which the existing multilateral institutions are being quietly reshaped to see how, brick by brick, such a blatantly inequitable international order is being built. The most obvious changes are taking place in the role and conception of the United Nations. In July 1995, the Halifax declaration of the heads of the G-7 industrialized countries made it unambiguously clear that these countries would like to see an end to the UN's economic functions, and to confine the organization mainly to humanitarian operations, dispute resolution and peacekeeping.[6] This was also the refrain of the Western Heads of State at the fiftieth anniversary celebrations of the United Nations.

Just how much the peacekeeping role has been expanded, may be judged from the fact that in its first seven years the UN undertook only two peacekeeping operations. In the seven years after 1988 it has undertaken twenty-two. But in the process the very concept of peacekeeping has been altered beyond recognition. It is worth remembering that the term peacekeeping is not even mentioned in the UN Charter. This role developed gradually, and with the exception of the Congo operation in the early 1960s, was carried out under Chapter 6 of the UN Charter, with the consent of both the belligerent governments or factions concerned. Then came the Gulf War, followed swiftly by Somalia, where the UN tried to impose a peace of the Security Council's liking on the contenders. The complete failure of the second intervention, followed by the UN's demonstrated impotence in Bosnia, have not slaked the thirst that was created by the swift and painless success of operation Desert Storm, among Western liberals and the media for a more active peacekeeping role for the UN. On the contrary, the pull-out from Somalia did more to discredit the Clinton administration in the eyes of the American establishment, than any other action it took in its first two years in office. The UN itself has been under relentless criticism for not taking overt military action against the Serbs in Bosnia.

For better or for worse, therefore, the concept of peacekeeping has changed once and for all. There is a now a far greater willingness among members of the Security Council to use it as an instrument of coercion against nation-states. This is particularly true of the use of economic sanctions. Indeed, the use of this weapon is tempered not so much by concern for the infringement of the sovereignty of nation-states that it involves, but doubts about its effectiveness, and impatience over its slowness and uncertainty. As for the use of force, after the Gulf War the issue is no longer whether the UN should impose peace through war, i.e. stray from Chapter 6 of the Charter into Chapter 7, but how severe the threat must be for the members of the Security Council to decide that this is worth doing.

Today an elaborate international institutional structure is also being set up to enable the present generation of highly industrialized nations to put pressure on others in a variety of economic matters. The chosen instruments for this are the IMF and the World Bank, and the recently established World Trade Organization. In the first two, control by the dominant Western industrial nations is assured by the fact that voting is proportional to the contributions made by a country to the funds of the organization, with the United States holding on to a 25 per cent share, and thereby its veto power on all decision-making in both organizations. Throughout the 1980s, the IMF and the World Bank increasingly made their lending policies conditional to changes in the recipient government's overall economic policies. More recently they have made a small beginning in attaching political riders, such as on human rights and adherence to environmental standards, to their loans. The principal new feature of the WTO, developed during the Uruguay Round GATT negotiations which set it up, is that it allows member States to indulge in cross retaliation for what they perceive to be infringements of fair trade practices. The purpose of drawing attention to these changes is not to suggest that the IMF, the World Bank or the WTO are misusing their powers, but to highlight the systematic manner in which the industrialized West has sought to gain control of the levers of economic power. In a world where the real economic power of these nations is diminishing, there is no guarantee that these institutions will always be wisely or equitably used.

One can argue that the globalization of political and economic concerns has made it necessary to move towards the creation of a global system of government. The real question, however, is not whether we need such a system, but whether it will be democratic, oligarchic or dictatorial. In their preoccupation with preventing it from becoming a dictatorial system controlled by the USA (a unipolar world), most people and governments have failed to notice that a democratic system has been quietly but decisively rejected in favour of an oligarchy. The oligarchies are the five veto-holding members of the Security Council. These five have so far rejected all suggestions for the democratization and expansion of the Security Council on the basis of some commonly accepted criteria formulated by the UN itself. Instead the UN set up a working group to study this question. To no one's surprise, the group suggested the expansion of the Council simply to include Germany and Japan as permanent members. Thus if the oligarchies have their way the Security Council is likely to have seven permanent members, of whom five will be members of the G-7.

Three of these seven members will be from the European Union. The USA, which has as large a population and GNP as the whole of the EU, has only one vote, but significantly, it is willing to go along with this blatant inequity. It has neither suggested that the European Union retain only one, or at most two seats, nor that the seats so released should be filled by one or more of the increasingly powerful newly emergent industrial countries of Asia or Latin America. Clearly, there is something else that the United States has in common with the EU that makes it unnecessary for it to demand parity with it in the Security Council. That 'something' is its perception that the institutions they are building will work for their common good.

To enforce their writ the highly industrialized countries need to back the quasi-legal sanction of UN institutions with an effective threat of coercion. That need is being realized at the conventional level by inducting German and Japanese troops into UN peacekeeping operations, and at the nuclear level by the nuclear five's recently cemented permanent monopoly of nuclear weapons. By no coincidence the only five countries allowed a nuclear-weapon capacity in perpetuity by the Nuclear Non-Proliferation Treaty signed in New York in June 1995, are the permanent members of the Security Council. Among them the only country that does not belong to the Western club is one whose rise was not foreseen when the Charter of the United Nations was framed in 1945. In hearings at the International Court of Justice and elsewhere, the Western members of the nuclear club have refused to consider committing themselves to a no-first-use doctrine, and have refused to forswear the use of nuclear weapons even against non-nuclear powers. Such is the confusion in the chancelleries of the newly industrialized countries, that none among them has realized that in their quest for nuclear peace they have ceded the unrestricted right to indulge in nuclear blackmail to the permanent members of the Security Council. This point was brought home to them by China, which exploded a bomb the day after the NPT was signed and France, which announced a new series of nuclear tests only weeks later. Subsequently, in hearings before the International Court of Justice, four out of the five nuclear powers have refused to renounce the right of first use of nuclear weapons. The same four have also refused to renounce the right to use nuclear weapons against non-nuclear powers. The lone exception is China.

A SECURITY STRATEGY FOR SOUTH ASIA

If conflict is inevitable because no industrialized country can even contemplate opening up its home market to foreign labour, and cannot, therefore, prevent the resulting flight of capital to the low-wage countries, then what form will the conflict take? And what should South

Asia's strategic aims be? The answer emerges from the following perception: Among countries that are fully engaged with each other in global trade and financial flows, the likelihood of the conflict overflowing the realm of the economic into the military is small. But in dealing with countries that are marginally involved in the global economic system, the West will not hesitate to use military force. Two examples stare us in the face: Iraq was attacked militarily when it sought to take over Kuwait. China on the other hand has not been touched despite heavy pressure on the United States and other G-7 governments and by non-governmental and human rights organizations to apply sanctions on it. The difference is not solely because of their respective sizes. China is far more strongly integrated into the global system of exchange described above than Iraq, whose main linkage is as one, but not the only, supplier of a crucially important raw material. Outside that Iraq has followed autocratic economic policies for decades.

This prescription does not depend for its validity on just two recent examples. A global market; i.e. an area of the world containing many countries among whom trade and capital movements are free, is not entirely a post-World War II phenomenon. It existed for most of the nineteenth century and before World War I, primarily between the countries of North and South America and Europe. Just how strongly the international market economy protected its members from war can be judged from the fact that while the nineteenth century saw an unprecedented amount of violence perpetrated against countries outside this charmed circle, in various colonial wars, and an equally single-minded suppression of ethnic insurgencies within even the countries inside the charmed circle, the seven major powers of the epoch were at war among themselves for a total of only eighteen months during the entire century from 1815 to 1914. How sharp a change this was from earlier centuries, may be judged from the fact that in the previous two centuries they indulged in as many as sixty to seventy wars per century among themselves.

The reason, as Karl Polanyi pointed out, was the restraining influence of international engagement, mediated by Haute Finance.[7] Today the degree of economic interlinkage between nations is profoundly greater than it was in 1941 (After the disruption caused by the two wars and the Great Depression, the trade-to-GDP ratio of 1914 was attained once more, as far back as in 1980). Thus the potential for preventing military conflict through international engagement is also correspondingly greater.

The most important step that South Asia must take, therefore, is to open its economies to transnational investment by large global companies. The more tightly South Asia is linked with the global system of exchange the larger will be the number of companies all over the world, and the number of shareholders in these companies who will be adversely affected if, for instance, economic sanctions are applied to one or all the countries of the region. The prescription to open up the economy and 'go global' is not new. It is being followed with varying degrees of enthusiasm by all the South Asian countries. But the rationale given for it has so far been purely economic. It is the contention of this paper that the political rationale is every bit as strong as the economic.

South Asian countries can simultaneously increase their attractiveness to foreign investors and their bargaining power with them, if they also open up their own markets to each other. The recent formation of the SAARC Preferential Trading Arrangement (SAPTA) is a welcome step in this direction, but only a small one. The lead in further unification of markets should be taken by India, which can afford by virtue of its size and industrial depth, to extend non-reciprocal tariff concessions to its neighbours, for a mutually agreed period of transition.

Security strategies for South Asia need, therefore, to be formulated at not one but two levels simultaneously. The first is the promotion of regional peace through economic integration. The second is the adoption of political and economic strategies that strengthen the region's bargaining power in its relations with the industrialized countries. Needless to say, success in the first will make the second palpably easier to achieve.

NOTES

1. The following quotations from the United Nations, *World Investment Report 1993* sum up the reasons why private investors are moving to developing (and some relatively lower wage developed) countries. 'As trade barriers fall, as communications technologies improve, and as international competition intensifies, firms are turning to outsourcing for parts of their value-adding operations' (p. 4). According to a widely accepted theory, TNCs go to a particular economy, because of its locational advantages. 'The main locational advantages include market size and growth, availability of skilled (low cost) labour, natural resources, infrastructure, a favourable policy environment, and proximity and access to other larger markets' (p. 173). 'One factor facilitating the development of an integrated system is the emergence of a global labour force' (p. 174). United Nations, *World Investment Report 1993: Transnational Corporations and Integrated International Production*, UN, New York, 1993, Doc. No. ST/CTC/156.

2. Official statistics of the Government of Hong Kong, as reported in the *South China Morning Post*, 1 June 1995.
3. UN, *World Investment Report 1993*, p. 13. See also, B.S.G. Scott Vaughan, *Private International Finance and Environment* (a UNEP summary paper, May 1995). The paper points out that private capital flows to developing economies and economies in transition increased fourfold between 1989 and 1994 from around $43 billion to $170 billion.
4. See UN, *World Investment Report 1993*, Table 1.4, p. 16; and UN, *World Investment Report 1994*, Table 1.4, p. 14.
5. UN, *World Investment Report 1994*, pp. 126-7.
6. An article by Nancy Landon Kassenbaum, Republican Senator from Kansas and a member of the Senate Foreign Relations Committee, and Lee Hamilton, Democratic member of the House of Representatives, and seniormost minority member of the House International Relations Committee, published in the *Washington Post*, 26 June 1995, suggests that the United States should withhold funds from all but three of the United Nations' seventy specialized agencies, the IAEA, the UNHCR and the WHO. Clearly most of the others are 'Third World agencies' whose only purpose is to put pressure for international cooperative action on donor nations like the United States, for worthy causes, or to act as a free think-tank on issues like trade, social standards and environmental legislation, which are rapidly becoming the new standards under which rich-country protectionism is being reborn.
7. K. Polanyi, *The Great Transformation*, Beacon Books, Beacon Press, Beacon Hill, Boston, 1957, ch. 1.

Political Economy of Trade Liberalization: Experiences of India-Bangladesh Trade Relations

ABDUR ROB KHAN

WHILE THE regional economic trend in South Asia in recent years has been characterized by deregulation of industry and liberalization of trade, the trend has not been consistent. The pattern of intra-regional economic relations is a replica of what is happening at the global level. An incipient globalization of the world economy with integration of the economies and concomitant tendency of lowering the national borders coexists with intense economic nationalism and regional trading blocs behind protectionist barriers. Intra-industry *collaboration* for sharing the benefits of technological developments coexists with fierce *competition* for market shares.[1] In other words, the contradictory tools of liberalization and protectionism are simultaneously used to gain access and market share for the final product on the one hand, and to protect and expand the domestic production base on the other. The contradictory tools and policy goals have their political resonance because not only some degree of political sovereignty is involved in these policy options, but also different interest groups within and across the political boundaries are affected differently. The dialectics of these economic and political processes with varying degrees of security implications constitute the political economy of trade liberalization.

A number of factors need to be taken into account to put discussion on the political economy of trade liberalization in South Asia in perspective. First, trade liberalization came mostly as a part of national programme in the form of a package of World Bank and IMF-sponsored structural adjustment policy, rather than as conscious efforts towards regional or bilateral cooperation. One characteristic of externally induced structural adjustment and trade liberalization programme is its orientation more toward macro-economic considerations rather than

The author is grateful to Prem Shankar Jha, for his valuable comments on an earlier draft.

expansion of mutually advantageous trade relations; another is the role of the multinational corporations (MNCs) which are taking the lead in the globalization programme. This, however, places the host countries in an interesting contradiction. The MNCs target the domestic markets primarily, and the markets in the neighbouring economies secondarily. For both they need a protected market and hence, support a tariff regime. Thus, taking advantage of trade liberalization and investment opportunities, the MNCs create a base and then advocate or at least prefer a protected market in the host country but easy access and hence, less trade barriers in the target economies. Moreover, it is in the nature of the MNCs to develop a product in one country, acquire finance from one source, set up production plant in another country and export to yet another country. In the process, they control the production and marketing process in a manner that the developing countries where the MNCs operate are not adequately benefited from the market liberalization process.[2]

Secondly, in the regional and inter-regional context, the benefits of trade liberalization are inequitably distributed. It is argued:

> While the restructuring of the regional economies on the basis of their dynamic comparative advantages is yet to take place, given the present imbalances in the economic structures, the market forces are likely to aggravate the resource flow deficits for the smaller countries. . . . Under the circumstances a policy of *laissez faire* is likely to be largely beneficial to India who can afford to take an essentially passive attitude towards regional cooperation by placing faith in the efficacy of the market mechanism to promote the growth of regional economic cooperation. In response, the potential and perceived apprehensions in the smaller South Asian economies of being dominated by a powerful Indian bourgeoisie will lead to a variety of artificial barriers to trade and investment, which will interfere with the free play of market forces.[3]

Thus, one is confronted with a paradoxical situation: at least in the short and medium terms, dependence on unhindered market forces and externally induced trade liberalization programme will lead to inequitable distribution of benefits in a manner that may witness a backlash of protectionism. Despite neoclassical wisdom suggesting otherwise, the question remains whether in the long run, efficient flow of resources will lead to maximization of national as well as regional objective functions.

Thirdly and relatedly, there are caveats to the operation of the market forces themselves. In most cases, market forces in matters of trade liberalization are allowed to operate only partially. The domestic market is protected and export is subsidized. A study sponsored by the Ministry of Commerce in Dhaka suggests that ceramic glass, bicycle, medicine, electrical ware, and textiles are being subsidized by such countries as India, China, Japan and Australia, and are exported to Bangladesh causing distorted and unfair competition.[4]

Finally, while trade liberalization under circumstances as depicted above creates its own dynamics of generating apprehensions and misgivings spilling over to the political arena, political interactions themselves inseparably tend to link up with the economic interactions. An analysis of the dialectics of these tensions and frictions in the economic and political arena—the former being the outcome of economic forces and the latter, State process—is the subject matter of this paper. The analysis will be carried out in the specific context of India-Bangladesh trade relations.

One may argue that the analysis smacks of the traditional State-centric notion of security and bilateral politics in an era where new conceptions of security—much broader and fundamental—are occupying the centre-stage of security discussions. But given the lack of regional content of trade liberalization, on the one hand, and absence of any substantive textural change in South Asian politics in the wake of the global changes on the other, the middle range objective of the paper is considered to be realistic. At another level, the argument goes that the issues to be discussed are matters of hard-core economics and there is little that a political approach may achieve. But that until trade liberalization comes as a part of structured bilateral and regional cooperation process, it is argued, a political approach will release the right kind of political signals for economic interactions. Table 1 presents figures for intra-regional SAARC trade in comparison with its total trade.

TRADE LIBERALIZATION PROGRAMME IN BANGLADESH

Bangladesh has been following the market liberalization approach since the early 1980s. The impetus, however, came from the donors. Bangladesh agreed to reduce the list of controlled items of import from 193 to only 139 to meet one of the conditions of the Industrial Sectoral Adjustment Credit-2 (ISAC-2) of the World Bank under which Bangladesh was provided with a credit of $105 million.[5] Subsequently, the list was further reduced to 112 and finally to 39 in June 1994 as contained

TABLE 1. INTRA-REGIONAL TRADE IN RELATION TO TOTAL TRADE OF SAARC COUNTRIES (US$ mn)

Country/Year	*Intra-Export*	*Total Export*	*% of Total Export*	*Intra-Import*	*Total Import*	*% of Total Import*	*Intra-Trade*	*Total Trade*	*% of Total Trade*
Bangladesh									
1986	54	889	6.1	91	2550	3.6	145	3439	4.2
1992	46	2040	2.2	378	3731	10.1	424	5772	7.3
India									
1986	277	9135	3.0	78	15051	0.5	350	24186	1.4
1992	587	20683	2.8	188	23638	0.8	779	44321	1.7
Maldives									
1986	5	25	18.8	9	78	11.0	14	103	13.6
1992	11	77	14.8	14	179	8.0	25	256	9.8
Nepal									
1986	51	134	38.2	102	314	32.2	153	448	34.1
1992	23	332	6.9	95	499	19.1	118	831	14.2
Pakistan									
1986	109	3383	3.2	95	5367	1.8	204	8750	2.3
1992	359	7267	4.9	139	9375	1.5	498	16642	3.0
Sri Lanka									
1986	58	1163	5.0	144	1829	7.9	202	2992	6.7
1992	47	2570	1.8	329	3661	9.0	376	6231	6.0
Total South Asia									
1986	554	14729	3.8	514	25189	2.0	1068	39918	2.7
1992	1073	32969	3.2	1143	41084	2.8	2220	74053	3.0
Annual growth rate of SAARC trade:									
1986-92 (%)	11.6	14.4	—	14.2	8.5	—	13	10.8	—

Source: IMF, *Direction of Trade Statistics Yearbook, 1993.*

in the Import Policy Order of 1993-5.[6] The World Bank prescribes free trade strategy in compliance with the principles of the General Agreement on Tariffs and Trade (GATT).

The agenda for trade liberalization moved forward in three phases—1981-6, 1987-91 and the third phase since 1992. The first phase, which coincided with the initiation of the New Industrial Policy of 1981 envisaged export diversification and import liberalization.[7] Tariffs were reduced, tariff structure was simplified and the import process was deregulated. A short 'negative' list of import replaced the previous big positive list specifying the items to be imported without prior government sanctions. In the second phase, the export sector was further invigorated through a newer range of incentives and import liberalization. The number of negative import list was further reduced, a process which was accelerated in the third phase. In this phase, thc government undertook concrete measures to open the economy by fostering trade liberalization, inducing industrial deregulation, expanding the private sector and inviting foreign investment in Bangladesh.

The process of liberalization of trade regime advanced significantly during 1993-4 through rationalization of the tariff structure and reduction of tariff and non-tariff barriers. By 1994, the share of free import items rose to 94 per cent of all HS-8 line items and only 4 per cent remained banned.[8] Apparently the pace of liberalization in the import of intermediate and capital goods moved faster than for consumer goods. For example, the share of intermediate and capital goods in items for import of which no government permission was needed rose to 97 per cent and 93 per cent in 1994 compared to 76 per cent and 73 per cent respectively in 1987. The share of consumer goods freely importable rose from 43 per cent to 80 per cent during this period. Non-tariff barriers and procedural complications have, however, been so high that import of consumer goods faced less effective tariff rates than the intermediate and capital goods. In the process, the economy has been opened to reap the benefits of free trade without considering the competitive strength of the local producers.[9] Consequently, the local manufacturing sector has been badly hit and the country has been flooded with foreign goods even where there is no dearth of local production capability.

TREND IN INDIA-BANGLADESH TRADE

A chronic feature of Bangladesh-India economic relations is unremitting growth of huge trade imbalance against Bangladesh. Trade deficit began to pile up right from the beginning of bilateral trade relations. Thus, during 1972-6, exports to India were only 12.45 per cent of Bangladesh's imports from India. A sharp upsurge occurred since the early 1990s with the liberalization programme. During 1991-3, total exports to India were $43 million and imports $753.85 million. In 1994 alone, imports from India were estimated to be $500 million compared to an estimated export of $20 million, according to trading sources.[10] During the five-year period 1988-9 to 1992-3, India's total exports rose by 164 per cent while its exports to Bangladesh rose by 293 per cent. The account presented here does not include Indian earnings from invisible sources of about $400-500 million annually on account of medical treatment, education and tourism originating from Bangladesh. The volume of informal merchandise trade—smuggling—is about $1.5 billion, which also is characterized by the same imbalance as official trade.

Bangladesh's share of exports in Bangladesh-India trade during 1980-92 has never been more than 32 per cent, and in 1991-2 it went down alarmingly to a mere 1.45 per cent.[11] Also, while imports from India have been relatively stable, exports have been quite erratic both in volume and composition.[12] Again, Bangladesh's trade balance with India, which until 1987 was only 5 per cent of Bangladesh's global trade balance, has in recent years gone up to 16 per cent (see Table 2).[13]

India mainly imports fertilizer, newsprint, raw jute, video cassette, hilsa fish and jamdani sarees from Bangladesh and exports to it raw cotton, dyes, chemicals, spare parts, machines, fabrics, tyres, tubes, cement and leather. The bulk of Bangladesh's imports consist of cotton yarn and fabrics, which accounted for 47 per cent of Bangladesh's

TABLE 2. BANGLADESH'S TRADE WITH INDIA 1980-94 (US$mn)

Year	*Export*	*Growth Rate*	*Import*	*Growth Rate*	*Trade Balance*	*Bangladesh-India Trade Balance*		
						Growth Rate	*As % of S. Asia*	*As % of World*
1980	8.0	—	55.6	—	-47.6	—	170.7	2.61
1981	20.2	152.5	64.0	15.11	-43.8	-7.98	73.8	2.35
1982	20.3	0.5	43.3	-32.34	-23.0	-47.49	247.3	1.39
1983	6.9	-66.01	37.9	-12.47	-31.0	34.78	—	1.97
1984	28.3	310.14	60.1	58.58	-31.8	2.58	—	1.8
1985	29.6	4.59	64.9	7.99	35.3	11.01	323.8	2.31
1986	7.7	-73.99	54.2	-16.49	-46.5	31.73	125.0	2.12
1987	11.0	42.86	74.4	37.27	-63.4	36.34	87.3	2.88
1988	8.7	-20.91	90.0	20.97	-81.3	28.23	84.8	4.63
1989	10.7	22.99	120.7	120.7	-110.0	35.3	99.8	4.69
1990	21.7	102.8	170.3	41.09	-148.6	35.09	78.6	7.71
1991	22.8	5.07	189.5	11.27	-166.7	12.18	96.6	9.73
1992	4.2	-81.58	283.9	49.82	-279.7	67.79	84.2	15.63
1993	13.0	209.52	380.0	33.85	-367.0	31.21	—	—
1994	17.9	37.69	429.9	13.13	-412.0	12.26	—	—

Source: IMF, *International Financial Statistics*, various issues; IMF, *Direction of Trade Statistics*, various issues.

imports in 1992-3,[14] followed by engineering goods, chemicals and allied products, coal and fruits and vegetables.[15]

The issues in Bangladesh-India relations are outlined below from the perspectives of the two countries. An attempt will be made to find a meeting ground, if any.

ISSUES IN INDIA-BANGLADESH TRADE RELATIONS: BANGLADESH PERSPECTIVE

Colossal Imbalance. Bangladesh's main concern is the sky-rocketing annual trade imbalance which should be reduced by twofold policy measures by New Delhi: importing more commodities from Bangladesh, and reducing tariff restrictions on Bangladeshi products. On average, there exist about 80-90 per cent import duties in India on consumer goods and some imports are totally banned. Bangladesh, on the other hand has a liberal tariff structure with average rate of duty only around 20 per cent. The imbalance is glaring and is seen not to be an outcome of normal trading relationship. That is why it is argued that the imbalance must be given special treatment.

Lack of Reciprocity. Trading circles in Dhaka believe that, leave alone special treatment, some reciprocity itself may ameliorate the situation a lot. Thus, measures such as granting zero tariff to selected products from Bangladesh may reduce the gap. Nepal, which has similar facilities available, does not suffer from adverse trade imbalance with India.[16] Sri Lanka was also recently granted tariff reduction facilities but Bangladesh was declined on grounds of GATT provisions.[17]

A second aspect of the lack of reciprocity is the residual treatment of Bangladesh, which is in fact a major partner of India. The Bangladesh side is reported to have told the fourth Joint Economic Committee (JEC) meeting in December 1993 that the Indian market is virtually closed to Bangladesh products either due to the existence of a negative list or high tariff or restrictions.[18] It is the expectation in Bangladesh that India and Bangladesh are natural partners in matters of trade. And partnership presupposes reciprocity.[19]

Infant Industry Argument. An important concern of the Bangladeshi traders and industrialists is that cheaper—and often inferior quality—goods from India are swamping Bangladeshi markets and destroying the domestic industry. The goods include books, electric items, consumer items, toiletries like toothpaste and engineering goods. It is estimated that Indian books worth $5-6 million enter Bangladesh markets annually, adversely affecting the publishing industry. The production cost of books in India is much less because the cost of paper production in India is almost half that in Bangladesh.[20] An industry related with the backward linkage of the publishing industry is the printing ink industry. In recent years this industry attracted some foreign investment from China, Japan and Britain. Because of higher tariff on import of raw materials but lower tariff on printing ink, the import of ink is cheaper and the foreign investors are contemplating to withdraw their investment. Another area where the infant industry argument is already evident is the production and sale of detergents in which Bangladesh was more or less self-sufficient. The industry is currently under severe threat.

Informal Trade or Smuggling. Smuggling or informal trade is accentuating the trade imbalance rather than mitigating it.[21] On the basis of a survey of India-Bangladesh trade relations sponsored by the Metropolitan Chamber of Commerce and Industry (MCCI) conducted by a senior consultant of India, it has been found that goods worth about $10 million find their way into India from Bangladesh and reach such places as Calcutta, northern West Bengal, Assam, Tripura, Meghalaya, Nagaland, Arunachal and Manipur.[22] Trading circles put the volume of informal trading between the two countries at double the official trade.[23] While informal trade is believed to be responsive to market forces, Bangladesh's complaint is that smuggling takes out valuable capital and intermediate and input type commodities, including items imported by Bangladesh itself, and it only brings in cheap consumer items and floods the market, as is the case with official merchandise trade.

Market Access. As already pointed out, Bangladesh traders argue that there are commodities which could profitably be imported by India and for the sake of reciprocity these should be allowed to get access to the Indian market. Items suggested by Bangladesh that could be sold to India if tariff were reduced are: among primary products jackfruit, pineapple, tea (for blending purposes); and among manufactured goods ceramic tableware, melamine products, electric bulbs and fluorescent tubes, garments, electric cables, soft drinks, aerated water and leather goods.[24] Items in which Bangladesh has well established comparative advantage are: newsprint, jamdani saree, jute carpet, urea, writing and printing paper, finished leather, sanitary ware, insulator and fish—all of which face high tariff in India.[25] If tariff is reduced, toiletries, terry towels and medicines could also be exported.[26]

Apart from the plea for removal of tariff and non-tariff barriers, the other suggestions Bangladesh has made concern joint ventures in Bangladesh together with buy-back arrangement. Several large joint venture projects in cement, fertilizers and sponge iron with buy-back guarantees had been discussed in the early 1970s, but none of them materialized.[27] In the meantime, a new trading environment emerged with privatization and economic liberalization. While there are joint venture schemes in garments, trucks and three-wheelers, they have no buy-back arrangements. Of late, Indian private firms have shown interest in setting up joint ventures in textiles, cement, fertilizers and newsprint with buy-back facilities. Progress, however, is extremely slow. While competitive production structure and more or less similar labour productivity could apparently be the main reason behind the lack of Indian interest, from the point of view of creating a dynamic trade regime, specially in the sub-regional context, joint venture projects have a bright future and Bangladesh puts much weight on this prospective field. In the study cited above, it has been argued that exports from Bangladesh to India are unlikely to exceed $100 million annually by the year 2000 unless Indian investors team up with Bangladeshi counterparts to set up manufacturing units in areas where Bangladesh has a clear edge over India in the availability of raw materials.[28]

To summarize, the colossal trade imbalance has political resonance and, therefore, has to be dealt with in all seriousness. While Bangladeshis would expect special treatment, they insist on reciprocity in tariff concession and no less importantly, that smuggling should be curbed. Only recently, however, India has agreed that all non-tariff restrictions on exports from Bangladesh would be withdrawn while 50 per cent tariff on 14 broad categories of items would be reduced. This was disclosed while the visiting Indian External Affairs Minister called on the Bangladesh Commerce Minister. At an informal dialogue under the auspices of the Centre for Policy Dialogue in Dhaka, the Indian Minister said this was the beginning and on some commodities from Bangladesh, there would not be any duty at all.[29] The details would be worked out at official level meetings which are in progress in New Delhi.[30] The Indian Minister also assured that Rs 100 crore worth of Indian supplier credit would be provided for promoting industrial investment in Bangladesh, which among other things, would include BMRE of Chittagong Steel Mills.[31]

ISSUES IN INDIA-BANGLADESH TRADE RELATIONS: INDIAN PERSPECTIVE

The Indian response to the Bangladesh point of view has many facets. It is argued that trade imbalance with an individual country should not be a matter of concern. What matters is the concerned country's global balance of trade.[32] Moreover, trade liberalization, even if done unilaterally cannot be harmful because in the long run it leads to efficient resource allocation. Secondly, both India and Bangladesh are pursuing nationalist agenda and thus Bangladesh cannot expect any special considerations. Besides, it would go against the GATT spirit. Thirdly, even if zero tariff is granted to some Bangladesh commodities, it will not have substantive relief on the balance of trade deficits. The then Indian Commerce Minister Pranab Mukherjee was in favour of expansion of trade between the two countries, which he believed was the best way to sort out the trade imbalance. He also suggested that joint ventures in industrial fields with buy-back arrangements could also improve the situation.[33]

The major plank of what Bangladesh can do, in the Indian view, is to allow the use of Chittagong port facilities for Indian commerce using a transit route over Bangladesh. The revenue thus generated could compensate for the trade imbalance. When the then Finance Minister, Manmohan Singh was visiting Dhaka in 1994, he was asked how the huge trade imbalance could be mitigated. He replied that Dhaka could expect preferential treatment in two years when India would be able to complete the general tariff reduction system. But granting of Chittagong port facilities, he said, would make at least 40 per cent compensation. He continued:

> If you have normal transit routes you will find that Bangladesh's balance of trade with India will increase dramatically. If our trade regime becomes liberal, in the long run [Chittagong] can become a better place for joint venture production for supply of goods to our north-eastern states than shipping them from Bombay. I have a vision that transit routes and liberalization of trade policies will offer vast opportunities of industrialization for Bangladesh, helping the north-eastern states of India also to flourish.[34]

The then Indian Foreign Minister, Mr I.K. Gujral was more eloquent and optimistic:

> Bangladesh-India trade gap is about Tk 2,000 crore. How to wipe that out should be a major concern for Bangladesh. . . . I had told your previous government, during my meeting with the former Foreign Minister, that opening up of the Chittagong port and passing of Indian goods for the north-eastern states alone can

give you nearly that amount and wipe out that deficit. So who is the loser? If you gain Tk 2,000 crore every year for the people of Bangladesh, will it add to your prosperity, or will it not?[35]

The Indian proposal went beyond the trade-and-transit link possibly since the beginning of the 1990s with the rapid change in the scenario in the north-east. Gujral's remark in this connection is significant:

Nearly ten years of losing Tk 2,000 crore per year and *also not getting water, who gained*? Think of the industries, jobs and wealth you could have produced with all that. No two nations can have only one-issue relations. (emphasis added)[36]

The major thrust of the Indian position is on the provision of transit facilities about which, however, Bangladesh remains reticent.[37] The imbalance continues to pile up in the meantime. The clouded political relations originating from the stalemate in sharing of waters of common rivers only adds to the stalemate.

IS THERE A WAY OUT?

It was recognized during two rounds of India-Bangladesh dialogue on economic cooperation—first held in February in New Delhi and next in Dhaka in May 1995—that Bangladesh's trade imbalance with India was not just an economic issue but it generated 'strong political resonance' which was inimical to cordial bilateral relations.[38] While the trade imbalances were not matters of special concern, the India-Bangladesh trade imbalance needed special treatment. In particular, it was strongly felt that all tariff, para-tariff and non-tariff barriers applying to Bangladesh's exports to India should be removed as fast as possible. At the very least, Bangladesh products should be allowed to compete with Indian products without any government-created impediments like tariff and non-tariff barriers.[39] Such a plea reinforces the argument of reciprocity in trade relations. If market forces are allowed to play a free hand in one case, they should be allowed to do so in the other. This should constitute the first step.

A question remains to be resolved. Access to Indian goods in Bangladesh, it is argued, takes place as part of Bangladesh's national policy applicable for all nations of the world and if Bangladesh's products do not have access in India it is also because of uniform national policy of India. But it may be argued that India does offer special preferential treatment to Nepali products, which is why trade imbalance between India and Nepal is not as serious as with Bangladesh.[40]

Breakthrough in Outstanding Water Issue. One has to recognize certain bottom lines. One is that no government could provide transit facilities or other trade concessions to India, regardless of benefits, without settling the water issue.[41] One may remember that even late Sheikh Mujibur Rahman did not restore the facilities which India enjoyed prior to the 1965 India-Pakistan war. The point that is made here is that the water issue is the major stumbling-block to improving India-Bangladesh relations and a breakthrough is needed here. Following the recent changes in Bangladesh and India, the climate of India-Bangladesh relations has changed for the better. The possibility of a breakthrough has become brighter.

Reciprocity—Key to Managing Imbalance. A second bottom line concerns Bangladesh's limitations on the supply side. It has been projected in the MCCI-sponsored study that Bangladesh's export is unlikely to exceed $100 million by the year 2000, when Indian exports to Bangladesh will exceed $1.5 billion. So a balanced trade is out of the question and none of the sensible business community in Dhaka expects that. What is needed, however, and that is felt and expressed, is a genuinely two-way trade, a feeling of reciprocity and visible Indian stake in bilateral trade.[42]

Internalizing and Legalizing Informal Trade. Another way out is internalizing the informal trade through a series of rationalizing measures to make informal trade unprofitable. It has been observed that one important loophole that makes smuggling profitable is the lengthy time involved in formal trading while some of the traded commodities might be needed very urgently. Reducing time gap is a recommended measure to discourage informal trade. A more effective measure will be to introduce border trading with a differential tariff structure for the bordering regions. One has to recognize, however, that smuggling is an ingenious and profitable pursuit that cannot be eliminated totally. To that extent a way out will be to provide some legitimate cover to smuggling so that there is some control over the movement of goods and people and at the same time, respective governments are not deprived of some revenue.[43]

SAPTA—Long-term Framework of Regional and Bilateral Trade Cooperation. The concern for reciprocal and structured trade relations can be accommodated within the framework of the SAARC Preferential Trading Arrangement (SAPTA) effective since January 1996. SAPTA has identified 200 items for which there will be tariff reduction. India has indicated 106 items for which the concession will be around 50 per cent. Other SAARC countries have indicated 120 items with proposed tariff reduction ranging between 7 per cent and 20 per cent. More concessions to the least developed countries of the region will be available.[44] At the bilateral level, Bangladesh asked for concessions in 59 items of which 3 have been agreed to, while India asked for 106 items of which 10 have been granted.[45] Although SAPTA is in a nascent stage and it would not be realistic to pin much hope on it at this stage, it remains the only available framework of structured relations both in the regional and bilateral context. Within trade an element of reciprocity and control of smuggling will in the short term, and joint ventures with buy-back arrangement in the medium term, help promotion of the cause of SAPTA.

To summarize, threefold suggestions are made: reciprocity and control of smuggling in the short run, joint venture with buy-back arrangement in the medium term, and promotion of SAPTA in the long run. The key is possibly held by issues beyond trade. It is believed that the possibility of a breakthrough lies in the resolution of outstanding issues like the water sharing dispute.

NOTES

1. See Debapriya Bhattacharya, 'South Asian Regional Economic Cooperation in the 1990s: Challenges and Prospects' in Anisuzzaman, *SAARC Cooperation: A People's Perspective*, AAPSO, Dhaka, 1993, p. 72.
2. See comments by Abdul Gafur on Bhattacharya, ibid., pp. 83-4.
3. See Bhattacharya, ibid., pp. 75-6.
4. See *The Daily Star*, 5 November 1995.
5. See S.M. Jasimuddin, 'Trade Liberalization vs Industrialization', *Holiday* (Dhaka), 10 June 1994.
6. Ibid.
7. See Government of Bangladesh, *The Industrial Policy*, 1982.
8. See Centre for Policy Dialogue, *Independent Review of Bangladesh's Development 1994/95*, 12 April 1995, p. 3.
9. See Jasimuddin.
10. See Sayed Kamaluddin, 'India Dangles the Carrot of Joint Venture while its Market is Virtually Closed to Bangladeshi Products', *Holiday*, 7 January 1994.
11. See Mahendra Lama, 'Bangladesh-India Trade Relation: Some Critical Issues', in S.R. Chakravarthy (ed.), *Foreign Policy of Bangladesh*, Har-Anand Publications, New Delhi, 1994, pp. 116-17.

12. Ibid., p. 117.
13. Ibid.
14. See Muchkund Dubey, 'Indo-Bangladesh Economic Relations' in ibid., p. 100.
15. Ibid.
16. See S. Kamaluddin, 7 January 1995.
17. S. Kamaluddin, *Holiday*, 14 April 1995.
18. Ibid.
19. See S. Kamaluddin, 7 January 1994.
20. See Lama, pp. 133-4.
21. An example is the smuggling of hilsa fish across the border. In 1995, 2,800 tons of fish worth $4.8 million have been taken out. In return, arms and drugs including heroin and phensidyl syrup are coming in. See *Daily Inquilab* and *Daily Janakantha* (both in Bengali), both dated 14 October 1995.
22. See S. Kamaluddin, 'Official vs Clandestine Trade', *Holiday*, 7 April 1995.
23. See Lama, p. 133.
24. Ibid.
25. Ibid., p. 124.
26. See Achintya Sen, 'Will Indo-Bangla Relations Ever Be on Even Këel?', *Holiday*, 24 July 1994.
27. See *The Independent*, Dhaka, 8 September 1996.
28. See S. Kamaluddin, 7 April 1995.
29. See *The Daily Ittefaq*, Dhaka, 8 September 1996.
30. *The Independent*.
31. See ibid.
32. See Dubey, p. 101.
33. See S. Kamaluddin, 14 April 1995.
34. See Achintya Sen.
35. See *Daily Star*, 5 September 1996.
36. See ibid.
37. Shahnaz Karim, 'Security Imperatives and Economic Benefits of Transit Facility: A Bangladeshi Perspective' in this volume, has discussed the issue in greater detail.
38. See feature article on the dialogue, 'Exploring the Potentials of Indo-Bangla Economic Cooperation', *Holiday*, 9 June 1995.
39. Ibid.
40. See Lama. See also S. Kamaluddin, 'India Dangles the Carrot'.
41. Ibid.
42. See S. Kamaluddin, 'Indian Businessmen Treat Bangladesh as a Dumping Ground for their Inferior Products', *Holiday*, 14 April 1995.
43. An example is 'import' of cows into Bangladesh from India. The people who bring cows from across the borders through designated routes report to the border posts where the cows are declared ownerless and hence auctioned. The cow traders themselves buy the cows and in the process, the consignment is legalized. It is gathered that there is tacit understanding with the officials across the border because only cows that carry some sort of identification or slips are processed in this way.
44. See *The Statesman*, 30 August 1995.
45. See *Daily Inquilab*, 2 September 1995.

Security Imperatives and Economic Benefits of Transit Facility: A Bangladesh Perspective

SHAHNAZ KARIM

THE IMPORTANCE of regional cooperation, particularly in the economic field, has assumed great importance in recent years. Against the backdrop of renewed global emphasis on regional cooperation, the South Asian countries are also increasing their efforts to strengthen cooperation among themselves. Cooperation can be facilitated to a great extent by the provision of appropriate regional infrastructure including efficient, easy and cheap transportation and communication network. Removal of burdensome and time-consuming transit formalities also facilitates regional economic cooperation. Efficient transport and communication networks along with uncomplicated border formalities are not only a prerequisite for a nation's economic development but are also essential for meaningful economic cooperation amongst nations. The countries of the South Asian region would gain in numerous ways through enhanced regional cooperation in land transport and communications. Improving as well as optimally utilizing existing land transport and communication linkages are likely to increase intra-regional interactions.

Transportation provides a crucial link among other sectors of development and, hence, it cannot be planned and managed in isolation. It is an essential input for mobility and access on which depends the success or failure of the development effort. It is an area which contributes towards creating the infrastructure for cooperation. There are various modes of transportation and the choice of a specific mode will depend crucially on the cost, performance, and development impact of alternative modes along with the geography and resources of the nation. The subcontinent's transport network is quite inadequate; resulting in high transport costs and handling charges, as well as delays in the delivery of goods. Inadequate transit facilities have demonstrably been a hindrance to the expansion of intra-regional trade. This has brought about an increasing awareness among the South Asian countries to support the development of transportation and communication linkages to increase trade in the region.

This paper first looks at the background and technical aspects of transit arrangements between India and Bangladesh. In this regard it examines the existing land transport networks between the two, what hurdles need to be overcome in order to facilitate transborder movement of traffic, how existing facilities can be upgraded and what benefits India, Bangladesh and other sub-regional neighbours stand to gain if transit facilities are improved. Next, the paper attempts to throw light on the security implication of this economic venture, specially highlighting Bangladesh's apprehension in this regard and India's response. Lastly, an attempt is made to see how these apprehensions and constraints can be overcome in order to attain a cooperative, complementary and integrative future for all concerned.

BACKGROUND

At partition, the unified economy of India had imposed a certain structural pattern on all sectors in all regions of the subcontinent. But less than a decade after partition saw a dramatic collapse of India-Pakistan trade and structural changes in the trading pattern. Transit arrangements between north-east India and the rest of India via then East Pakistan were, however, still operational up to the 1965 war, after which all economic links were broken off.

In newly independent Bangladesh, India sought to regain the transit facility. This was reflected in the India-Bangladesh Friendship Treaty of March 1972, one clause of which specified that Bangladesh would give India transit facilities through its territory for sending Indian goods to its north-eastern states. But soon relations between the two neighbours began to sour. Various contentious issues increasingly contributed to the deterioration of relations. Bangladesh began to perceive India as an 'all-pervasive threat' and explored the limited options open to it to counter this threat. One way was to deny India transit through Bangladesh territory. And Bangladesh has been denying India this access to date. The creation of Bangladesh, therefore, altered not only the political geography of the region, but also caused the severance of traditional markets, communication arteries, and transit routes.

In recent years, the issue of transit has once again been brought to the forefront as a way of enhancing economic cooperation between the two neighbours. Both agree that the present system of transhipment of goods traded between India and Bangladesh at the border is time-consuming and contributive to corruption. The general feeling is that such delays should be minimized, if not abolished, by allowing vehicle transit, under prevailing international norms, to facilitate flows of traffic originating in India, Nepal and Bhutan for goods entering or crossing Bangladesh.

EXISTING TRANSPORT LINKAGES AND POSSIBILITIES

Economic relations constitute a very significant aspect of the overall relations between India and Bangladesh. They are extensive, including trade relations, credit arrangements, joint ventures, and transport. They benefit both countries and have an overall stabilizing effect on political relations.

The existing transportation linkages between India and Bangladesh date back to the Mughal era when Sher Shah Suri constructed the original Grand Trunk Road. Further development of the surface transportation network—consisting of roads and railways—continued during the British period for strategic as well as developmental and trading purposes. In the context of the present discussion, land transport refers not only to the availability and quality of road and rail facilities, but also border formalities which are an important consideration in making road and rail linkages viable. The existing transportation linkages between Bangladesh and India can be considered under three main categories: railways, road and inland waterways.

Rail Linkages. Bangladesh has a total 2891.83 km of railway tracks, of which 978.82 km are broad gauge and 1912.91 km are metre gauge. The system may be divided into two sections by the rivers Jamuna and Padma. The two sections are linked by ferries at two points on the Jamuna.

A broad gauge link connects Calcutta in India with Paradaha in Bangladesh with interchange points located at Gede (India) and Darshana (Bangladesh). A metre gauge rail track links Radhikapur (India) to Parbatipur (Bangladesh). There is another metre gauge link from Gitaldah in India to Lalmonirhat in Bangladesh. A third metre gauge rail track links Maishashan in India with Dhaka in Bangladesh, passing through Kulaura.[1]

Highways. Bangladesh's road network may be categorized in the following manner: national highways, regional highways, feeder roads and *upazilla* (subdistrict) roads. The national highways link the capital Dhaka with divisional headquarters and important regional centres. The regional highways join district headquarters with industrial and commercial centres of the country. The remainder of the road network links all the district and subdivisional headquarters in the country.

The Indian national highway (NH) 34 from Bangaon to Petrapole (India) links Dhaka via Jessore (Bangladesh). NH 31 starting from Siliguri (India) links Dhaka via Dinajpur and Bogra (Bangladesh). NH 44 from Shillong to Agartala links Dhaka with Coutal. NH 51 connects Dalu (India) with Dhaka via Sylhet.[2]

Inland Water Transport. This is one of the oldest forms of transport in Bangladesh. The navigable waters are some 8,372 km in length during the monsoons, and some 5,152 km in the dry season. The main waterways are on the rivers Jamuna, Brahmaputra, Meghna and Padma.

India and Bangladesh have an inland water transport link. The Central Inland Water Transport Corporation (CIWTS) of Calcutta runs regular services on the Calcutta-Khulna and Calcutta-Narayanganj routes. The corporation also operates services on the Calcutta-Guwahati and the Calcutta-Karimganj routes in Assam which pass through Bangladesh. The river transport system linking Calcutta with north-east India was also a major communications artery up to 1965.[3]

IMPEDIMENTS

Many obstacles exist in the transit arrangements between India and Bangladesh. No through passage is allowed across the western border of Bangladesh with India to vehicles or trains. Transhipment arrangements too are extremely unsatisfactory. It has not yet been possible to reach an agreement for through passage of motor vehicles between the territories of the two countries. It was reported that during his January 1994 visit to Dhaka, the then Indian Commerce Minister Pranab Mukherjee suggested the construction of a highway from Dhaka to Calcutta with a lane reserved exclusively for automobiles to facilitate speedy and uncomplicated passage of cargo and passengers. But there has been no response from the Bangladesh side yet.[4]

The rail link across the Jessore border which existed till 1965, linking the Indian railway system with the broad gauge rail system in Bangladesh west of the Jamuna, is yet to be activated. A rail link from the Indian border to northern Bangladesh, which existed before but had been lying in unused and damaged condition was opened only recently. Its viability depends very much upon the commencement of, and progress in, the construction of the Jamuna bridge, as it would be mainly used for carrying boulders from India to the construction site of the proposed bridge.

As regards the inland water transport system, the river route linking Calcutta with northeast India, which was a major communications artery and an important foreign exchange earner for Pakistan up to 1965, is yet to be reactivated.

IMPROVING COMMUNICATION LINKS

With improved roads, waterways, and railways infrastructure and network Bangladesh can offer services to its regional neighbours, and hence, significantly enhance its foreign exchange earnings. India and Bangladesh could jointly develop infrastructure capabilities and share facilities in order to improve transportation linkages. India is interested in seeking an outlet to the sea for Tripura by construction of a 4 km railway link from Agartala to Akhaura and then on to Chittagong by Bangladesh Railway. The alternative of linking Agartala to Dharmanagar, the nearest Indian railhead en route to Silchar-Guwahati, by a metre gauge line is estimated to cost about Rs 450 crore. Even if this partly commenced line is completed, the journey to Calcutta will be long and circuitous. India is also reportedly willing to invest in the upgrading and the expansion of Chittagong port facilities. It was recently reported in a Dhaka daily that Chittagong port, after a break of five years is again being used as a transit port for shipping cargo to Nepal. Official sources have said that 100,000 metric tons of DAP fertilizer are to be transported to Nepal via Chittagong port by a Bangladesh private company.[5] Again, the Bangladesh section is part of the missing link in the 10,784 km Asian Highway network stretching from Bazargan in Iran down to Ho Chi Minh city in Vietnam.[6] Collaboration is already underway with regard to India's forging road links with Myanmar. India could assist Bangladesh to upgrade the latter's road, rail and waterway system to support the growing needs of both countries.

Such internal transport network system could aim towards building a common system to feed into the bigger regional communication grid. The costs of developing this system could be shared as the benefits would be mutual. The economic and political gains from improved communication and transit, to both India and Bangladesh, would be very high. Bangladesh would benefit enormously in infrastructure development and employment generation through economic collaboration with India. The creation of jobs and services in Bangladesh would also be extremely beneficial. Once such infrastructural and industrial developments have taken place, the sub-region would be more attractive for national, regional and international investments.

Transit facilities would further promote people-to-people interaction, in ways already proposed by the South Asian Association for Regional Cooperation (SAARC). The government of West Bengal especially is very keen on developing movement of passenger as well as freight traffic to and from Bangladesh.[7] India is interested in promoting two-way tourism between the two countries by road. This calls for permission to bus tour operators and private cars registered in either country to move freely in both countries with valid tourist visas. A proposal made by the government of West Bengal to this effect some time ago is awaiting consideration by the government of Bangladesh.[8]

Using the Jamuna bridge for transit facilities seems an attractive proposition for India, and also for Bangladesh and beyond to the north-east. Such mutuality of interests would also serve to improve the rate of economic amortization of the Jamuna Multipurpose Bridge investment.[9] The development of Mongla port plus its hinterland which can serve the trade of Nepal and Bhutan, is also an important opportunity for Bangladesh. This would help these countries to diversify their trading outlets, for which Nepal is willing to invest in the expansion and modernization of Mongla port facilities. Of course, for this prospect to be realized, traffic movements across Indian territory would need to be greatly improved.

Looking Beyond South Asia. A Japan International Cooperation Agency (JICA) report has stressed that Bangladesh has tremendous potential for becoming more competitive in many economic areas.[10] With adequate foreign investment Bangladesh can emerge as the epicentre of a Bay of Bengal industrial triangle, embracing Sri Lanka, eastern

India, Nepal, Bhutan, Myanmar, down to Malaysia/Singapore and up to China. The development of the sub-region must thus be increasingly viewed within a broader regional context. Similar possibilities exist for forging an economic community stretching from eastern India and Bangladesh through Myanmar and Thailand to south-west China.

To avail of such opportunities, Bangladesh needs further investment to improve its infrastructure. Chittagong's port facilities are five times cheaper than those of Singapore[11] and also more accessible to south-west China than many Chinese ports. If port facilities are improved and expanded and related services made more efficient, Chittagong port will once again become an attractive choice for servicing not just the north-east region of India, but could, via the Jamuna bridge, service Nepal and Bhutan, and could even be a cost-effective link for the Yuan and Sichuan provinces in China as it would be their nearest outlet to the sea.

SCOPE OF IMPROVEMENT

It is true that any programme of cooperation between India and Bangladesh is likely to remain closely related to the climate of political relation. Given the political realities of the region, some would argue that unless these political differences are resolved no meaningful co-operation in the areas of land transport and communications would take place. For them, the experience of the economic cooperation within the European Union should serve as an eye-opener. Regional cooperation in Europe was successful because there existed close interaction among the economic, political and cultural fields, even though disputes were not altogether absent. But above all, there was the ever present political conviction that the costs of non-cooperation would be higher than the costs of cooperation, be it economically, politically or culturally.[12] Political differences were kept aside in the European Union while the agenda for economic cooperation remained in the forefront. The European Union is certainly not a perfect model for India and Bangladesh but it can offer many ideas and inspirations for future cooperation strategies.[13] It is high time that they learn from the experience of the European Union and other regional groupings how conscious efforts have to be made to promote regional integration through cooperation in the land transport and communication network, and streamlining of the transit facilities. The long shadow of mutual suspicion cannot be removed overnight but it is possible to make a distinction between economic and political issues and to work out a system to safeguard individual interests while concomitantly promoting collective welfare. What is required most is vision and courage.

As a first step both India and Bangladesh should streamline transit facilities. Standardization of fleet and improvements in wagons are essential for cooperation in rail linkages. Standardizing roadside movement of vehicles, particularly pertaining to load and axle weight requirements, is essential for the smooth flow of traffic. An agreement regarding such standardization should be formulated.

Both India and Bangladesh face serious difficulties at the interchange points because of complex customs clearance regulations which are due mainly to security reasons. Customs formalities should be made easier and more convenient to facilitate the movement of goods.

Lack of modern cargo handling facilities and poor management practices also lead to delays in clearance. Such facilities should be upgraded to avoid unnecessary delays.

The trans-border movements of goods can be facilitated and promoted by adoption of a Transit-Transport Modality or convention governing commercial traffic.[14]

Visa problem and border formalities regulating the entry and exit of foreigners constitute a serious bottleneck in the region and have been a major hindrance in the growth of tourism. The governments should take steps to make these arrival and departure formalities easier and more convenient in order to promote people-to-people interactions.

BENEFITS OF PROVIDING TRANSIT FACILITIES

Any transit deal would provide immense economic benefits not only to Bangladesh but also to the entire northeastern part of the South Asian subcontinent. It would have beneficial linkage effect on infrastructural development, wider market access, economic collaboration on a sub-regional basis, and also on the potential for 'a western anchor of a great new Golden Triangle'.

If the four countries of the sub-region—Bangladesh, Bhutan, India and Nepal—can develop an integrated transportation and transit network between themselves, all four stand to gain immensely and there will be no loser. Bangladesh, for one, could earn considerable revenues from both north-south and east-west communication with India, Nepal and Bhutan, at all points. The four neighbours stand to gain the following benefits, among others:

1. At current calculation, Bangladesh will earn about Tk 720 crore per annum by way of freight and other charges leviable on Indian goods. This includes earnings from facilities provided at the Chittagong port for the transhipment of Indian goods.
2. Bangladesh could develop an export trade of US$50-100 million annually with the north-eastern Indian states. Bangladesh's export earning to Nepal could also increase by US$50-100 million annually because of the provision of transit facilities by India.
3. With the granting of transit facilities by India for trade between Bhutan and Bangladesh, there will be an increase in the two-way trade between the two countries. Bangladesh would earn also a considerable amount from freight and other charges leviable on Nepalese and Bhutanese goods. Nepal's earnings from exports to Bangladesh and to destinations beyond are also likely to increase.
4. India will be able to send goods to its north-eastern states at a cost which will be a fraction of the present cost. India will be prepared to invest some US$200 million for the expansion of Chittagong port to enable it to handle the additional volume of Indian cargo. Nepal is also willing to contribute to the investment for expansion of the Mongla port in Khulna. India would also be willing to invest in the upgrading of the Bangladesh railway system.[15]

For any programme of cooperation to take root the mutuality of benefits must be made apparent. These will imply concessions on both sides, and in both India and Bangladesh, there appears to be a growing recognition of the enormity of gains from such cooperation. Progress, however, remains remarkably slow mainly because of apprehensions, mistrust and diffidence at the political level.

APPREHENSIONS OF BANGLADESH

Considered purely on its own, and delinked from other issues, mutual granting of transit facilities is solely an economic matter. But not even a purely economic aspect of India-Bangladesh relations is free from political undertones. The most important factor conditioning Bangladesh's attitude towards cooperation with India is the apprehension of being dominated. Among the roots of discord, the most fundamental is that relating to the burden of the past. Cultural commonality makes its own contribution to distrust.[16] India often has stressed that South Asia is one cultural unit. Bangladesh believes that too much stress on commonality may block the preservation and growth of its separate identity as a nation. The powerful elements of cultural commonality also tend to create serious problems along borders through the migration of culturally homogeneous people across them. This often leads to turmoil and conflict and in turn, contributes to tension. Differences in security perception further deepen distrust. Hence the pattern of economic relations too could not escape such a legacy.

Opinion is divided in Bangladesh on allowing transit to India through Bangladesh territory to northeastern India.[17] One view is that transit should be treated as a trade-linked infrastructural issue since two-way reciprocal transit facilities would help in increasing bilateral trade. It goes further and stipulates broadening the scope of transit facilities to cover India-Bangladesh-Nepal-Bhutan routes.

The other section of the Bangladesh opinion is clearly reluctant to provide the transit facility to India.[18] Even though recently there appears to have been some softening of overall Bangladesh view on the issue, transit facility is widely regarded as a leverage that Bangladesh should retain to put pressure on India to resolve the crucial water issue.

The other ground for reluctance regarding transit to India relates to the weaknesses and low capacity of the Bangladesh port, railways, river and road system to take the additional load. Also, Bangladesh is unsure of the means of strengthening the existing infrastructure. Considerable cross-border informal trade exists. It is suspected that the volume of informal trade could be larger than the official trade. Bangladesh fears that the grant of transit facilities to Indian vehicles would further facilitate trans-border informal trade.

Fears of economic domination are compounded by political and security considerations. Bangladesh is haunted by the fear that the growth of the transportation network may ultimately result in the establishment of Indian hegemony in Bangladesh. The fear has deep roots in the psyche of Bangladesh, exacerbated by its experiences *vis-à-vis* India in both the distant as well as the recent past. Bilateral disputes are a major hindrance to the growth of cooperation. In fact, the slow growth of economic relations is the result of unresolved bilateral disputes regarding such issues as Farakka, Talpatty, demarcation of the maritime boundary, population migration, tribal insurgency in the Chittagong Hill Tracts, charges of Indian interference in the internal affairs of Bangladesh, etc.

In the prevailing political milieu, where the dark cloud of mutual suspicion casts its shadow over every aspect of India-Bangladesh relations, 'emotive and highly charged politics' get precedence over economic considerations. Bangladesh is apprehensive at the very least of the adverse impact that granting transit to India might have on its security. The insurgency in Chittagong Hill Tracts is a case in point. Bangladesh alleges that India has been providing support, including training and supply of weapons, to the insurgents who are locally known as the Shantibahini. Bangladesh fears that granting transit to India will make it easier for the latter to provide the insurgents with assistance. Similarly, it is suspected that easing of restrictions in the movement along the borders will help India in its widely quoted 'push-back' operation against Bangladeshis who are allegedly residing in India illegally. Bangladesh also fears that easing of border formalities would imply a weakening of border security and would leave the problem of demarcation of boundaries unresolved, placing India in added advantage.

OVERCOMING APPREHENSIONS

Mistrust, political discord, and entrenched inhibitions are preventing progress in the opening of transit facility and also overall strengthening of economic relations between Bangladesh and India. The political and security considerations are basic and real, and cannot be wished away. The economic costs of slow cooperation on transit issues are high for both sides, and there are numerous gains to be realized in terms of employment, investment, and income generation. It is both possible, and feasible, to substantially improve such links, to each other's mutual economic benefit. This must be kept in mind by both governments in making what will always be politically driven decisions on this subject.

No region in the world is free from feelings of insecurity between component States. Experience of other regions has shown that it is quite possible for countries riven by bilateral conflicts or disputes to cooperate for certain common purposes. Such cooperation must, however, be backed by a growing feeling of mutual confidence which can evolve only if the two governments have the political will and courage to do so. The burden of improving the political climate lies on both countries, but as the bigger neighbour and stronger trading partner, more on India.

In the India-Bangladesh scenario, steps should be taken to overcome the differences in security perception through dialogue at various governmental and non-governmental levels, transparency and mutual sharing of information. Increased people-to-people contact can play a crucial role in removing prejudice against neighbours and promoting confidence. The media can play a significant role by highlighting possible areas of cooperation including transport and communication. Parliamentarians and politicians of the two countries should meet more frequently. Greater interaction between the private sectors of the two countries can strengthen cooperation by developing shared stakes.

Granting transit facilities should not mean weakening of border security, rather it should merely mean coordinated transportation arrangements and uncomplicated border formalities. There already exists an inland water route which India uses to ship goods. Movement of Indian traffic on this route has not weakened border security. Hence, there is no strong justification to assume that land transit routes will weaken border security. It needs to be realized that trade and transit do create interdependence and this interdependence increases security rather than decrease it. There should be an improved infrastructure for transhipment of goods and promotion of people-to-people interaction.

CONCLUSION

In spite of many historical, civilizational, social, linguistic and cultural linkages, India-Bangladesh relations have been conspicuous for the high level of tension and conflict and very low level of bilateral cooperation and development. The economic and political processes of integration, that characterize the post-Cold War international relations in several parts of the world, have yet to take root in South Asia. It is being increasingly recognized, however, that long years of non-cooperation have not served the interest of either party. The time has come for both India and Bangladesh to leave behind the legacy of distrust and conflict, and strengthen bilateral and regional cooperation conducive to development, peace and security in each other's country. India and Bangladesh should take steps forward towards enhancing cooperation, keeping in mind that sub-regional and regional integration is a vital instrument for ensuring security in the contemporary world. In the new realities of regional groupings, based on geo-economic considerations, a cooperative and complementary sub-regional transportation network should be considered an additional advantage for both Bangladesh and India. Policies should not be influenced by the unfortunate legacies of the past but should rather be informed by the needs of the present and the requirements of the future.

NOTES

1. Ashfaque H. Khan and Annice Mahmood, *Comparative Advantages and Benefits and Costs of Regional Cooperation in Land Transport and Communications,* Friedrich Ebert Stiftung, Islamabad, 1993, pp. 80-1.
2. Ibid., p. 84.
3. Ibid., pp. 44, 84.
4. *Dhaka Courier*, 7 January 1994.
5. *The Daily Star* (Dhaka), 25 October 1995.
6. Khan and Mahmood, p. 74.
7. Charan Wadhva, 'Report on Bangladesh and Indian Perspectives and Consensus in the Dhaka Dialogue on India-Bangladesh Economic Relations' (May 1995), p. 13.
8. Ibid.
9. CPR-CPD, 'The Dhaka Dialogue on India-Bangladesh Economic Relations' (May 1995), p. 10.
10. Ibid.
11. Ibid., p. 11.
12. Christian Wagner, 'Regional Cooperation in Europe and South Asia: Can the European Union Serve as a Model for SAARC?' *Nepal Foundation Paper 4*, Nepal Foundation for Advanced Studies, Kathmandu, 1994, p. 24.
13. Ibid., p. 26.
14. Khan and Mahmood, p. 129.
15. Muchkund Dubey, 'India-Bangladesh Economic Relations', in S.R. Chakravarty (ed.), *Foreign Policy of Bangladesh*, Har-Anand Publications, New Delhi, 1994.
16. V. Kanesalingam (ed.), *Political Dimension of South Asia Cooperation*, Friedrich Ebert Stiftung, Colombo, 1993, p. 7.
17. Ibid., p. 5.
18. Ibid.

Regional Economic Trends: Security Implications for the Maldives

MOHAMED JALEEL AND AHMED SHAHEED

IN EXAMINING the relationship between regional economic trends and security of the Maldives, this paper will first identify the relationship between security and economic issues. It will then identify the major economic trends in the South Asian region. Six issues are highlighted: poverty, uneven economic performance, problems of sustainability, economic liberalization, the emergence of new and revitalized relationships, and regional cooperation. After the importance of these issues to the region is analysed, their relevance to the Maldives is examined. The latter is discussed in relation to the overall economic situation of the Maldives. Finally, the implications of these trends to the security of Maldives are discussed.

Security is often conceptualized in military terms. With the end of bipolarity, however, as many would argue, during the 1970s, economic issues began to creep on to the security agenda of the great powers. Economic competition amongst Japan, the USA and Germany together with the energy crisis and stagflation of the 1970s, clearly became important issues of national security. Protectionist measures in international trade, continuing adverse terms of trade for the Third World, burgeoning national debt, famine and starvation in Africa ensured that economic matters remained on the security agenda of States. In the 1980s and 1990s, these have been joined by concern over pandemic disease and increased political awareness about the implications of environmental degradation. At the same time, as the UN Secretary-General Boutros Boutros-Ghali stated on the occasion of the fiftieth anniversary of the UN, the world is facing a new dialectic, between increasing globalization and rapid fragmentation. Both these trends have implications for national security, for, as he stated, both are trends which the nation-state is not particularly suited to deal with. Given these perceptions, in the post-Cold War world, there is now a much wider appreciation of the argument that security is a very broad term encompassing military, economic and social aspects, amongst others.

For the Third World, security has been dominated by concerns of economic, political and social development. This is not to deny that in some cases, countries have sought military solutions or have made military conquest or capabilities the pre-eminent concern. The Third World has been the primary battleground during the Cold War. Whatever the causes of these conflicts, the Third World is worse off for them. The linkage between war and economic woes (poverty, indebtedness, resource depletion, etc.) was reaffirmed in a recent study that found that: there were wars in 65 of the 126 developing countries listed in the 1993 *Human Development Report*.[1] That is, there was war in over 50 per cent of Third World countries. Of these, 10 were among the top third of the Third World countries, measured by HDI; 24 were in the middle third; 31 were in the poorest third. The most violent of these conflicts were associated with the poorest. Of 32 such cases, 4 were among the top third; 12 in the middle third; and 16 in the poorest third.

The study also examined the relationship between indebtedness (and adjustment loans) and war. Of 71 Third World countries that had received adjustment loans, 50 were conflict-ridden countries (70 per cent). Of the top 25 Third World debtors, 22 countries or almost 90 per cent were experiencing conflict. Alternatively, of 65 Third World conflict-ridden countries, 80 per cent or 51 countries carried major debt burdens. Focusing on the Third World countries plagued by violence, of which there were 33 the study found that 90 per cent or 31 countries carried major debt burdens.

While identifying causation is a complex issue, especially whether war causes poverty or poverty causes war, these findings leave little doubt that poverty and war are correlated, as are development and peace. Indeed, by contrasting two snapshot pictures of 1988 and 1993, the link between indebtedness and war is made more ineluctable. By 1993, 85 per cent or more of the top debtors in 1988 were also carrying a heavy burden of violence. Therefore, our focus on South Asian security, a region where economic underdevelopment is widespread, must bear these correlations in mind.

THE SOUTH ASIAN CONTEXT

In South Asia, too, inter-State wars have been fought. Military expenditure is high. Consequently, it remains a region of intense arms racing and nuclear competition. At the same time, South Asia is also an arena of all the other kinds of security threats identified earlier. Many countries remain concerned about the threat of political disintegration; some countries have experienced years of ethnic instability. Many are also concerned about the strength of civil society or its ability to sustain a stable, democratic political order; in some cases, multi-party democracy is under severe challenge; others feel that civil society has not yet reached this stage; while others are taking only faltering steps in this direction. Economic backwardness is also imposing a heavy toll on the region, with a large segment of the South Asian population living in abject poverty. Pandemic disease poses serious threat to many communities and societies in the region, while deforestation, sea-level rise and flooding pose grave hazards to the region. At the same time, rapid modernization combined with globalization is eroding traditional values, perhaps far too rapidly and pervasively than local cultures and society can cope with. All of these are then matters of insecurity, even if we discount the armies facing each other on the Himalaya or the bands of thugs and mercenaries roaming around the Indian Ocean.

Despite all these security concerns, for years the military dimensions have gained more attention. In part this is because of the Cold War, with the Indian Ocean becoming a major arena for East-West competition. In 1977, Geoffrey Kemp, in an article in *Survival*, argued that the Indian Ocean was at the centre of what he called the 'new strategic map', with competition for naval bases from Mombasa to the Malacca Straits, and from Asmara to the Cockburn Sound. Between Soviet Admiral Gorshkov's advocacy of command of the sea and President Reagan's maritime strategy, there was little scope for even local disputes. Indeed, rather than the 'Zone of Peace' the UN called for in 1971, for the next fifteen years the zone was more appropriately described as an 'arc of crisis'.

Today, however, military competition at the global level has been replaced by a focus on economic development, human rights and regional cooperation. The end of the Cold War has also been accompanied by several trends of economic interaction that provide both opportunities and constraints. Given the promise heralded by the termination of the Cold War, and the focus on economic exchanges, it is appropriate that a fresh look be taken at South Asian security, especially in the context of predominant economic trends. Indeed, a broad spectrum of international-relations theorists argue that increased mutual benefits will enhance international stability, and in the South Asian case, will ameliorate several intra-national security concerns. In identifying these trends, this paper focuses on the old and the new. From an economic perspective, six such predominant trends can be identified which will now be examined.

1. Pockets of Poverty. Poverty is a major problem in South Asia. Most countries in the region are included in the list of the least developed countries drawn up by the United Nations Committee for Development Planning (CDP).[2] Except for Sri Lanka, the exclusion of some other countries in the region is because their population exceeds the identified limit, and not because of their level of development. With the exception of Sri Lanka, all South Asian countries are well below the cut-off point for income level and the newly employed composite index called the Augmented Physical Quality of Life Index based on life expectancy, per capita calorie supplies, combined primary and secondary school enrolment ratios and adult literacy rates. In all cases, there are problems of uneven distribution of wealth. Indeed, in most cases, the welfare benefits for the general population are so poor that they attain a very low rank in the UNDP's Human Development Index.[3] In fact, despite an overall per capita growth rate for the region averaging at 3.1 per cent over the past decade, estimates of the poor in the region varied between 330 million and 440 million in 1991.[4] It is not surprising, therefore, that the Independent South Asian Commission on Poverty Alleviation argued that: 'When coupled with the multifaceted crisis currently facing South Asian countries, the problem is becoming unmanageable, not only putting democracy at risk, but also posing a threat to the fabric of South Asian societies.'[5]

Poverty in the region however has attracted attention at the highest regional political level. The Dhaka Declaration of the SAARC Summit meeting in 1993 reflected this: 'Conscious that the sheer magnitude and complexity of South Asian poverty constituted a major political and economic challenge, the Heads of State or Government reiterated their commitment to continue to accord a high priority to its eradication from the region in the shortest possible time.' This has materialized in the SAARC poverty alleviation programme.

2. Uneven Performance of the Economies. The South Asia region encompasses economies as large as that of India, those that have sustained high rates of growth such as Sri Lanka and small economies such as the Maldives. Their rate of growth varies widely. Such variation and the imbalances in the size of the economies have hindered regional cooperation. Perhaps more striking is the uneven performance of various sectors of individual economies. Even where growth has been achieved, such uneven performances have raised concern over the allocation of resources across sectors. Generally, economic growth has been lop-sided: a modern services sector with a partially developed tertiary sector and an under-invested and inefficient primary sector. Hence, the different sectors of the economy are ill integrated, and the modern sector operates almost like an enclave, with the benefits of growth in this sector not trickling down.

3. Problems of Sustainability. Sustainability affects the region in two ways. The first is the problem of demographic pressure. Although several countries in the region have now pursued successful policies in population control, South Asia still remains one of the most populous regions in the world. In most countries the youth comprises the largest segment of the population. At the same time, given the populousness of the region, even small increases in the rate of growth translate into significant numbers. In addition, reduction in infant mortality and morbidity rates acts as another pressure on size of population. As a result, the ability of economic growth to deliver its benefits to a wider segment of the population is hindered. This in turn affects the quality of life index for the countries concerned, which, in conjunction with the prevalent market development strategies, imposes additional short-term pressures on the delivery of welfare benefits and poverty alleviation programmes, unless high economic growth rates are sustained.

The second problem of sustainability is related to ecological concerns. In part, these are related to demographic pressures, in terms of population/space ratio and resource utilization. Sustainable development and ecological conservation are major problems for many countries, such as Nepal, Bangladesh, and the Maldives, in particular.

4. Liberalization of the Economies. The end of the Cold War and the extravagant borrowing of the previous fifteen years compelled all Third World countries to turn to Western donors, including the IMF and the World Bank. At the same time, failure of the so-called 'third way' strategies or models accelerated the march towards economic liberalization in most parts of the world. Although South Asian imperatives are not exactly similar to those mentioned above, most countries in the region have begun to pursue more liberal policies. In the process, they have registered some economic successes, such as in achieving and sustaining the economic growth mentioned earlier.

Indeed, substantial economic reforms aimed at removing restrictions and distortions have been underway in the South Asian region since the late 1970s. Liberalization policies in the region were pioneered by Sri Lanka with the introduction of the economic reforms package of 1977. Trade liberalization measures have been intensified in the majority of the countries in the region since then, and restrictions on domestic and foreign private investment are being dismantled. India introduced major trade and investment reforms during the mid-1980s which, by providing momentum, seemed to be contagious, as neighbouring countries accelerated reforms to keep apace. Liberalization policies in Pakistan, Bangladesh and the Maldives followed along similar lines; restrictions on imports were relaxed in all of them. Countries of the region have also adopted policies to reform the financial sector, covering broad issues of interest rate structures, improving efficiency of financial systems through institutional reforms, and formulation of monetary policies which would achieve macro-economic objectives through indirect controls. Some countries have shown progress in improving the incentive framework, mainly deregulation in areas such as industrial licensing, lowering restrictions on direct foreign investment, and waiving entry barriers in most sectors. These have been accompanied by public sector reform such as tax reform, expenditure restructuring, improving the performance of public enterprises by increased competition, privatization, and wider distribution of share ownership.

As part of this liberalization process, South Asian countries have accelerated their search for outside markets. Exports have grown by 7 per cent per annum in the 1980s, which is twice the rate of the preceding decade, allowing their share in the domestic output to double.[6] Indeed, in comparison to the 1970s, intra-regional trade was 76 per cent higher during the 1980s. Intra-regional trade flows are, however, still considerably small in comparison with the trade of the region with the rest of the world.[7]

5. New and Revitalized Economic Relationships. With the liberalization of the economies of the region, relationships with countries of the developed West have become widened and revitalized. South Asia in general has traditionally maintained significant trade and economic relations with the outside world, particularly the West. These links received a new boost when India began to attract US and other Western investment as a result of a range of policy measures introduced by New Delhi since 1991. These measures simplified rules and procedures and terms offered to foreign capital, bringing them in line with current global practices. The success of these measures can be gauged from the fact that foreign investment proposals approved from the announcement of the new policy to the 1993-4 budget totalled nearly US$3 billion.[8] Interest in India has continued right through, with high-level trade delegations visiting the country from the United States, the UK, Japan and Singapore. Even other countries, such as Pakistan, Bangladesh and Nepal, in part led by domestic political developments, have now become more attractive for US investment.[9]

With the re-entry of South Africa into the family of nations, commercial relations have also begun to emerge between South Asian entrepreneurs and their South African counterparts. More important, perhaps, is the interest of other Western countries. All these developments augur well for the economic advancement of the region. They have formed the basis for calls for closer cooperation in the broader Indian Ocean region.

6. Evolution of Regional Economic Cooperation. Beginning in 1988, SAARC has paid greater attention to cooperation in core economic and related areas of finance, trade and development planning. Cooperation is also underway in areas of poverty alleviation through strategies of social mobilization, empowerment of the poor, promotion of agriculture and small-scale industry and the development of human and financial resources.

In the process of evolving regional cooperation, numerous institutions or vehicles have been created over the years. The first institution in the area of economic cooperation, the Asian Clearing House (ACU) was established in 1974 (prior to the formation of SAARC) to facilitate a multilateral payments arrangement for the region. More recently, to help promote and increase the region's economic self-reliance, attempts have been made to identify areas for harmonizing national economic policies (including areas of trade cooperation) in a regional cooperative framework. Such attempts include the endorsement of the SAARC Preferential Trading Arrangement (SAPTA) in 1993, and the establishment of the Economic Cooperation Committee. In addition, there are also a few other networks of regional cooperation such as the South Asian Development Fund and the South Asian Fund for Regional Projects.

These are the major discernible trends in the South Asian region. These trends have differing impacts on the security perceptions of different countries, in large part dependent upon the impact of the trends on each nation. Some characteristics are more applicable to certain States, and the extent of benefits from these trends, as may be expected, differs across the region. In the rest of this paper, the economic trends in the Maldives will be examined with a view to identifying the security implications therein, and the relevance of each of the above trends to the Maldivian context.

THE MALDIVIAN ECONOMY: RECENT PERFORMANCE

More than any other country in South Asia, the past two decades have seen rapid and sustained economic development in the Maldives. The liberal policies pursued by the country have generally stimulated economic growth. During the decade 1979-88, the gross domestic product grew at 7.9 per cent per annum.[10] Between 1987 and 1992, GDP grew in real terms by a remarkable 58 per cent, or at an average annual rate of around 9.5 per cent. Such growth has been seen in nearly all sectors of the economy, save fisheries and agriculture, which achieved below average rates of growth.[11]

Such rapid economic growth has been fuelled by a booming tourist industry. High rates of growth were also achieved in most other sectors of the economy. For example, the services sector has grown between 6.7 and 8.5 per cent during the 1990s. Industry, too, registered impressive growth rates between 8.4 and 9.8 per cent. In both cases, rates of growth have been above the average rate of growth of GDP, which has varied between 5.9 and 7.6 in the 1990s.[12]

Growth has also been underpinned by public sector investment in infrastructure. This includes projects such as harbour expansion, land reclamation, construction of government buildings, schools and road upgrading projects.[13] As a result, government investment in recent years has reached 40 per cent of GDP. Public investment in fisheries alone in the 1980s amounted to around \$70 million. The government also invested heavily in tourism with the construction and improvement of the international airport (\$100 million).[14]

Such economic growth has been part of a strategy of modernization of the country, in terms of economic activity, social relations and political development. In some senses, while economic 'transformation' is an appropriate term to describe the economic history of the Maldives in the past two decades, such transformation has also been accompanied by notable problems.

One of the biggest problems the country faces is double-edged. On the one hand, human resources comprise the most productive resource the country possesses. At the same time, demographic pressures, caused by increased urbanization and one of the highest birth rates in the world, are imposing problems on the delivery of the benefits of such economic development to the population. Such pressures are also aggravating some of the weakness of the economy, such as growth based on fiscal expansion, and creating socio-economic concerns with some security implications. Quite precisely what these implications are may be ideological, depending on one's conception of security and objects of social policy and equity issues. There are three kinds of demographic problems the country faces: high birth rates, dispersal of population with very thin density in areas outside the capital and inadequate human resource development.

High birth rates mean that a substantial proportion of the population are under-aged, thereby requiring a large share of the resources before that population becomes economically active. High birth rates also cause problems to the delivery and social services, and to institutional capacity to deal with problems. At the same time, these are also tied with issues of sustainability, as the population-space ratio is affected, with implications for various infrastructure and urbanization services.

This is compounded by the fact that as a result of the dispersal of the population and the limited size of such centres, there are uneconomic overhead costs involved in replicating essential infrastructure service for all population centres. Only three of the 200 inhabited islands of the Maldives have a population of more than 4,000. As many as 162 islands have less than 1,000, and there are ninety islands with fewer than 500 inhabitants. Overhead costs in servicing such small population are joined by high transportation costs as a result of the geographic dispersal of the population centres.

Inadequate human resource development is another problem. There is a shortage of skilled labour, necessitating dependence on expatriate skilled workers. This results in considerable loss of national income through remittances abroad. At present, the gross national product is only 70 per cent of GDP.

Together with these problems of sustaining development to meet socio-demographic pressures is the question of the sustainability of the environment. The Maldives, as a low-lying archipelagic State, is faced with a grim future as a result of sea-level rise caused by global warming and climate change. Perhaps after the most apocalyptic visions were questioned, there has been some complacency on this issue. But recent reports show that low-lying States could face dire consequences even with the most conservative estimates of emission of greenhouse gases to the atmosphere. Already, most of the islands are facing constant problems of conservation. In as many as thirty-five islands, erosion is causing severe problems. One needs hardly point out the threat of complete submersion as one of the worst forms of insecurity a nation can have.

Another important issue is the problem of capital flows. During the 1980s, the debt service ratio climbed to 7.2 per cent as the share of government expenditure financed by net official capital flows increased. The ratio of official flows to government expenditure rose to 13.8 per cent by 1993 and the ratio of external debt to GDP stood at 60 per cent between 1989 and 1992. Due to the large concessional element in official borrowing, however, the debt service ratio declined to 4.8 per cent in 1993. As already noted, public sector investment has played an important role in the economic expansion. Nevertheless, problems of budgetary imbalance are imposing restrictions on the ability to sustain public expenditure at the levels of the 1980s.

REGIONAL TRENDS AND SECURITY OF THE MALDIVES

How does the economic situation of the Maldives and regional economic trends relate to the country's security? Here we need to recall the discussion on security. We argued that security is much more than mere military security. Security must include the protection of a nation's core values, whether in terms of society, the functioning of the economy and the polity. Society is important because it determines a nation's core values, such as freedom and justice. Economy is important because its robustness is related to the ability to attain goals both at the individual and collective level. The stability of a polity is closely related to its effectiveness in meeting the expectations and demands of the populace. Having identified these conceptual pointers, we can then establish the relationship between the current economic trends and security in the Maldives.

Although rapid economic development is considered to have the potential of increasing income differentials, there is no convincing evidence that this is a serious problem in Maldives. Maldives does have the problem of people living below the poverty line, but poverty in the Maldives is different from some other areas of the region. Although malnutrition may be a problem in some parts, starvation is non-existent, calorie intake is increasing and access to basic services is rapidly expanding. These warrant the middle level of human development ranking of the Maldives in the Human Development Index produced by the UNDP. Indeed, the triennial CDP review of developing countries in 1994 placed the Maldives well above the graduation point in the Augmented Physical Quality of Life Index, unlike many of its South Asian neighbours.

In terms of performance over time, the economy has maintained steady growth rates during the entire period of economic expansion. As we have noted, the Maldivian economy has registered high growth in most sectors. Concern persists, however, over the performance of the fisheries sector and about the scope of the agricultural sector. Some concern has been expressed about the internal allocation of resources away from the fishing industry towards economic activities with a higher return.[15] In this regard, as in the case with other countries of the region, there is a need to strengthen linkages between and across different sectors of the economy.

Sustainability is a major concern in terms of the ratio between economic growth and population growth. Continued success in human development requires that demographic growth does not swamp out gains in economic productivity. Over the past decade or so, the rate of economic growth has been able to absorb the high rate of population growth. But in addition to undermining efforts at human development, such population growth has implications for the sustainable use of resources.

Indeed, even without a high demographic growth rate, sustainable exploitation of resources would still remain a key policy concern. For an economy that has relied on the tourist market for growth, tourism is seen as the hen that lays the golden egg. Over-exploitation may destroy the ability to continue to reap benefits from tourism. Therefore, in official policy on tourism, for example, as expressed in the Tourism Master Plan under discussion, concern about ecological issues takes a high profile. In fact, awareness about the dangers of ecological degradation is high, especially since the main marketing appeal of the Maldives tourism product is the country's pristine natural environment with a rich diversity of marine life. The focus, therefore, has been on 'ecotourism': that is, tourism that markets and protects an unspoiled natural environment.

Equally important, if not more, is the problem of conservation of fish stocks. Although many observers point out that fish stocks in the Indian Ocean are still more bountiful than in other regions, the Maldives shares the concern of coastal States about sustainable methods and levels of fisheries. For a country with little natural resources, marine resources, especially tuna, become especially important. Although Maldivians adhere to fishing practices that are sustainable, such as fishing by pole and line rather than by purse-seining, distant-water fishing fleets that operate illegally in the country's Exclusive Economic Zone use methods of fishing that have led to over-fishing in other regions. Therefore, while developments in international law have enabled the country to extend its Exclusive Economic Zone, illegal fishing by foreign fishing trawlers remains a major concern for the country. This problem is compounded by the fact that the country has only very limited surveillance ability against poaching. As experience has shown, even marginal increases in surveillance ability have resulted in major increases in the number of vessels apprehended for poaching in Maldivian waters.

In addition, as already noted, trends of ecological degradation are a concern to the Maldives. One of the major threats arises from global warming and the sea-level rise that is expected to follow. As low-lying coral atolls, the entire country could be submerged by sea-level rise of only a few metres. Even a more modest rise in sea-level would have catastrophic implications for the country's ability to sustain human life.

For most parts of the past ten to fifteen years, the Maldives has maintained a relatively open and liberal economic policy. There is no exchange control legislation and the economy is free from restrictions to international payments and trade. The dominant role of the private sector has contributed significantly to the socio-economic development of the country. These characteristics of the economy have helped the rapid economic growth witnessed in the past many years. Recognizing some of the structural weaknesses inherent in the economy, however, Maldives is currently pursuing macro-economic reform policies, including a reduction in fiscal deficits and monetary policy reform. These policies have been accompanied by addressing areas of public enterprise and financial sector reform and attempts to remove disincentives for foreign private capital flows through reform of the legal and regulatory system.

Liberalization is also important for the Maldives in view of the constrained budgetary situation and the need to attract private capital.

Especially, given the low levels of domestic savings and limited availability of credit, the attraction of foreign private investment must play a major role. Here, of course, the Maldives is competing with the larger economies of the region and elsewhere, in the short term. For attraction of increased levels of foreign investment, the Maldives needs to enhance its institutional machinery. Here, there is scope for legal and administrative modernization as also scope for provision of finance sector support services. As the Government of the Maldives and the international community, particularly donors, observe, institutional improvement is essential to attract the much needed private and foreign investment to finance the development of the economy, especially the fisheries sector.

The Maldives has benefited from increased integration of the region into the world economy, as witnessed by the increased interest by Western companies in the region in the post-Cold War era. The re-entry of South Africa into the world community has benefited the Maldives, as South Africa has quickly become an important market for tourism and an important source of imports. Other links have ensured a modest diversification of trade and tourism. In tourism, occupancy rates have increased even during the traditional 'off-season'. With the break-up of the Soviet Union, newer relations with some of the former Republics, as well as growing links with States in South-East Asia and the Far East have become important. Closer contact and increased commercial and other bilateral exchanges with SAARC member countries have aided the country in a variety of ways, such as in promoting trade and functional cooperation.

Except for the obvious and meaningful political spin-off effects of enhanced regional cooperation, benefits for the Maldives from SAPTA, in the short term, will be limited. The Maldives' major export and other trade markets are extra-regional. Hence, the Maldives, along with the other small less developed countries in SAPTA, has the least to gain from tariff concessions offered through SAPTA as it has a limited number of export items. Nevertheless, as the Maldivian Minister of Trade and Industries, Abdulla Yameen, recently stated, gains to small LDCs accrue on the import side. They may therefore wish to seek concessions on whatever non-tariff measures that may prevail in the economies concerned. Easier and faster trade-related procedures, competitive prices and freight rates, relaxed immigration rules and offer of expertise in human resource development are the areas in which LDCs in SAPTA have much to gain.[16]

As regards other projects of regional economic cooperation, there is a need to streamline activities to avoid duplication. For small countries like the Maldives, duplication of efforts results in an unaffordable use of limited resources and administrative capacity. Many of these regional economic trends have minimal impact on the Maldives in an economic sense. Over time, however, these advantages are likely to be increased, especially if SAARC maintains its impetus. More importantly, in the long term, the Maldives stands to gain economically from the increased openness of the region to foreign capital and commerce. Even at present, the country relies on the free movement of labour within the region, and will continue to do so for the foreseeable future.

On the other hand, continuing economic problems, or indeed, political problems in the region are likely to endanger the economic prospects of the Maldives, given its high external dependence. For example, 40 per cent of the tourist traffic of the Maldives passes through Sri Lanka. As experience shows, growth in the tourist industry is closely related to political stability.

IMPLICATIONS FOR SECURITY OF THE MALDIVES

In thinking about the security scenario of the Maldives, one is struck by the pervasive influence of the country's small size. Indeed, all small States may be seen to share generally similar threats. These include conventional and irregular military threats, economic hazards, pandemic disease and ecological threats. Although small States are vulnerable to conventional threats, as Brigadier Mohamed Zahir, Chief of Staff of the Maldives National Security Service, has pointed out, conventional threats are not the most serious threats that small States face.

On the other hand, as Zahir points out, irregular military threats have always been a problem for small States. These include bounty hunters (Bahamas in 1975 and New Hebrides/Vanuatu in 1980) and mercenaries (as in the Indian Ocean Island States). Recently their kind have been joined by drug-traffickers, terrorists, gun-runners and money launderers. Given the scale and nature of their operations and the vulnerability of small States, the activities of these thugs pose considerable threat to the fabric of society, political stability and national security of many small States.

Special mention must be made of those who poach the natural resources of States unable to guard them by running the expenses that diligent surveillance operations require. Illegal fishing is a major problem for small States. Even where licensing arrangements may be in operation, deficiencies and difficulties in the monitoring systems lead to considerable loss of resources and potential income.

The threat from such activity is compounded by the employment of illegal methods of fishery. These include drift-net fishing. Nets tantamount to 'walls of death' several miles long, kill any and every marine life in their path. Such fishing methods, therefore, constitute a major threat to the sustainability of fish stocks and marine life. World-wide concern over the issue has been expressed, and a decline in fish stocks has been registered in nearly all fishing grounds of the world. Related to these are other activities detrimental to the environment. The ecosystems of the small States are very fragile. The livelihood of these States is often based on the natural beauty and sustainability of their ecosystem. Dumping of toxic and nuclear wastes adds to the environmental problems caused by ecological degradation: climate change, greenhouse effect and sea-level rise.

A final security concern for small States is that of political instability. Small States of the world have a mixed record in this regard. In the Indian Ocean, concern for political stability has been compounded by the continuing activities of mercenaries. Mercenaries have always threatened the stability of the legitimate government in the Maldives throughout its history, the latest round being the attack in November 1988. Today, with a population which has over 50 per cent under 20 years of age, drug traffickers also pose a significant threat to the country. Likewise, the spread of contagious disease is both a threat to the nationals as well as to its most important export, the fickle tourist. Inability to guard its marine resources is also a grave concern.

These threats notwithstanding, the assessment of the trends in the country suggests a comparatively benign situation in the Maldives. The insularity of the island provides strong bonds of nationhood built upon years of social, political and economic interaction based on ethnic homogeneity. The society and the economy have remained unscathed by the bitter colonial experiences which occurred elsewhere in the region. The economy has been developing at a sufficient rate to ensure that demographic growth is absorbed. Benefits of development have been dispersed widely. Accordingly, the security threats to the Maldives are much less intractable than for many others.

This is not to advocate complacency. In terms of economic insecurity, three areas of concern must be stressed. First is the problem of fiscal imbalances. Experience in the rest of the world shows that insolvency creates social and political unrest, in addition to economic problems. As a country which experienced rapid economic growth spurred on, in part, by fiscal expansion in addition to private sector investment, restraining debt will be the main challenge with implications for socio-economic stability. The second related concern is that of equal access to social amenities by all segments of the population. Failures of the distributive process clearly undermine progress on human development. If social harmony and political stability are to be enhanced, equity must be ensured in the process of distribution of economic benefits. The third area of concern is that of human resource development. In addition to being the key to further development, failure to achieve adequate progress in this regard has socio-political implications. This is particularly so, given the age structure of the population.

From these security considerations, certain policy implications follow. Here, national policy-makers must pay attention to prioritizing objectives and designing policies to achieve specific targets within an overall integrated framework. As we have noted, the rate of economic growth in the recent past has been able to absorb the growth in population size. Nevertheless, its sustainability is in question. Previous Development Plans could afford not to accord this aspect immediate priority. The current Plan does pay adequate attention to this question, and it would be important to restrain the growth rate to less than 2 per cent by 2005, as currently projected.

Macro-economic reforms, including reform of fiscal policy and improvement of the balance-of-payments position are part of the current economic priorities. Demographic pressures and development priorities, focusing on human resource development and improvement in the standard of living, however, apply continuous pressures on the national budget. Dispersal of the population and its age structure as well as shortage of supply in the labour market are particularly important. In light of this, new sources of public finance have to be considered and other means of expanding revenue need to be examined.

Accordingly, adequate policies to ensure sustainability need to be matched with ways of attracting foreign private capital. This would require strengthening of the legal framework and the institutional machinery to attract foreign investors. At the same time, further diversification of economic activity, and expansion of existing ones such as fisheries, would yield desirable benefits.

Above all, the focus on human resource development needs to be maintained. This would result in the exploitation of our best resource, expand the economic productivity of labour, increase the supply of skilled labour, and diminish losses through remittances by expatriate workers. It would also provide many social benefits fundamental to sustaining the march towards modernization and socio-political stability. To these ends, the Maldives must utilize regional cooperation for the mutual benefit of all its partners.

CONCLUSION

This paper has argued that security is related to economic performance. In light of this, it has analysed the various predominant trends in the South Asian region, and examined their relevance to the Maldives and drawn security implications and policy inferences. With respect to the security situation of the Maldives, the main argument of the paper is that the Maldives enjoys a comparatively comfortable security scenario, specially in terms of internal socio-political and economic dimensions. Other kinds of threats that it faces, namely military vulnerability with respect to looming threat of mercenaries and sea-level rise, are not related to the economic trends in the region. Moreover, the country has experienced sustained economic growth, the socio-economic benefits of which have been distributed with reasonable degree of equity.

Looking into the future with an economic perspective, however, the country needs to address certain issues to sustain its current positive socio-economic status. These are sustainable development, both in terms of resource exploitation and human development, public finance and private investment, and the development of organic linkages across different sectors of the economy.

NOTES

1. Dan Smith, 'War, Peace and Third World Development', *UNDP Human Development Report Office Occasional Papers*, no. 16, UNDP Human Development Report Office, New York, 1994.
2. See United Nations, Committee for Development Planning, 'Report on the Twenty-Seventh Session, Official Records of the Economic and Social Council', Supplement no. 2, 1991, pp. 2-62; Supplement no. 2, 1994, pp. 52-62; and Udo E. Simonis, 'Least Developed Countries—Newly Defined', *Internationales Asienforum* 23(1-2), 1992, pp. 5-19.
3. See UNDP, *Human Development Report 1994*, p. 223. Only Sri Lanka and the Maldives are listed as having attained a middle level of human development.

4. UNDP, Concept Paper for the UNDP Sub-regional Projects on 'Institutional Development at the Grass-roots for Poverty Alleviation', p. 2.
5. Ibid., p. 1.
6. E. Stern, 'Developing Asia: A New Growth Pole Emerges', *Finance and Development*, June 1994.
7. S.S. Colombage, *Payments and Monetary Cooperation*, Friedrich Ebert Stiftung, Colombo, 1993.
8. International Forum on the Indian Ocean Region, *Current Economic Characteristics and Economic Linkages in the Indian Ocean*, Working Paper no. 2, Perth, pp. 46-7.
9. See Statement by Robin Raphel, Assistant Secretary of State for South Asian Affairs, House Foreign Affairs Subcommittee on Asia and the Pacific, Department of State, Washington, 11 August 1994.
10. Ministry of Planning, Human Resources and Environment (MPHRE), *State of the Environment*, Male, 1994, p. 6.
11. *Perspective Plan 2000: A Vision for the Future*, Male, October 1995, p. 3.
12. United Nations, Economic Commission for Asia and Pacific, *Economic and Social Survey of Asia and the Pacific 1995*, New York, 1995, p. 22, Table II.2.
13. MPHRE, p. 7.
14. *Republic of Maldives, Sustainable Human Development—Constraints, Plans and Strategies* (vol. 1), Document prepared for the Round Table Meeting, Male, October 1994, p. 4.
15. See John Kaminarides, Lino Brugiglio and Henk Hoogendonk, *The Economic Development of Small Countries*, Eburon, Delft (The Netherlands), 1989.
16. *Haveeru* (Male), 21 October 1995.

Economic Trends, Security Issues and Nation's Dilemma: A Nepalese Perspective

LOK RAJ BARAL

THE THREE issues encapsulated in this paper have their own universe, but two of these—economic trends and security issues—can hardly be dealt with separately. The third issue relates to the operational problems facing the South Asian countries, whose new economic policies are being implemented in a not too friendly environment. On the one hand, the countries in the region have adopted policies for market economy; on the other hand, they are also increasingly coming under pressure from the native lobbies against privatization. Security issues remain high on the agenda, specially in India and Pakistan because of their perpetual conflict relations and in Sri Lanka because of domestic compulsions. As a result, their defence expenditures in these countries and their regional neighbours—Bangladesh and Nepal—have remained constant or have risen, draining funds from development.

What is security and how is it being redefined and connected with other areas of security? Mahbub Ul Huq, a former Pakistani finance minister and advisor to the United Nations Development Programme (UNDP) has given new imperatives of human security and states that 'we are entering a new era of human security where the entire concept of security will change—and change dramatically'. Now security would be interpreted as:

- — security of people, not security of territory;
- — security of individuals, not just security of their nations;
- — security through development, not security through arms;
- — security of all people everywhere—in their homes, in their jobs, in their streets, in their communities, in their environment.[1]

Such an exhaustive agenda of security and encompassing strategies of development is gaining currency at a time when South Asian countries are going through a major economic transformation process including

Structural Adjustment Programme (SAP). Security of individuals and development of social sectors are equally important aspects of the new political economy approach to resolving the endemic crises bedevilling the region. For, development has to be understood 'not as a conveyor of consumerism for a few, deprivation for many, and pollution for everybody, but as a process of social graduation from inequality and injustices for many to equality and justice for all, including the coming generations'.[2] If the new economic trend is too capital-centric, not paying serious attention to labour, the SAP becomes highly parochial because of its preoccupation with owners of land or capital, thus giving rise to an 'epistemological problem'.[3] The present paper focuses on the emergent economic trends and their impacts on security issues as put forth by the new debates. While dealing with the selected issue areas, an integrated approach would be taken with reference to member countries of the South Asian Association of Regional Cooperation (SAARC).

THE REGIONAL CONTEXT

South Asia has not remained unaffected by the sweeping post-Cold War global economic changes. Its effects were more evident in Eastern Europe and those developing countries which started moving from an authoritarian political and autarchic economic system to pluralistic and market economy. The newly industrialized countries (NIC) spanning the entire Asia-Pacific region had demonstrated successes through economic liberalization regardless of size, resource endowment, level of development, extent of market imperfections, and political conditions. The Soviet Union, a 'bastion' of communism with a highly centralized economy collapsed, paving the way for both political and economic liberalism despite the problems of implementation in different historical, political and economic settings. The South Asian nations are also trying to keep pace with global liberalization, albeit confused and uncertain of the direction of change.

How do we comprehend economic trends in present-day South Asia? Most of its countries had adopted planned economic models impressed by the 'success' of the Soviet Union. Accordingly, most of them were impervious to market economy that espoused deregulation and competition. Joining today's wave of liberalization can take the following forms: 'moving from quotas and non-tariff barriers to tariffs, lower tariffs, and making the exchange rate more realistic (which in almost all cases means a real, as opposed to just nominal, depreciation)'.[4]

Moves towards liberalization have mostly been taking place under compulsive circumstances such as the international pressure for SAP to overcome a country's macro-economic instability and weakening of international creditworthiness.[5] The insular nature of most South Asian economies as also of the world polarized into two opposite ideologies stalled the liberalization process. Notably, most South Asian nations started to adapt to the new trends quite late, while a politically closed China had started them in the late 1970s. Thus, by the time the South Asian nations found that they would be sidelined if they failed to adopt new economic reforms, China had made considerable progress in both social sectors and economic growth. China began the economic reform process much early because Deng Xiaoping and his colleagues were not satisfied with the sluggish economic progress since the communist take-over in 1949. Agriculture, the backbone of the Chinese economy, suffered because the countryside was neglected. As a remedial measure, the system of household farming was made popular, prompting the farmers to cultivate plots of land individually. Several such incentives resulted in increased agricultural production. While experiments with industrial reforms had been going on for several years the focus was also moved to other vital economic sectors, specially to strike a balance between rural and urban development.

If China offers its own model of economic reform systems, the experience of enviable economic growth in the rest of East and South-East Asia, specially the 'Tigers', is of considerable relevance to the South Asian countries. Although there is always a correlation between politics and governance, it is also widely accepted that the selection and implementation of appropriate economic policies is just as critical to a country's economic success as its resource endowment, labour force, and so on.[6]

It would appear, therefore, that authoritarian settings did not necessarily prevent policies favouring liberalization. South Asian countries other than India and Sri Lanka were not rated as democratic before waves of pro-democracy movements started blowing in Bangladesh, Nepal and Pakistan in the late 1980s and early 1990s. These countries had, however, already initiated the trend of liberalization by adopting SAP in the 1980s. Nepal first adopted such policies in 1985 though without fully opening the door of privatization. The latter step was taken by the Nepali Congress government that came to power for the first time following the 1991 parliamentary election. India started liberalization only when it faced an acute foreign exchange reserve and balance-of-payments crisis in 1990-1, necessitating a departure from its State-controlled economic thrust to a more market-friendly approach. Other countries have also moved towards market economy, departing from their traditionally practised regulated economic policies.

The linkage between economy and security in South Asia has far-reaching implications for intra-SAARC economic cooperation. The underlying proposition is 'security through regional cooperation'. Strengthening of intra-regional interdependent relationship will also contribute to the region's cooperation with other regions. This is consistent with the current global wave from which the region can hardly remain isolated. Moreover, 'regional cooperation is dictated by the economics of neighbourhood as well as by own close linkage with global interdependence and inter-regional cooperation'.[7]

The SAARC approach to economic security may be viewed in light of its Integrated Programme of Action (IPA) dealing with a variety of areas of cooperation such as agriculture, communication, education and culture, environment, health and population activities, meteorology, prevention of drug trafficking and drug abuse, rural development, science and technology, tourism, transport and woman in development. The economic cooperation agenda covers the recently launched SAARC Preferential Trading Arrangement (SAPTA), for promoting intra-regional trade among the member countries on the basis of reciprocity. Under the arrangement, preferential trade is to be negotiated step by step on all commodities, with special attention given to the needs of the least developed States. Tariff preferences are to be negotiated initially on a product-by-product basis, with provisions left open for further expanding activities through trade liberalization measures.[8]

If this arrangement works, the region is likely to transform itself into a Free Trade Area notwithstanding asymmetries in the size, strength and potential of the economies of the individual countries. The negative implications of lingering political divergences and disputes cannot, however, be underestimated. Cooperation in even some non-controversial areas—poverty alleviation, regional development fund, food security reserve—remain sluggish due to lack of trust between SAARC members. A new breakthrough also seems unlikely.

In addition the smaller countries have their own specific economic problems and approach to development which may not be conterminous with the general SAARC approach including SAPTA. Land-locked Bhutan, for example, has adopted a cautious strategy of economic liberalization. Learning from Nepal's experience, Bhutan has become wary of inviting foreign capital and labour as they, in the Bhutanese calculation, may jeopardize the Bhutanese society, polity and economy. Moreover, stratified as the region is, the SAARC strategy has to be both universalistic and country-specific. Countries like Bangladesh, Bhutan, Maldives and Nepal, which belong to the category of less developed nations, they need preferential treatment for upgrading their level. 'If such a strategy of economic collaboration is adopted, the immediate aim would be the promotion of economic collaboration among member States in the context of rational specialization.'[9] The spirit of collective self-reliance and cooperative security can be sustained if such conditions can be created promote intrinsic interest and commitment to the regional system among all members. A challenge of this nature cannot be viewed in isolation from the region-wide economic reform process which is mainly externally induced. A Bangladesh economist, Rehman Sobhan says:

> Governments in the region remain bound by their own social constraints, political compulsion and external obligation in redirecting their development priorities. If in fact the governments of South Asia remain committed to an extraneously driven reform agenda, we must presume they have good reason to do so since our top policy makers are no less aware of the issues . . . than any of us. What is thus important is that the renewal of debate on the reform agenda must take place before a broader civil constituency who must be conscientized about the importance of widening the terms of reference of a reform agenda for South Asia.[10]

Sobhan identifies the following key issue areas to be addressed by the regional intelligentsia:

(a) The efficacy of the prevailing reform agenda.
(b) The nature and problems of redirecting the reform agenda towards sharing growth.
(c) The role of governance as an integral part of the reform agenda.
(d) Shared growth for sustaining democracy.
(e) Sharing growth for sustaining peace and cooperation within South Asia.[11]

So far, these agendas have been sidelined, giving the impression that the governments are not committed to developing a more coordinated approach to the region's development. Political considerations and endemic mistrust among the member States, especially India and Pakistan, have stultified regionalism regardless of summits held every year and study groups created for forging regional cooperation. With past prejudices and time-worn political and strategic considerations still casting their shadow among the countries of the region, the actual implementation of shared growth or enhancement of complementarity in line with the objectives of SAARC Charter becomes difficult. Even if these countries move towards liberalization either collectively or by integrating their domestic economy with regional and global economic regimes, the South Asian challenge looks as formidable as ever. For a region where intra-regional trade remains as low as 3 per cent of the total trade volume, obviously formal agendas and debates alone are not enough for bringing about a change in the regional perspective.

CHALLENGES OF ECONOMIC REFORMS IN SOUTH ASIA

The dilemma facing South Asian countries is between the perceived necessity of new agendas of economic reforms and circumventing their immediate negative impact. In Pakistan, for example, most public enterprises privatized in the past fifteen years were closed, thus presenting privatization as

> a vehicle for extracting resources from the State and from the people without contributing either to growth in investment or productive efficiency. . . . A decade of sponsored structural adjustment has brought little more than stagnation, with mass poverty remaining pervasive.[12]

In India and Nepal there is debate on whether to embrace the market economy and privatization with open arms or whether due consideration should be given to their impact on employment and social sectors which are traditionally viewed as the domain of the State. Recently, at an international seminar on Gandhi, community-oriented issues and welfare schemes were powerfully advanced by many participants. Questions were raised whether the ongoing global economic trends of liberalization were compatible with the Gandhian approach to the alleviation of poverty and other forms of social and economic disparities. But given the ground realities, it seems difficult to extricate from the global trend. India was in the midst of deep economic trouble in 1990-1 when it opted for the economic liberalization process. As a quick step to salvage the economy, the Narasimha Rao government initiated such policies as delicensing and deregulating enterprises along with an invitation for direct foreign investment with about 50 per cent equity. Although it was still a restrained form of liberalization, several foreign and multinational firms and investors came to India, seeing India as one of the big emerging markets. Other supporting factors like India's liberal political climate helped the process.

Nepal's liberalization measures were manifested in a number of areas. These include privatization of selected industries, promotion of foreign investment and one-window policy (1992), move towards convertibility of currency, and measures to increase the domestic and external competitiveness of Nepal's products. The expectation was that these policy measures would help increase productivity by mobilizing resources and facilitate inflow of foreign capital, modern technology, and management and technical skills. Only defence-related industries, cigarettes and bidi and alcohol were left out of the scheme.

These economic policy changes, adopted by the Nepali Congress government (1991-4), received a severe jolt following the Communist Party of Nepal (Marxist-Leninist) take-over in December 1994. The new government committed itself to continuing the policy of liberalization, while at the same time giving contradictory signals regarding privatization of industries. The communist government took several populist measures with an eye on the mid-term elections in case it lost the support of the parties that helped form the government. Its political agenda was top-heavy with economic promises and slogans such as 'build your village yourself', distribution of land to the landless, old age pension and allocation of half a million rupees to each village and Rs 1.5 million for each of the 205 constituencies.

The financial status of public sector enterprises which were privatized earlier had deteriorated, but the government did not explicitly acknowledge the problem.[13] It criticized the modalities of the previous government's privatization efforts but did not make clear whether the new government was likely to place greater weight on selling State enterprises to cooperatives or to workers or would allow management contracts while retaining State ownership. Further betraying lack of direction the Deputy Prime Minister and the General Secretary of the party said in his speech at the non-aligned summit in Indonesia that democratically elected governments ought to follow whatever economic model made sense, rather than being forced into a mould by donors.[14]

Meanwhile, the corporate sector became a liability rather than an asset, while the trade deficit kept mounting, featured by slow growth of export. During the first nine months of FY 1994/95, Nepal's foreign trade increased by 16.8 per cent, of which export constituted 22.9 per cent and import 77.1 per cent. Trade deficit during this period increased by 50 per cent. Major exports—garments and carpets—declined due to restrictions on products using child labour and the new quota system imposed on ready-made garments by the United States.[15]

The chronic trade deficit with India has been mounting relentlessly, despite measures adopted by the government in 1992-3. Measures introduced to encourage investors from India, on joint ventures in areas crucial for Nepal's development are in the offing. The reasons for Indian investors' lack of interest for investing in Nepal include their own assessment of risk involved in investing in Nepal. No less inhibiting is the Nepali suspicion that the dominant Indian economy may benefit more from such joint ventures than the weaker partner Nepal. At the same time, Nepal's agro-based industries, water and human resources, have remained sidelined in the process of integration of the economy into the world market, resulting in a decline of their productivity. The traditional export items—rice and jute, etc.—have been significantly replaced by garments and carpets, which are also facing new competition in the international market. Even these two major sources of foreign exchange are not likely to promote sustainable development if the earnings generated from them are not used in the productive sectors.

How such emergent issues could be tackled in the increasingly challenging context of internationalization and regionalization and other forms of economic bloc configurations needs to be examined seriously by the developing countries. Whether regionalism is contradictory to globalism is not clear, given that the developed countries themselves display an 'infatuation' with Free Trade Areas. As the *Economist* sees it, it is wrong to see these regional developments in terms of trade.

> The EU is much more than a trade agreement. APEC [Asia Pacific Economic Cooperation] has as much to do with maintaining security in the Pacific as with economic initiatives. And moves for a transatlantic trade alliance are part of a broader effort to bind America and Europe that the Cold war has passed.[16]

The World Trade Organization on its part may add to tensions as developed countries may be inclined to withdraw their quota and concessions given to the less developed countries.

SOCIO-ECONOMIC CHALLENGES: SOUTH ASIAN SECURITY DILEMMA

The *Human Development Report 1994* has stated: 'Future conflicts may often be within nations rather than between them—with their origins buried deep in growing socio-economic deprivation and disparities. The search for security in such a milieu lies in development, not in arms.'[17] South Asian nations are confronted with this dilemma on taking ahead the agenda of development along with on-going conflict, mistrust and competition for armaments. The smaller countries may not be engaged in bilateral or multilateral competition for asserting their status as powerful nations but they too are entangled in domestic crises which divert their attention to military build-up in order to stem multifarious crises emanating from ethnic conflict, economic conditions, problems of governance, environment, population increase and so on. All countries of the region, whether big or small, are beset by disintegrative trends, demonstrating a steady erosion of the secular legitimacy of governance. Parties which had all along been clamouring for secular democracy are falling prey to populism and all sorts of parochial tendencies with a view to continuing or capturing power through formal but not entirely free and fair elections. All these have coalesced to transform into crises of both domestic and external security implications. Added to these are the declining governing capability of South Asian leaders whose nexus with corruption and unscrupulous elements is being increasingly highlighted.

Thus, the South Asian leaders are seemingly becoming *ad hocist* in their regular functions, neither able to fully embrace the on-going global economic trend, nor having the courage to find a proper mix between market economy and regulated economic system that could meet the specific needs of their countries. At the same time, South Asia continues to be grilled by the traditionally inherited conflicts as well as by the new strategic competition between India and Pakistan. Rivalry between these two has both conventional and nuclear dimensions, draining resources which could be of much greater significance for enhancing people's security. The manner in which India and Pakistan are steadily increasing their expenditure on armaments suggests that the South Asian security scenario is not likely to be extricated from such trends. Military expenditure as percentage of GDP of India and Pakistan is 3.1 and 6.5 per cent respectively. During 1994-5 India allocated 15.15 per cent of the central government's expenditure for defence, and Pakistan 34.52 per cent. Other countries of the region also have not brought down their defence spending, thus diverting resources from development. Yet, pressure to maintain the momentum of arms spending continues. India's missile programme, for example, is being criticized for not receiving adequate attention because 'key decisions on missiles and other defence-related issues' have allegedly fallen 'victim to the wimp factor in policy-making'.[18]

While the Indian security view is basically determined by three factors—China, Pakistan and its self-perception as a big power deserving a seat in the United Nations Security Council and a role in the Asia-Pacific region—Pakistan is paranoid about the India factor. India's justification for keeping its nuclear option is based on its rejection of the possession of nuclear weapons exclusively by some powers for all time. But we find a synchronization of India's security concern over China and that of the Western powers, especially the United States, Japan and other countries of the Asia-Pacific region, who want to contain Chinese influence. The United States sees China as a threat to its security and to the rest of the world. For the United States, the robustly growing Chinese economy is a more serious threat than military and political threats. Expressive of this viewpoint it has been noted: 'how to deal with a resurgent China is one of the biggest challenges of today's world. Unfortunately, far too many people still see China's thrust toward superpower status as a political and security problem and overlook the importance of economics.'[19]

The recently improved India-China relations are, in Indian thinking, no guarantee to its future security. With Pakistan armed heavily with Chinese weapons including the M-11 missiles, both Pakistan and China dominate India's security agenda. Coming close on the heels of this agenda is the recent American decision to maintain traditional strategic relationship with Pakistan, making India paranoid. These plus the backlogs of history have led the two countries to military postures which are moving increasingly towards offensive-defensive doctrines.[20] Possibly, the high degree of strategic competition witnessed in India and Pakistan can be reduced if only both move towards effective confidence-building measures.

The conventional thrust of security and the interpretation of development purely in terms of economic growth are now looked at within a broad framework, as outlined at the outset. Countries dependent on foreign aid and loans cannot survive if they fail to develop their own intrinsic capability. Moreover, aid and other forms of financial assistance flow only to those who acquiesce in the policies and strategies of the rich nations. Analysing the pattern of flow of official development assistance (ODA) to the poor countries, Huq says that 'two and a half times as much per capita ODA goes to high military spenders as to low military spenders. Even today, strategic allies get preference over poor nations'.[21] It also means that the present world trend remains highly biased, entrenching the old rich-poor dichotomy. It is a manifestation of a new international political disorder in the offing.

It is now increasingly recognized that security is meaningless without taking development in its totality into consideration. The role of government, the State and the market has to be properly defined and practised. The government can adopt policies it thinks appropriate, thus taking a major role in 'initiating and facilitating market-reliant economic growth'. In addition, it has to ensure that its policies yield public welfare.

In response to animated public and intellectual debates on the positive and negative sides of the ongoing market-oriented economy, many South Asian governments have been under pressure to adopt measures specially addressed to distributive aspects. These include land reform, literacy and basic education, social security, decentralization of both economic and political power, gender balance, health care, etc. Without public sector role in these sectors, economic growth in South Asia is likely to remain a cliche as in the past. It may be noted that even the World Bank seems to have changed its previous stand and has recently come out with a postulation of a new approach to economic development. It says: 'Economic growth alone is not sufficient to address the needs of South Asia's poor . . . evidence suggests that pattern of public spending and in particular, spending on basic services like education, health, nutrition, and family planning and safety net programmes has an important effect on living standards.'[22] The countries of South Asia are not, however, yet clear how they strike a balance between market economy and the social prerequisites. The experiences of China and other East Asian countries could be of considerable relevance in this context.

CONCLUSION

If the conventional security considerations continue to receive priority for the South Asian rulers, human-centric development approach that gives equal importance to a substantial improvement in social indicators and economic development is also gaining acceptance in Asia. The growth of population due to lack of education and awareness is a stumbling block for development and a variety of socio-economic and political crises.

National security is not uni-dimensional as the conventional gurus of security suggest. It is as much determined by international developments as by domestic factors and by a variety of socio-economic and political measures taken on the home front. The South Asian strategic and security climate has not changed much even after the tumultuous developments in the international system, and it is still preoccupied with the old security agendas and lingering bilateral disputes. On this account, threats to security are increasingly becoming complex if not insurmountable. What is more worrisome is the eroding performance-legitimacy of democratic rulers who behave as captives to age-old attitudes rather than visionary and committed leaders. Unless they address the domestic problems concerning the people at large, their countries 'remain vulnerable to dismemberment, intervention, instability and internal conflict in a way not normally experienced by States in harmony with other nations'.[23] Interconnectedness between domestic and external sources of security in South Asia—Kashmir, the Punjab or the Tamil problem in Sri Lanka, to mention a few—cannot be underestimated. But progress in ensuring long-term stability and security in South Asia would depend on how the countries of the region define and address the new and emergent security issues and development challenges postulated in this paper.

NOTES

1. Mahbub Ul Huq, *New Imperative of Human Security*, Rajiv Gandhi Institute for Contemporary Studies, New Delhi, 1994, p. 1.
2. Keynote Address delivered by Devendra Raj Pandey to a National Seminar held at Kathmandu on 30 May 1995.
3. Ibid.
4. Andras Koves and Paul Marer, 'Economic Liberalization in Eastern Europe and in Market Economies' in idem (eds), *Foreign Economic Liberalization: Transformations in Socialist and Market Economies*, Westview Press, Boulder, 1991, p. 16.
5. Ibid.
6. David G. Timberman, 'Introduction' in idem (ed.), *The Politics of Economic Reform in Southeast Asia: The Experiences of Thailand, Indonesia and the Philippines*, Asian Institute of Management, Manila, 1992.
7. Kant Kishore Bhargava *et al.*, *Shaping South Asia's Future: Role of Regional Cooperation*, Vikas, New Delhi, 1995, p. 71.
8. See Agreement on SAARC Preferential Trading Arrangement (SAPTA), SAARC Secretariat, Kathmandu, Nepal, as cited in ibid., p. 118.
9. Fakhruddin Ahmad, 'Global Developments and South Asian Security', in Mubashir Hasan, *South Asia: Vision and Dialogue*, Lahore, 1994, pp. 256-66.
10. See Rehman Sobhan, 'Redirecting South Asia's Development Agenda', in Mubashir Hasan, p. 184.
11. Ibid., p. 186.
12. Rehman Sobhan, 'Country Report on Bangladesh', in ibid., p. 323.
13. See *Budget Statement of the Fiscal Year 1995-96 for Public Information*, Ministry of Finance, Kathmandu, 1995.
14. See for details, *Economic News* (US-AID/Nepal, 6(2), 30 April 1995).
15. See for details, *Economic Survey: Fiscal Year 1994-95*, Ministry of Finance, Kathmandu, 1995.
16. *The Economist*, 16 September 1995.

17. UNDP, *Human Development Report 1994*, Oxford University Press, New Delhi, 1994, p. 1.
18. See Brahma Chellaney, 'India's Missile Programme: Behaving Like a Wimp', *Indian Express*, 12 October 1995.
19. *International Herald Tribune*, 26 September 1995.
20. Kanti P. Bajpai and Stephen P. Cohen, 'Introduction' in idem (eds), *South Asia After the Cold War: International Perspectives*, Westview Press, Colorado, 1993, p. 12.
21. Mahbub Ul Huq, p. 10.
22. World Bank, *World Development Report 1995*, as cited in *Rising Nepal*, 8 October 1995.
23. Barry Buzan, *People, States and Fear: The National Security Problem in International Relations*, Harvester Press, Brighton, Sussex, 1983, p. 47.

Economic Trends, National Security and Defence Spending in Pakistan

PERVAIZ IQBAL CHEEMA

FOLLOWING THE end of the Cold War and subsequent disintegration of the Soviet Union, important breakthroughs were witnessed in many trouble spots of the world such as the Middle East, southern Africa, Latin America, Northern Ireland, etc. In addition, the overthrow of authoritarian regimes in many areas of the world heralded an era of democratic processes in which people's participation was greatly enhanced. But trouble spots still remain. The civil wars in Somalia, former Yugoslavia and Afghanistan, closely trailed by massive human rights violations in different parts, are among the grim reminders of man's inability to rectify self-created complex problems.

During the Cold War era political imperatives influenced policy formulation processes powerfully, and economic imperatives were relegated to the background. Perhaps the most significant trend to emerge after the Cold War is the increasing importance and continuous strengthening of economic imperatives. In some areas, however, it seems that a tug-of-war is still going on between the economic and political imperatives. One such area is South Asia. More specifically the continuing Indo-Pak hostility appears to be somewhat untouched by the stupendous changes of the post-Cold War period. The main focus of this paper is on Pakistan. It tries to identify some important economic trends, then discusses the problems of national security and defence spending, and finally attempts to highlight why the emerging economic imperatives are still not able to overcome political impediments.

RECENT ECONOMIC TRENDS IN PAKISTAN

During the last five years Pakistan has embarked upon a course of economic liberalization. Many economic reforms have been introduced, and still are being introduced periodically. In consequence, Pakistan's economy has been undergoing a qualitative management change, transforming an over-regulated inward-looking system into a more open, deregulated and market-oriented economy.[1] To be able to open up, Pakistan initiated a process of deregulation, denationalization and privatization. Deregulation was intended to encourage both trading and manufacturing sectors by easing official procedures. A concept of one window was adopted, primarily curtailing the large network of regulations governing investments and trading. This was specially intended to attract foreign investors. Such deregulation has been continued by successive governments, with varying emphasis on procedural aspects. The result was that foreign private investment registered a steady increase. According to one source foreign private investments increased from US$443.2 million in 1992-3 to US$642.7 million in 1993-4 and touched US$1540.8 million in 1994-5.[2]

Closely trailing deregulation was the concentration on building and extending infrastructure. Large-scale projects like the construction of a motor-way were initiated and the Ghazi Brotha project for energy generation was given momentum. Concerted efforts were directed at encouraging foreign investments in the energy sector, which as a result has been able to attract memorandums of understanding (MOU) from a large Hong Kong-based firm (Consolidated Electronic Power of Asia) and US-based energy conglomerates. Japan has signed an agreement on a gas pipeline linking Turkmenistan with Pakistan via Afghanistan, a gas pipeline from Qatar to Pakistan involving $3.2 billion, and a pipeline from Iran to Pakistan.[3] Projects relating to infrastructure development inclusive of road transport, pipeline linkages for gas transmission, electricity generation, and extending the network of telecommunication have been initiated and a series of future projects planned. Development efforts in the energy sector have forged ahead with the recent flow of foreign investments.

Denationalization and privatization is the other major aspect of economic reforms. Though late in joining the global bandwagon like most other South Asian countries, Pakistan has departed substantially from the policy of promoting nationalization followed since the early 1970s. The government has also been encouraging joint venture projects with special emphasis on technology transfer. Encouraging joint ventures and foreign investments is an important strategy of the government for accelerating economic development. In some areas such as the investment sector the results have been quite encouraging. During 1994-5 private fixed investment increased by 15.5 per cent as compared with 11.6 per cent in 1993-4.[4]

The impact of all this in terms of economic gains for the people has, however, remained limited. The people's purchasing capacity has not kept pace with the rapidly increasing cost of living. Despite repeated assertions to the contrary, neither has the debt burden been reduced significantly nor has the tax collection base increased. Some are of the opinion that the government's policy of high taxation, increasing inflation and rising cost have taken a high toll of the purchasing capacity of the general public.[5] The former caretaker Prime Minister specifically stressed that earnings from the expanded programme of privatization should be spent only on reducing public debt, which is consuming around 40 per cent of government's revenue to service.[6]

Defence is the other major source consuming a large portion of government resources. But to understand the compulsions for continued defence spending one needs to discuss the concept of national security and how Pakistan perceives security threats.

NATIONAL SECURITY: A COMPREHENSIVE APPROACH

National security, to many, means national defence which they often equate with a nation's military preparedness. They perceive it as being ensured or protected through the existence of particular institutions such as the armed forces. They believe that well-disciplined armed forces equipped with latest military devices can provide the requisite level of security and ensure national survival. Many dwell rather heavily upon that aspect of national security which is directly concerned with the threats emanating from the changing international environment or the dynamic nature of inter-State relationships. This many indeed be a very important aspect of national security, but not necessarily the only one. What about internal problems like revolution, subversion, violent struggle for power, *coup d'etat*, internal disorder ranging from ordinary crimes to a full-scale civil war? It has often been observed that many minor internal disturbances snowballed into a conflict situation where they became indistinguishable from international conflict and thereby acquired what these scholars term as the characteristics of a national security problem. Does this imply that one should wait and watch until the so-called insignificant internal disturbance magnifies and becomes unmistakably threatening? By then, it may be too late. Besides, what about threats emanating from economic insecurities?

There are others who regard heavy reliance upon the means of violence (i.e. armed forces and police) as detrimental to society. They project the institutions of armed forces and police as potential threats to man's liberty in society.[7] They advocate the obsolescence of military and other violent means, and stress that alternatives must be found to replace this traditional method of national survival. The ideologies of this group, while dwelling rather heavily upon the criticality of sanctimonious means of violence, suggest that security must be perceived essentially in non-military terms such as the provision of education, employment, social welfare housing, health and sanitation facilities, protection of environment, the establishment of a just international economic order, etc. To me this notion seems to be a logical extension of an old idea that security lies in the defeat of the major evils of society such as want, disease, ignorance, squalor and idleness. But assuming that one has been able to get rid of these societal evils and acquired the much desired cultural refinement and economic prosperity, would it not then be right to assume that the principal concern of that State would become the preservation of what has been achieved? Experience shows that economically prosperous and well-established States also have to seek security in the traditional method of building up their military machine. It defends them, deters aggression, provides effective support for political and diplomatic bargaining, gives them confidence and serves as an index of their power and prestige.

Both groups seem to be obsessed with just one aspect, though a very important one, of national security, and underplay the other equally important aspects. For instance, the exponents of armed forces are over-protesting the utility of military means and are obsessed with regional and international considerations only. They tend to focus exclusively on external threats, ignoring those which emanate from within. They accord almost negligible respect to those aspects of security which stem from the economic prosperity of a nation. Similarly, the advocates of military obsolescence are making the same mistake by over-emphasis on the economic aspect of security and relegating military utility to a lesser level.

A comprehensive definition of national security must take into account external and internal threats as well as threats emanating from economic insecurity and inequalities. National security is a national public good producing collective outcomes. Collective outcomes are those whose use or enjoyment cannot be denied to any potential consumer within a State and whose consumption does not reduce their availability to other users. In the economists' terminology these characteristics are called 'non-excludability', 'indivisibility' and nonrivalness'.[8] Collective outcomes include many of those services which national governments furnish to their citizens, such as the defence of the country, preservation of territorial integrity, police and fire protection, sanitation facilities, anti-pollution controls, etc. It is not surprising, therefore, that one hears of various ministries squabbling for increased allocation of resources, all in the name of security. However tenuous the connection between a particular ministry's proposals and the security of a nation, the claim that they are related indicates that references to security are expected to evoke a sympathetic response. For example, a people's educational level affects that nation's productive capacity which, in turn, affects its ability to protect itself.

National security can be viewed as being ensured through preparedness and vigilance of the armed forces, guaranteed protection against disintegration and subversion through the joint efforts of armed forces and the police and socially secured through ideological consolidation and economic prosperity. Admittedly, under the operative international political system, almost all States maintain that the fundamental goal of a State is to ensure its own survival as an independent and distinct political entity. But true security is generated only when real national interests such as survival, security, power, prosperity, freedom, peace and ideology are attained. The priority order of the essential goals of the State is somewhat debatable, but they certainly tend to overlap and be interdependent; peace is dependent upon prosperity and power, prosperity generates power and vice versa, and so on. The intriguing question that arises here is: has security any meaning when detached from survival, power, prosperity, peace and ideology? The answer would be in the negative. Hence, the notion of comprehensive security implies abilities to defend against external as well as internal threats; prevent disintegration that may have been commenced by internal strife; growth of power and prosperity accompanied by improved quality of life; and abilities to maintain desired level of peace and security.[9]

DEFENCE SPENDING: THE DILEMMA

Defence expenditure is a function of perceived threats and levels of domestic economic activity. Defence spending impinges on a country's resources. To comprehend the rationale for committing resources to the defence sector, three factors that predispose such decisions need to be discussed here: the availability of resources, threat perceptions and government's sectoral priority. To begin with, one has to assess the ability of the economy to pay for the envisaged defence cost. Pakistan's current budget can be broadly categorized into three sections of somewhat equal size: debt servicing, defence, and all other sectors. Around 35 to 40 per cent is allocated to debt servicing. While debt has been mostly used for developmental purposes, the efforts to reduce the debt burden appear somewhat unimpressive. The amount allocated to defence is less than that allocated for debt servicing. The debt incurred because of defence needs is not viewed as all that unmanageable.[10] But still defence consumes visibly much more than any other service sector. According to the Economic Survey of Pakistan, defence expenditure in 1994-5 was 29.4 per cent of the total expenditure and was 5.5 per cent of GDP whereas loan coupled with interest payment amounted to 5.7 per cent of GDP.[11] One major reason most often given to justify huge allocation to defence is the Indian factor. Since the major threats emanate from Indian policies and attitudes, the allocations are often raised as a reaction to meet the perceived Indian threat. Allocations for defence in Pakistan rarely remained less than what has been allocated in India in percentage terms. Even so, when in 1994-5 India increased its allocation to defence by 20 per cent, Pakistan raised its allocation by only 14.3 per cent.

Defence is a public service like all other services (education, health, etc.). Each public service sector competes for budgetary allocations. Every year the input and output of various public services are explained with the possible exception of defence sector. Since it is rarely explained what level of input had been made and what the outputs in the preceding year, it is very difficult to work out the opportunity cost of defence spending. To find out the opportunity cost and to find out what non-defence goods and services have been sacrificed to ensure a chosen level of defence activity becomes difficult in the absence of official statistical record of exact resource allocations to defence activity in general and to various arms of defence in particular. Besides, one needs to know what security-related items or units are being paid by other ministries such as para-military forces, etc.

In such situations one tends to make comparative analysis of central government expenditure on various sectors as percentage of total expenditure in order to find out the opportunity cost. This type of analysis could be misleading and present a somewhat distorted picture. For example, according to a World Bank report, Pakistan's central government spent more than 33 per cent of its budgetary allocation on defence in 1982 compared to 2-3 per cent on education and 1-2 per cent on health.[12] If true, this means that not only education and health paid a heavy toll in 1982 but that the then government attached low importance to these public services. But this is not a true picture because both education and health are also provincial subjects and a fairly reasonable amount is allocated to them by the provincial budgets. To ascertain the true opportunity cost, it is essential that a detailed budgetary statement be made to the National Assembly.

The second major consideration behind defence spending is threat perceptions. If a nation perceives a major external threat, it is unlikely to object to even higher allocations depriving other sectors. Pakistan has been facing external threat to its independence and territorial integrity right from its inception. Added pressures emanating from periodic domestic upheavals and internal subversions have further complicated the situation for security planners. Sandwiched between hostile India and unfriendly Afghanistan, Pakistan's security perceptions have largely been influenced by the evolving state of relationships with India and Afghanistan. More specifically, the single largest determining factor has been the Pakistani perception of continuous Indian threat. The Soviet invasion of Afghanistan in 1979 and the consequent massive refugee influx into Pakistan not only transformed what was initially an irritable relationship into a major threat on its western border, but also caused a rapid deterioration in its overall security environment. With the signing of the Geneva Accord and subsequent withdrawal of the Soviets from Afghanistan, the situation on the western border began to improve considerably. The current civil war among the various contenders for power in Afghanistan has once again made the situation on the western border somewhat alarming though many in Pakistan are convinced that this phase will also pass soon.

By far the major source of threats for Pakistan is India. The intensification of the Kashmiris' struggle for freedom during the 1990s and India's inability to manage the crisis situation brought the two countries to the brink of war. Despite having fought three wars and experienced countless border skirmishes the leaders on both sides seem hardly interested or determined to effectively check the drift towards war situations. The Kashmir dispute is so deeply caught in the cobweb of domestic politics that it does not need major efforts to secure the desired level of support. Both sides want to appear to have adopted tough postures. Perhaps they view this attitude as a dividend-paying pursuit. The former Indian Minister of State for Internal Security, Rajesh Pilot, hardly missed an opportunity to issue threats to Pakistan. In reaction, the Pakistani leaders also delivered equally strong statements. This is not a new development. Quick reaction to each other's strongly worded statements has been viewed as an appropriate response and a timely rebuttal ever since partition. The decades of the 1950s and 1960s reflected Pakistan's heightened sense of insecurity when concerted efforts were made to deter perceived Indian aggression. The decades of the 1970s witnessed a relative calm whereas the decade of the 1980s was largely influenced by security threats from western borders. The decade of the 1990s is once again witnessing an upsurge of threat perception from India primarily because of the on-going Kashmiri struggle for self-determination and India's alleged covert role in the Karachi situation.

The third aspect of defence spending revolves around sectoral priorities. Sectors with relative high priority are protected during periods of budgetary deficits; and during periods of growing budgetary surplus, that is, during times of ample availability of funds their budgetary shares tend to increase.[13] The government decides the level of defence allocation which in turn is determined by the national priority ladder. The place of defence in the priority ladder is often influenced by the threat perceptions of the incumbent government, and may vary with a different government. In democratic countries the placement of defence on national priority ladder is the product of existing national consensus coupled with government's own preferences. In the absence of democracy, the choice becomes the prerogative of the ruling group or the ruler himself.

The decision regarding how much should be allocated to defence and what sector should be subjected to cuts in order to meet defence requirements is extremely difficult and complex. If defence is viewed as a value to preserve other values that society holds dear, then a direct correlation between the values could be established. The final output of defence is national security which, in turn, generates a sense of security among the citizens. The feeling of security not only puts a man at ease but also provides a stimulus to increase productivity. Insecurity breeds discouragement and disappointment which is not conducive to healthy development of the economy. Despite the massive monetary input by the Americans via the Marshall Plan into Europe after World War II, the West European recovery programme did not take off until the Americans committed themselves to the defence of West Europe through the North Atlantic Treaty in 1949.[14] The major reason for the dismal West European performance was the West Europeans' sense of insecurity. A sense of security is therefore essential to accelerate economic development. But should a nation allocate so much resources that it begins to pinch economic development? The obvious answer would be in the negative. On the other hand, economic development will slow down considerably if the sense of security is replaced with insecurity. This is the dilemma facing decision-makers.

CONCLUDING REMARKS

Given the political situation in the region the trend in Pakistan seems to be in favour of top priority to defence in order to ensure a secure future for the people as citizens of an independent country. The possibility of reducing expenditure on the purchase of modern sophisticated weapons and equipment appears somewhat unrealistic in Pakistan. Despite repeated assertions by the donor agencies and organizations that Pakistan has to cut down its defence expenditure, the successive governments find it difficult to effectively cut the defence budget. The task becomes even more daunting and complex when the ongoing disputes like the Kashmir dispute continue to occupy an alarmingly dangerous position. The threat from India is viewed as real, and contemplating reduction of the defence budget is seen as endangering national survival. The question persistently being asked is whether or not it is possible to reduce the defence budget without compromising the security needs of the country. Defence allocation is measured in terms of the magnitude of the threat confronting Pakistan, mainly from India. Since the major dispute haunting both countries is the Kashmir dispute which is the product of the Cold War days and both countries have remained enmeshed in the Cold War imperatives, the emerging economic imperatives of the post-Cold War era have not made an impact.

Perhaps the best way to secure the desired reduction in defence spending is to undertake a comprehensive defence review with the intention of plugging the sources of waste, obviating unproductive apparatuses and appendages, continuously assessing the emerging threats and subjecting the existing threat perceptions to objective and investigative yardsticks, shifting emphasis to cost-effective equipment, and opting for structural reorganization. The second important pursuit should concentrate on efforts directed to making the South Asians realize the significance of post-Cold War imperatives. Finally, the Kashmir dispute needs to be resolved. It cannot be resolved unless the leaders prepare and impress upon the general public in their countries that it is in the interest of both the peoples to resolve the problem. No dispute is likely to be resolved if approached in terms of win and loss.

NOTES

1. Pakistan, in fact, initiated a somewhat similar deregulation programme during the 1960s, specially with respect to the industrial sector. But the process did not continue primarily because of political changes. For details see Sartaj Aziz, 'The Unfinished Reform Agenda', *The Dawn*, 8 October 1995.
2. For details see G.H. Qamar Baloch, 'Financial Achievements and Reforms', in *Pakistan Times*, 20 October 1995.
3. See Rana Zulfiqar, 'Modern Economic Trends', in *Masawat* (in Urdu), 16 October 1995.
4. For details see State Bank of Pakistan, Annual Report 1994-5; a shortened version of the report was published in *The News*, 10 October 1995.
5. See *The News*, ibid.
6. For a detailed discussion see Shahid Javed Burki, 'Qureshi's Agenda of Economic Reforms', in *The News*, 23 August 1993.
7. See Pervaiz Iqbal Cheema, 'The Imperatives of National Security: A Case Study of Pakistan', in *Asian Defence Journal*, November 1983.
8. Ibid. See also David Greenwood, 'Economic Constraints and National Defence Efforts', in *European Military Institution: A Reconnaissance* (Scotland Universities Study Group Report 1970-1), pp. 71-91.
9. During the Cold War the promotion of preferred ideologies was also viewed as part of the notion of comprehensive security. The Cold War having ended, it appears that the level of emphasis that was placed by the communist states on ideologies during the Cold War no longer remains operative.
10. See Pervez Tahir, 'Futility of Defence Spending Debate', in *The News*, 28 August 1995.
11. *Economic Survey of Pakistan 1994-95*, Government of Pakistan, Finance Division, Islamabad, p. 57.
12. For details see Pervaiz Iqbal Cheema, 'Arms Build up in South Asia: Impact on the Process of Peace and Development in the Region', in L.L. Mehrotra, H.S. Chopra and Gert W. Kueek (eds), *SAARC 2000, and Beyond* , Omega Scientific Publisher, New Delhi, 1995, pp. 42-64.
13. For details see Robert E. Looney and David Winterford, *Economic Causes and Consequences of Defence Expenditure in the Middle East and South Asia*, Westview Press, Boulder, 1988, pp. 193-208.
14. For details see Pervaiz Iqbal Cheema, 'Growing Defence Expenditure and its Implications for Economic Development in South Asia' in Sridhar K. Khatri (ed.), *Regional Security in South Asia*, Centre for Nepal and Asian Studies, Tribhuvan University, Kathmandu, 1987, pp. 111-23.

SAARC and New Realities in the Indian Ocean Region

AMERA SAEED

SAARC'S DECADE OF DOUBTS

As NEW factors have emerged which have changed the ground realities of the global order, one is tempted to state that SAARC's decade of a doubtful existence is also over. This does not mean that the challenges facing the member States of SAARC have disappeared and that it is going to be easy sailing. With the end of superpower rivalry, smaller and/or underdeveloped nations have the opportunity to become more openly realistic about their ground realities, now that they are no longer tied to the apron strings of the superpowers. The latter, by virtue of the role they played in World War II, were also in a position to dictate the imperatives of their specific national interests as the norms of the world order they had helped to shape. Powerful nations have not disappeared, nor need they disappear. Their advancement provides an impetus to greater human creativity. With the birth of new nation-states, what is fast emerging on the global scene is a new world order of economic regional blocs. In this new context, SAARC has multi-dimensional opportunities and possibilities before it.

The emergence of region-based economic trends lends another perspective altogether to security issues, and both are much more closely intertwined in this new scenario than ever before. New opportunities bring with them other challenges—the dilemma of which directions to take; the difficult decisions of what options to exercise; tough political choices over which national interest to subsume, perhaps, in a larger organizational strength and the ever-present need for a resilient awareness as to how to make it happen with the widest possible acceptability both at home and externally. What it implies for the SAARC member States is the focus of this study.

A brief overview of SAARC's first decade in existence would be in order, to see its organizational strengths and weaknesses in proportion to what has been considered as successful yardsticks in other parts of the globe, as well as against the potential inherent to it independent of these factors. To further highlight the great potential which exists in SAARC, the case study of recent efforts at developing an Indian Ocean-based regional forum will also be discussed, to see what it means to the member States of SAARC.

What were the foundations on which regional cooperation in South Asia emerged? What were the positive factors which cemented together the common perceptions into that broad-based agreement? Economically, the South Asian region, inhabited by more than 900 million people is one of the poorest in the world. A survey done by the Marga Institute of Colombo on Economy, Resources and Prospects in South Asia made the following observation that graphically captured the regional context. The economic situation of the region was characterized by

> the persistence of the problems of the low rates of economic growth, high rates of population growth, heavy pressures of population on land, scarcity of natural resources . . . under-utilization of large manpower resources and high incidence of poverty, income inequalities, illiteracy and infant mortality, low expectations of life at birth, lack of safe water supplies for large proportions of population, recurring food shortages in spite of the predominance of agriculture in the economies of the region, excessive dependence of agriculture on weather, adverse terms of trade, heavy balance of payments deficits, governments' expansionary fiscal and monetary policies and inflation remaining at double digit figures in most countries.

Ten years later the scenario has not changed in any phenomenal manner. Added to this, the political dissensions and tensions prevailing in the region have deepened. It may be recalled that the working paper circulated by Bangladesh to the member countries, which was the basis for the founding of SAARC, referred to the common historical heritage, ethnic origins and social and cultural affinity. It stated that

> the countries of the region have cooperated with one another both bilaterally and regionally under the umbrella of such forums as ESCAP, the Non-Aligned Movement and the Commonwealth. The efforts have not fully exploited the vast potential of regional cooperation that exists and the consequential benefit that this will bring collectively and individually to the countries of the region.

The working paper expressed the hope that regional cooperation would be a positive factor in generating a climate of harmony conducive to a better perception of what countries have in common and that a regional approach would help advance their economic interests.

When SAARC was launched in 1985 it was stressed that the decisions within the forum would be on the basis of unanimity; that bilateral and contentious issues would remain outside the scope; and that regional cooperation would not be a substitute for bilateral and multilateral cooperation but would complement them. Despite the rising expectations, the modesty in approach was clear and understandable. Notably, this was the period of heightened superpower tensions because of the Soviet invasion of Afghanistan, with Pakistan experiencing the full impact of the consequences of refugees and fearing security threats from the Soviet Union. To that extent South Asian security was a global concern. Therefore, any development taking place in this region drew immediate attention, as the setting up of SAARC did. Given the factors of rather negative economic conditions, prevailing intra-regional political discord and the volatile external security environment due to the Soviet invasion, while the idea of regional cooperation in the region was generally welcomed, it was not considered sustainable at all.

The process of cooperation under SAARC has, however, continued despite all predicaments. Not only that, there is a growing recognition in the region that potentials of cooperation could be realized in the region even if in small ways. SAARC has survived recurrent setbacks caused by continued political differences between member States including postponement of high-level meetings on more than one occasion. Core areas of economic concern like trade under the recently launched SAARC Preferential Trading Arrangement (SAPTA) and food security under the SAARC Food Security Reserve Scheme are being increasingly included in the cooperation agenda. In fact, SAARC did play an important role, although indirectly, in defusing some regional tensions at tense times. For example, informal talks between the Indian and Pakistani Prime Ministers at the Bangalore summit, at a time when the Indian troops were massed along their common borders, led to the two sides agreeing to resume the process of normalization of relations and to work out detailed measures to control illicit border crossing, drug trafficking, smuggling and terrorism. Later, at the Kathmandu summit, the Indian and Pakistani leaders initiated measures to discuss border controversies and conflicts, including the issue of the Siachen Glacier and a process that led to the decision not to attack each other's nuclear installations. At Kathmandu, a particularly significant event was the signing of two SAARC Conventions, one on the Suppression of Terrorism and the other on the Prevention of Trafficking and Abuse. Although their effectiveness may be debated, these developments indicate the potential of SAARC in bringing disputed issues into the agenda and facing them frontally.

INITIATIVES FOR AN INDIAN OCEAN REGIONAL FORUM: THE CONCEPTS

A notable post-Cold War trend is the rise of region-based organizations, in various parts of the world. Two significant initiatives were launched in 1995 to establish a trade-oriented economic grouping in the Indian Ocean Region. In March 1995, the Mauritius government hosted a meeting, known as the Indian Ocean Rim Initiative (IORI), in which Australia, India, South Africa, Oman, Kenya and Singapore participated. The second was held about two and a half months later on 11-15 June 1995. Hosted by Australia, it was a relatively more broad-based effort, with a three-tier participation, in which the government, business and academia from twenty-two countries met at Perth to discuss the possibilities of establishing an International Forum for the Indian Ocean Region (IFIOR). Both meetings attempted to give an all-encompassing, regional image to their deliberations. A strong impression they left behind was the effort by some countries of the region to shroud their desire for greater unilateral advantage in some palatable concepts that other countries of the region would swallow. This was to be expected at these initial, exploratory stages.

Meaningful interaction among the countries of the Indian Ocean region is not only a desirable but a highly practicable idea. It is a region richly endowed with material and human resources, and a number of sub-regional organizations have been in existence in the various sub-regions of this area, some since the 1960s. A larger, all-inclusive, regional bloc would, therefore, have the basis of available experience of interaction at these sub-regional levels. The proposal for establishing an Indian Ocean regional bloc for greater economic interaction merits a close scrutiny to ensure that the currently less developed littoral countries, the small island States and the land-locked countries, are not left behind through non-participation in decision-making.

The Cold War period is generally known for dividing the world into two major zones of political influence of the two major powers, with their antagonistic social, political and economic systems. The same period, however, also saw the rise of regional blocs in many parts of the world. Smaller countries grouped together for mutual economic safeguards outside the arena of superpower struggle for domination.

Two notable and more successful groupings were the European Economic Community (EEC), now transformed into European Union (EU), and the Association of the South-East Asian Nations, or ASEAN. Evidently, being located in the zones of direct superpower influence, the member States of these blocs could not entirely escape the impacts of the Cold War confrontation which imposed direct and indirect constraints on national development objectives of individual States. It was largely this perception which helped forge these region-based economic blocs aimed at offsetting such disadvantages, and to find greater economic leverages through a collective approach. The commonality in the external threat perception of member States—Soviet and Warsaw Pact threat in the case of EEC and the expanding Indochina conflict in the case of ASEAN—is considered to be an important factor behind their success in consolidating regionalism. On the other hand, the functioning of these economic regional blocs, as well as of those in other parts of the world underlined exclusivity as an important principle. Competitiveness based on protectionist principles *vis-à-vis* other regions also remained perceptible.

The larger economic benefits for the member States arising out of the establishment of these blocs, inclusive of the relative stability which their collective approach fostered, now provide the motive force for the current explorations by some of the Indian Ocean Region (IOR) countries to establish their own region-based economic grouping as well. The similarities within the EEC and the ASEAN economic blocs were largely in terms of subsuming national development objectives, in order to gain the advantages of the framework of a larger economic bloc. There were also inherent differences between them in terms of levels of economic development and objectives, and basic motive forces, not too different from the kind of difficulties to be encountered in the setting up of a region-based economic organization among the countries of the Indian Ocean region, and in its evolution from an idea into some practicable organization.

On the side of similarities, both the EEC of the earlier decades and ASEAN emerged as exclusivist, region-specific organizations. Their outermost territorial limits were determined by their geographical setting and the factor of contiguity, and on the basis of political boundaries established more or less as an outcome of World War II. With the passage of time, when the need was so felt, extra-regional countries were given either 'observer status' or made a dialogue partner, on account of the political and/or economic clout they wielded. Hence,

Japan and the USA found themselves being associated with both blocs in such capacities. The member States of both these regional organizations were also members of various other international organizations alongside their dialogue partners. The difference lay in that through their region-specific organizations, the member States of these regional blocs managed to acquire some measure of economic and political leverages specific to their geographical location. The blocs to which they belonged enabled them to establish a bypass system through which to cope with such international developments as they could not have handled effectively as single entities. These also provided the basis of a collective inter-State interaction through which international economic competition was better contained for promoting mutual interest. Through the pooling of expertise, and the establishment of complementarities, the broader economic objectives of the regional organizations provided the umbrella cover, in tense times, to pursue negotiations among themselves on how to deal with international pressures, as well as to carry on their economic development activities, without succumbing to external pressures. What was true as the rationale for the founding of the EEC *vis-à-vis* the superpower-dominated international environment, was also the basis behind the establishment of ASEAN *vis-à-vis* the industrially advanced nations of the world.

Differences between the two are no less significant. The EEC grouped together industrially and technologically advanced economies of countries which had also been former colonial powers; ASEAN represented the underdeveloped, highly populated countries, largely former colonies of the pre-World War II days. While both regions had been battle theatres during World War II, the EEC was established as a post-War phenomenon. When ASEAN assumed organizational shape the Vietnam war was fully on, and the superpower contention and the Cold War was at its zenith. The founding of the EEC followed the setting up of a collective military cooperation structure, the North Atlantic Treaty Organization (NATO), which included all the EEC member States as well as the USA. ASEAN, on the other hand, was established when its member countries faced economic adversities as a fallout of the on-going Vietnam war in Indochina with the spectre of a possible expansion of the war into their countries. This was also at a time when they were facing ethnic confrontations internally with many an incident of cross-border violations in their areas. Despite these problems, the South-East Asian countries avoided any security pact among themselves so as not to be drawn deeper into the superpower contention, beyond allowing the leasing out of military bases to the USA, which provided them a security cover against the Soviet Union's bases in Indochina, particularly in North Vietnam. It was with the demise of the Soviet Union, and the withdrawal of the American forces stationed in the Philippines in 1992, that the ASEAN countries have felt the need to set up a security forum as well. Coincidentally, the ASEAN Regional Forum (ARF) came into being in July 1994, at a time when these countries have all achieved enviable economic development.

The territorial expanse of these two economic blocs provides another interesting aspect to consider. In both, geographical contiguity determined which countries qualified for grouping in their respective configurations, while shared political perceptions established where the outermost limits ought to lie. As a scrutiny of the countries constituting ASEAN and the EU bears it out, this latter delimitation was determined by a mutually perceived commonality of the more general socio-cultural aspects which, despite political boundaries, allowed for a certain comfortable feeling of homogeneity as a friendly interactive environment. This perception encompassed mutually acceptable and common economic development objectives, not at variance with the 'national interests' of the individual member States. Furthermore, the political boundaries specific to these nations, of the EU and the ASEAN, provided both their landward and the seaward delimitations as the territorial extent of their respective blocs. Also to note here is the fact that both these organizations were set up prior to the passage in 1982 of the United Nations Law of the Sea Convention, known as UNCLOS III. The impact of this latter development is all-pervasive in the initiatives underway to establish an Indian Ocean economic zone and will be discussed later in this assessment. Internationally, UNCLOS III has added a significant and an entirely new dimension to inter-State relations as a whole, and to 'regionalism' in particular.

These groupings worked out their regional commitments in cooperation among themselves through the decades of the Cold War, to find themselves in the 1990s, confronting a post-Soviet Union global scenario, in which the numbers of sovereign nations have gone up, and notions of 'regionalism' are being furthered, with a specific colouring of interests, depending on which region these emanate from. Some newly independent nations have been born as regional blocs. Consider the quintuplet States of Central Asia—Uzbekistan, Kazakhstan, Kyrgyzstan, Tajikistan, Turkmenistan—which are also land-locked hinterland States of the Indian Ocean region. The other instance is post-apartheid South Africa, an Indian Ocean coastal State which is so endowed with resources, development potential, strategic location and ancient history as to have the wherewithal to claim a right of primogeniture, as it were, to be a leading State in its region.[1] The explorations for an effective conceptual base for an international forum in the Indian Ocean region are against this global backdrop, and will have to confront the multi-faceted ideas of 'regionalism' already in circulation.

REGIONALISM IN THE 1990s

Some recent developments provide a measure of insight on the perceived needs and current concerns behind the shaping up of concepts of 'regionalism'. Between 1993 and 1995, while existent regional blocs have changed their configurations, new blocs have emerged. Both the EU and ASEAN have increased their membership: the former now includes Austria, Sweden, Norway and Finland, is working towards a single currency and has forged a strategic security alliance with Russia through NATO's 'partnership for peace' proposal; the latter has already established the ASEAN Free Trade Area (AFTA) and has welcomed Vietnam as its member, with expectations that Cambodia and Laos would follow suit. The ASEAN Regional Forum (ARF) includes important extra-regional nations as 'dialogue partners'. The setting up of the ARF was considered a momentous development. Considering that South-East Asia was acknowledged to be 'an economically and politically buoyant segment',[2] with relative stability and largely cooperative international relations, it begs the question why the security forum was needed at all, especially since, with the formal disbandment of the Soviet Union, superpower contention had ended? Similarly, when the EEC was converted into the European Union (EU) in 1994, other economic groupings already existed comprising many of the member States of the EU. For instance, the European Free Trade Association (EFTA) was already in place. EU and EFTA negotiations resulted in the establishment of the European Economic Area (EEA) on 1 January 1994. All these groupings, ostensibly for economic purposes, make the European regional bloc system rather a complex entity. The multiplicity of groupings within the same regional setting with similar objectives, is a phenomenon that points to a rather cumbersome set of relations.

Regionalism got renewed impetus in other parts of the world too. The NAFTA—North American Free Trade Area—comprising initially the USA, Canada and Mexico was formally established in November 1993. Other notable regional bloc formations emerging in 1994 included the Group of Three (G-3) Free Trade Agreement comprising Colombia, Mexico and Venezuela for a ten-year period starting in January 1995. On 24 July 1994, twenty-five countries in the Latin American and Caribbean regions formally established the Association of Caribbean States (ACS), with the objectives of promoting a common approach to their respective regional economic and political problems, and working towards an eventual integration into a political union, such as the EU.

These developments provide an important backdrop to examine the shaping up of the IFIOR and other Indian Ocean-based initiatives as well as SAARC. When NAFTA was established in 1994, many views were expressed on the benefits or otherwise of the regional bloc. The London-based *Economist*, noting the vote for NAFTA, against the background of the GATT discussions underway at that point of time, and with the Asia-Pacific Economic Cooperation (APEC) summit meeting to take place in Seattle (USA), questioned whether big regional trading blocs would displace the multilateral trading order established after 1945, and whether on the basis of exclusivity barriers would be raised against outsiders. The article did not state whether it saw this principle at work in the EU and its affiliate organizations. It did note, however, that 'the big trend in the world economy is towards regionalism and the reassertion of economic geography . . . politics has made it possible, but market forces are driving it forward'. It went on to distinguish between 'benign regionalism' from 'the separatist sort'.

Noting that geography was at last getting its way the journal upheld the 'productive face of regionalism' in which there was

> voluntary exploitation of local trading opportunities rather than the compulsory restriction of exclusive trading blocks . . . Europe's economy was divided into halves by armies and ideology. Some East Asian countries grew rapidly, but their trade was largely with America and Europe rather than with each other or with the biggest countries in their midst: China and India. China shut itself off in Maoist poverty, India in nationalist poverty. And the Americas ought to be natural partners in trade, but Latin American countries shut their borders first through xenophobia and a belief in import substitution, later through debt-induced slump.

The journal argued that because trade moves in all directions, it needs a worldwide (not regional) set of rules, and a global (not regional) enforcement service, to prevent piracy on the high seas.[3]

In January 1995, the World Trade Organization (WTO) came into being formally, replacing and incorporating GATT and its legacy of trade regulations. In the process leading to the establishment of WTO, regionalism again became a concern for both developed and developing countries. This is a factor of importance in the context of IFIOR. One has just to witness the growing dimensions around the charge arising out of developed economies that developing countries were engaged in 'social dumping—competing unfairly by denying their workers basic rights', in total disregard of their own social conditions on the eve of their respective industrialization. The Indian Ocean region has a variegated economy, consisting as it does of industrialized nations such as Australia and South Africa, the newly industrialized countries (NICs) of ASEAN, as well as many of less developed economies and landlocked States and the greater number of the least developed countries (LDCs). The bottom line is that there are many instances of backward social conditions and varying levels of employment which can be whimsically categorized as violations of basic rights, by the better placed industrialized nations.

On coping with new competitors, the Western concern is that the established powers normally have difficulty coping with new competitors: France with Britain in the early nineteenth century, Britain with America later, and most recently the United States with Japan. Now, as a group, the industrialized democracies must integrate into the world economy not one but many developing countries, some with enormous economic potential. This process is producing acute concerns among established powers. Will jobs be lost, wages lowered, investment capital diverted? Can work-place and environmental standards be maintained, if not improved? It is suggested in some quarters that answers to two questions of considerable import will soon set the direction of the world economy: One, will the industrialized democracies cooperate to sustain an open, market-oriented world trade and financial order? To do so, they must rise above the different ways they practise capitalism and mounting domestic pressures for economic nationalism. Two, can these countries integrate into such an order those countries that are turning from State controls towards market capitalism? Noting the likelihood of political tolerance being in short supply because many Americans and Europeans share the apprehension that rising imports from Asia would eliminate domestic jobs, it is argued that a greater dispersal of economic power will mark the post-Cold War order. Different layers and categories of trade relationship—multilateral, regional, sub-regional and bilateral—will coexist. This web of relationships can incorporate newly transformed market-oriented economies into the global system in different ways and on different schedules and evolve on two broad tracks. One track would emphasize regional negotiations between such economies as well as between them and industrialized market economies. The other track would consist of efforts to strengthen international rules and organizations so that sub-global arrangements will be consistent with the non-discrimination and accountability required of open world markets. The bottom line concern is bluntly stated: as the world's largest exporting nation, the United States loses if regional blocs are allowed to become protectionist.

It is also argued that regionalism, not being a uniformly viewed concept cannot by itself be the organizing principle for a new global economic order.

> Regionalism does not answer how trade should be conducted among regions, nor does it ultimately provide a basis for integrating large economies like China, India and Russia into the global economy; . . . many countries will not likely be part of a major regional group in the near future. Finally, geographic regions are not necessarily natural trading areas.[4]

THE INDIAN OCEAN REGION

Assumptions based on the centrality of the United States as the sole superpower in the global economic system, miss the point that other countries of comparable attributes could also think the same way about themselves. Such viewpoints provide the existent realities which other existent and emergent regional organizations would have to confront. In this context, the IFIOR concept presents an entirely different situation. Here, the focus on the Indian Ocean as the regional basis of some future forum for economic interaction among the countries which lie within this region, visualizes the Indian Ocean as a unifying factor and not a delimiter. Geographically, therefore, the land aspect of this region includes not only the seabed of the Indian Ocean, the islands, and the littoral countries which have their coastlines directly on the Indian Ocean, but a hinterland region, which also has land-locked States directly affected by any development in the Indian Ocean region, and, therefore, fall within its regional geographical considerations.

Specifically, the Indian Ocean region comprises: Antarctica bordering on the Indian Ocean with parts of it under extra-regional ownership; southern Africa: South Africa and Mozambique as the coastal States and Botswana, Zimbabwe, Zambia, Malawi, Swaziland and Lesotho as the land-locked States; Eastern Africa: Tanzania, Kenya, Somalia and Djibouti (on the Red Sea) as the coastal States and Zaire (its borders along Tanzania are nearer to the Indian Ocean than to its own coastline along the Atlantic Ocean), Uganda, Rwanda and Burundi as the land-locked States; Saudi Arabian peninsula: South Yemen, North Yemen,

Iraq, Oman and the UAE (on the Persian Gulf) as the coastal States; West Asia: Iran (specifically because of its coastline stretch adjacent to Pakistan); South and South-East Asia: Pakistan, India, Bangladesh, Myanmar, Thailand and Malaysia as coastal States and Nepal, Bhutan, Afghanistan, and the five States of Central Asia as the land-locked States; Island States: Australia, New Zealand, Indonesia, Sri Lanka, Madagascar (Malagasy Republic), Mauritius (including Rodrigues Island), Maldives and Seychelles; Island territories: South Africa (Prince Edward Island, Marion Island); Tanzania (Zanzibar Islands); Oman (Kuria Muria Island); South Yemen (Socotra); India (Lakshadweep, Andaman and Nicobar Islands); Australia (Cocos Island, Christmas Island, Heard Island); France (Reunion, Amsterdam Island, St Paul Island, Crozet Island, Kerguelen Island, Island de l'Europa, Bassas da India, Tromelin, Mayotte); UK (the Chagos Archipelago, Mahe Island); and there are also the small islands of Pemba and Macquerie. The coastal and land-locked States, inclusive of those which have island territories, add to a total of forty-four Indian Ocean countries located in the region and two extra-regional ones, France and UK, with their island territories, making it a total of forty-six political entities in the Indian Ocean region. The land-locked States number seventeen. Of these, eight are in, or adjacent to, South Asia alone.

As is obvious, the Indian Ocean region has a number of natural sub-regional systems within it, and a number of regional formations already exist, some of them since the 1960s. These would have a direct and indirect bearing upon the development of IFIOR. Notable among these are, in East Africa: the Inter-Governmental Authority on Drought and Development (IGADD, 1986); the Indian Ocean Commission (IOC) and the Kagera Basin Organization which has the land-locked States of Burundi, Rwanda, Tanzania and Uganda as its members. In East and southern Africa: the Preferential Trade Area for Eastern and Southern African States (PTA, 1981); Common Market for Eastern and Southern Africa (COMESA, founded in the twelfth summit meeting of PTA). In southern Africa, there is Southern African Development Community (SADC, founded in 1992). There is also an informal grouping of seven front-line States bordering or close to South Africa, grouped together by their attitude to the erstwhile apartheid regime, namely, Angola, Botswana, Mozambique, Namibia, Tanzania, Zambia and Zimbabwe. In West, South and South-East Asia there is the Gulf Cooperation Council (GCC); the Economic Cooperation Organization (ECO); the South Asian Association for Regional Cooperation (SAARC); there is also Australia and New Zealand's pact with the United States (the ANZUS), the

Association of South-East Asian Nations (ASEAN) and the ASEAN Regional Forum (ARF), as also the ASEAN Free Trade Area (AFTA) and the Asia-Pacific Economic Cooperation (APEC).

It is against this background that this study compares the two major initiatives taken in early 1995 on developing an Indian Ocean economic community, and attempts to determine their major thrusts, analyses the motive forces, and on that basis to evaluate what the ground realities of the region dictate to be the criteria for a viable Indian Ocean-based regional forum.

THE MAURITIUS INDIAN OCEAN RIM INITIATIVE

An international meeting on the Indian Ocean Rim Initiative, described as a tripartite meeting of the government, the business and the academia, was held at Grand Baie, on 29-31 March 1995, hosted by the Government of Mauritius. Delegates from seven countries, namely, Australia, India, Kenya, Mauritius, Oman, South Africa and Singapore participated. A communique and a joint statement were issued at the conclusion of the deliberations. The joint statement stated that the main objective of holding discussions was to examine the possibility of enhancing economic cooperation amongst the countries of the Indian Ocean Rim. The meeting took note of the recent significant political and economic changes on the world scene and particularly noted 'the conclusion of the Uruguay Round of GATT Negotiations and the setting up of a World Trade Organization (WTO) *which promises to usher in a more liberal international trading system; the growing trend towards regionalism* and the increasing adoption of market-friendly policies by a growing number of countries' (emphasis added).

The meeting acknowledged 'the vital interests shared by the Indian Ocean region' in the expansion of free trade and investment, at the regional and global levels. It called for greater cooperation for a more effective utilization of human, natural and other resources of the IOR for sustained, accelerated economic growth, and for the improvement of the economic and social welfare of its peoples, who shared history, had close cultural links and long-standing trade relations.

The meeting set out the principles, objectives, scope of activity and future course of action to be undertaken by the 'core' group, namely those participating in the 'initiative'. The principles stated that 'in a spirit of open regionalism it seeks to build and expand understanding and mutually beneficial cooperation through a consensus-based, evolutionary and non-intrusive approach'. The underlying principles were identified as follows:

1. Cooperation within IOR's framework would be based on respect for the principles of sovereign equality, territorial integrity, political independence, and non-interference in internal affairs, peaceful coexistence and mutual benefit.
2. It would reinforce, not replace, bilateral and multilateral cooperation and be complementary to the latter and would be consistent with bilateral and multilateral obligations.
3. Eligibility for membership would be open to all sovereign States of the IOR. What constitutes the IOR was, however, left unspecified.
4. Decisions on all matters and issues and at all levels would be taken on the basis of consensus.
5. Bilateral and other issues likely to generate controversy and be an impediment to regional cooperation efforts would be excluded from the deliberations.

The objectives of the Indian Ocean Rim Initiative (IORI) would be to promote the 'welfare of the peoples of the participating countries' through carefully designed programmes to improve their standards of living; promote sustained and balanced development 'of the region and the member States'. The formulation of the economic cooperation programmes was envisaged through expansion of trade, tourism, direct investment, scientific and technological exchanges and human resource development. It considered lowering the tariff barriers for freer and enhanced flow of goods, services, investment and technology within the region, as well as through close interaction of the academia and trade and industry and the peoples of the member countries. It would serve as a forum for strengthening cooperation and dialogue of its member countries with international fora on global economic issues. Closer institutional links were envisaged for the development of human resources.

The scope of activity reinforced the notion of not dealing with any contentious issues, but focusing on those economic areas which provided ample opportunities to develop shared interests and reap mutual benefits. These were identified as trade facilitation through greater exchange of information and data on patterns of trade, investment and technology, and complementarities, as well as dialogue on standards, quality and customs procedures. Trade promotion, liberalization and investment promotion were considered the major areas for the initial interaction. The establishment of a trade-related infrastructure (mechanisms for consultation and cooperation, shipping, air service and telecommunications) was envisaged. Further areas in science and technology, tourism, and human resources development were also to be identified.

The meeting decided to set up a working group, comprising representatives of the seven participating countries and chaired by Mauritius, to formulate ideas and proposals in a report. It would have a tripartite structure—government, academia, and the private sector. Another intergovernmental meeting was to be convened by Mauritius within twelve months to consider the report. The Mauritius offer to establish a national coordinating unit to facilitate work on IOR issues and to provide support for the follow-up meetings was also noted. The private sector group's proposal to set up a networking mechanism in the form of an Indian Ocean Rim Business Forum (IORBF) and a Tripartite Focal Group was also accepted.

The communiqué, issued around the same time, reiterated most of the points made in the joint statement. It referred to the keynote address given by the Mauritian Minister of Finance, Ramakrishna Sithanan, in which he observed that the Indian Ocean was 'the only major region in the world which did not have a forum to debate issues of regional interest'. He stressed the need for concerted action by the countries of the region to avoid their marginalization from the mainstream of global developments. For this, he emphasized, there was need to concentrate on factors which united the participating countries rather than those which divided them.

The communiqué described the tripartite composition of the working group as its 'key characteristic'. It noted the global process of regionalization and stressed: 'it has become necessary for countries within specific geographical boundaries which share common characteristics and concerns to join forces in order to make their voices heard in international fora'. It was a little more specific than the joint statement as to what constituted the Indian Ocean region: 'it covers a large expanse of sea, spreads over three continents and includes established and emerging economic powerhouses'.

There was agreement on the principle that the IORI would be complementary to the objectives of existing regional groupings. There was consensus that the IORI could also be a consultative forum driven by economic cooperation issues with an outward looking policy, for which more preparatory work needed to be done. On the nature of this cooperation, the need for initiating a consultation process with a view to enhancing East-West cooperation in the IOR was stressed. The major thrust of the scope of action was identified as economic cooperation issues, 'specifically in the fields of trade and investment' and other sectors of mutual interest. Other areas with the possibility of yielding handsome dividends were in the field of science and technology, human resource development, air and maritime linkages, banking and finance, port management. The proposal of the academic group to draw upon existing networks and to extend their scope for data collection/dissemination, policy information, and the required training and development programmes was considered an essential underpinning. To that end, a proposal to establish a Chair in Indian Ocean Studies was welcomed; so also was the proposal to hold ministerial meetings to advance the initiative. The communiqué also mentioned Australia's intention to host a non-governmental Indian Ocean international forum in Perth in June 1995. What these public declarations did not disclose was the fact that for more than a year preceding the get-together at Mauritius, there had been much loud thinking on the possibility of establishing an India-Australia-South Africa axis, as the hub of an Indian Ocean economic bloc.

Just a year before the Mauritius meeting an article had appeared in the New Delhi-based daily, the *Pioneer*, dated 6 March 1994, on the same subject, written by Kenneth McPherson, Director of the Indian Ocean Centre for Peace Studies in Perth. It discussed an Australia-India-South Africa axis as the possible beginning of a new political and economic arrangement which could lead to an Indian Ocean zone of cooperation, very much 'on the lines of similar exclusive economic zones in Europe, North America and the Pacific'. It was argued that the challenge of the 1990s for the countries which border the Indian Ocean would be to seize the opportunity to develop a mechanism for regional cooperation which would advance the *economic and security interests of the nations of the region on a collective basis.*[5]

The obstacles in the way of such cooperation, according to the author, might be preoccupations with extra-regional power groupings, quarrels with neighbours, civil wars and parallel paths of economic development, differences in attitudes towards the USA, differing views on the NPT, relations with China and issues such as Kashmir.

As a counterweight to these contentious issues he posed a range of interests which could induce sufficient interest to provide the basis for regional cooperation in areas such as maritime security and resources, environmental concerns, trade, investment, technology transfer, communications, tourism and transport. He noted that the considerable cooperation between regional navies which had taken place had led to a 'healthier degree of transparency and hence confidence'. Within the framework of a regional dialogue he saw the possibility of a broadening regional and international cooperation in 'neutral' areas such as maritime security encompassing maritime boundaries, the Exclusive Economic Zones (EEZ), marine pollution, movement of drugs, contraband goods and illegal immigrants: 'all of these concerns impact upon the nations of the region and all are capable of immediate action on a collective basis'. He also saw the possibility of immediate regional cooperation focusing on fisheries, seabed resources and the equitable and sustainable exploitation of the marine wealth of the region. Fisheries was the most pressing concern: 'Extra-regional fleets are operating in the Indian Ocean with the sanction of regional governments and to the long-term detriment of both these individual governments and the interests of the region as a whole.' He argued that exclusivity would be futile but cooperation with extra-regional interests based on the region should be objective and this could only be achieved on the basis of regional planning and scientific investigation.[6]

Environmental issues, according to this viewpoint, were also best addressed on a regional basis. It was the question of trade and investment, however, which posed the greatest challenge to the concept of regional development since it was overshadowed by rivalry in pursuit of extra-regional development funds and markets. While the Indian Ocean region could not remain an isolated economic unit cut off from the rest of the world, the writer also held that the development of an increasing number of exclusive economic zones in other parts of the world ought to urge the Indian Ocean nations to look to their own interests and consider the 'scope for greater cooperation in searching out regional economic complementarities in the areas of markets for goods, cooperative industrial and resource development and regionally generated investment funds'. The economic blocs in other parts of the world impacted upon issues such as airlines, shipping, satellite communications, banking and tourism, binding the Indian Ocean countries to the economic interests and imperatives of extra-regional economies.

McPherson also referred to both an Indian and a South African perspective, drawing upon the visit to India in November 1993 of the South African Foreign Minister R.F. Botha. During this visit an agreement was arrived at to examine a proposal for creating an economic grouping of Indian Ocean rim countries. The news report attributed the proposal to Botha's initiative, for 'an economic grouping of Indian Ocean rim countries comprising India, Pakistan, South Africa, Gulf States and East African nations'. In a meeting held with the Indian Foreign Minister without aides, Dinesh Singh, Botha expressed his country's willingness to host such a meeting after the April 1994 elections. Such a grouping, it was reported, could effectively meet the challenge posed by emerging economic groupings such as NAFTA, ASEAN and APEC. Botha was also reported to have said that such a forum could help India and Pakistan to resolve or even take off the sharp edges from the Kashmir problem. The fact that the South African Minister felt it necessary to mention the Kashmir dispute, was as significant as the total absence eventually in the final communiqué of reference to any current disputes which have flared up in the Indian Ocean region which impinge upon its regional security environment. India's official governmental position thus managed to prevail, simply because other countries who could have posed a challenge were not included. Another core participant, the new South Africa, having emerged in its democratic splendour, was also facing its first territorial headaches in the Natal Zululand, demanding autonomy. Totally sidelined were all those regional, security-related developments which continue to nullify the best of economic regional development plans: the genocide in Rwanda; the unsettled Somalia, the war between North and South Yemen; the on-going international tensions centring around Iraq; the continued hostile Western suspicion of Iran; the on-going civil war in Afghanistan and demands for self-determination in Indian-occupied Kashmir; and internal insurgencies in many prominent countries of the region.

AUSTRALIAN PERCEPTIONS

Since the beginning of the 1990s, Australia's official policy has been marked by a reorganization and reorientation, focused on making Australia a major economic power in the Asia-Pacific region. It is the most populated region of the world and thus offers an immense market potential. Becoming a partner in an all-round regional development of this vast area gives any participating State a leading edge, particularly if it has expertise to offer, in addition to capital. Australia has both. In 1992, the Parliamentary Secretary to the Minister for Foreign Affairs and Trade, Stephen Martin spoke of the many advantages which Australia offered to qualify as the headquarters of a regional financial centre.[7]

The Asia-Pacific Economic Cooperation (APEC) was itself launched in Australia in 1989, and includes nations with the fastest growing economies, accounting for something like 40 per cent of the global trade and 50 per cent of the global GNP, making it the biggest regional grouping in the world so far—a market of two billion people producing half the world's output. APEC has acquired the stature of being the pre-eminent consultative body on trade issues, in the Pacific region.

A major trade and investment convention was held in Perth—the 'Into Asia' Convention—attended by some 500 government and business representatives from the region, on 16-18 November 1992. In the keynote address at the Convention, the Premier of Western Australia, Carmen Lawrence, noted with satisfaction that the state was at the forefront of a national transition to a more Asian-oriented economy. Not only did the state conduct 70 per cent of the trade with Asia, but this activity also provided 40 per cent of the jobs. With Asian Australians becoming increasingly involved in such trade initiatives, Western Australia, he said, could become a major gateway to Asia. He said, 'we have the strategic industries, we have the services and we have the cultural framework and the location to become a major gateway into Asia'.[8]

Following the Mauritius intergovernmental meeting and before the Perth Conference the Australian Foreign Minister, Senator Gareth Evans undertook an eleven-day visit to eight countries around the Indian Ocean: India, Pakistan, Sri Lanka, the Seychelles, Madagascar, South Africa and Mauritius. At an address he gave on 19 May 1995, at the India International Centre in New Delhi, he expressed his ideas on an 'Indian Ocean regionalism'. He referred to the 'important first step' taken at the intergovernmental meeting hosted by Mauritius, at which a broad agreement was reached to pursue the whole question of regional cooperation. His visit, he stressed, was in pursuance of that objective 'of looking at ways of building an indigenous Indian Ocean region-wide process of cooperation'.

He described Australia's overall goal in discussing and advancing an Indian Ocean regional policy as 'to ensure a stable and more prosperous cooperative regional environment which provides the maximum scope for economic development and trade, and where difficulties are resolved peacefully'. He noted that the Indian Ocean region being a diffuse one had made it difficult to work out a supportive regional institutional framework so far. What was important was his definition of the region:

> It contains, moreover, a variety of sub-regions. Its ethnic, cultural and religious diversity is extraordinary, as its economic disparity, not least when one extends the region—as one should—to the Gulf littoral. It contains sovereign States ranging in

size from India with over 900 million people, to Seychelles with less than 80,000 people. Economies range in size from over US$250 billion for our two countries, to less than US$400 million for Maldives and Comoros. Income levels range from US$15,000 per capita in Australia and the United Arab Emirates to less than US$250 in Mozambique, Tanzania, Madagascar and Bangladesh.

The Australian Foreign Minister noted that foundations for intra-regional trade had existed in the Indian Ocean region for at least 4,000 years, establishing a complex network of maritime trade routes, linking the earliest urban civilizations in the Middle East, the Gulf littoral, and South Asia. This led to a cross-fertilization of cultures, ideas, beliefs, politics and economy. South Asian and Middle Eastern merchant diaspora spread from Mozambique to southern China. On the nature of this trade he observed: 'Indeed before the arrival of Europeans in the late fifteenth century, the economic, political and cultural world of the Indian Ocean was largely self-sustained and interwoven.' This was a significant observation as such potential for regional self-sufficiency remains inherent in the region. Its enormous market still makes the Indian Ocean region an attractive arena for international competition, not as a peripheral supplier of raw materials as it was in the earlier times, but economically proactive with the strength of developing technologies in many countries of the region.

Equally relevant were the Australian Foreign Minister's observations on the geo-strategic importance of the Indian Ocean, because it lies at

> the strategic intersection of three continents; its underwater topography is ideally suited for locating submarine-based strategic nuclear system (at least those in service from the 1960s to the early 1980s); the bulk of the Western world's proven oil resources were, and are still, located in the recesses of its littoral; and its surface waterways carried, and still carry, the strategic raw materials and trade products of much of the industrialized world. For all these reasons, the Indian Ocean was accorded fundamental geo-strategic importance during the Cold War.

In his review of the tradition of formalized regional cooperation which could provide some sort of a foundational basis, he stressed the need for a 'broad, inclusive grouping'. Despite its critical importance in enhancing regional cohesion in and around the subcontinent the SAARC was considered insufficient because 'it does not have dialogue relationships with any outside countries', as, for example, the ASEAN and the ASEAN Regional Forum does. The Indian Ocean Commission (IOC), set up in 1982 as a result of a conference in Mauritius, was confined to the island entities and had 'not broadened its reach and capacity to carry forward a region-wide agenda'. The Indian Ocean Marine

Affairs Cooperation Council (IOMAC), initiated by Sri Lanka in 1985 and formally established in 1990, was 'slow to gather momentum, . . . (and) it is not yet clear that it is an idea whose time has come'.

Stressing the potential for growth in intra-regional trade and commercial interaction in an international atmosphere free from Cold War-oriented inhibitions, the Australian Foreign Minister noted that 'the emergence of global economy and global market-place means that the Indian Ocean region will not return to some kind of ancient economic self-sufficiency and internal cohesion'. At the same time, against the background of a rapid increase in the tempo of regionalism since the end of the Cold War, he recognized the 'continuing difficulty of developing a dialogue on economic, security or any other issues in the Indian Ocean region', since the sense of community was still weak among its littoral and island States. In the present-day scenario he observed that the regional relationships have developed new, diverse layers. Looking at successful regional arrangements he noted that the factors of success were: their inclusive approach, heterogeneous membership, multi-tracked efforts and a large degree of consensus. He argued strongly against any 'world-wide tribalism based on mutually antagonistic regional groupings', and suggested that 'globalization of the world economy means that inward-looking, self-sufficiency policies will inevitably fail to capture the enormous growth potential that interaction with other economies offers'. He also stressed a cautious and exploratory approach with emphasis in the first instance on data compilation, information dissemination and policy dialogue and on cooperative projects in specific sectors of economic activity, such as transport, infrastructure and telecommunications, and particular thematic areas like human resource development and small and medium enterprise development. At the same time 'no encouragement will be given to, or opportunity allowed for, the counter-productive airing of bilateral disputes or confrontational attitudes surrounding them'.

On security issues, the Australian Foreign Minister conceded that many sensitivities exist, 'not least in the subcontinent'. Though the security issues would occupy a small proportion of the conference agenda, the opportunity could be taken 'to advance a constructive, non-threatening and forward-looking agenda for the region', starting first with areas of likely broad agreement as a basis for approaching later, when greater confidence and understanding came about, to tackle the more difficult issues. He identified a list of apparently non-controversial security issues for discussion at IFIOR, such as: maritime resource protection; the safety of the sealanes and seaborne commerce; anti-piracy measures; the UN Agenda for Peace issues as they relate to the Indian Ocean context. This would be on the basis of experience elsewhere in developing the patterns of security dialogue at the regional level such as the ASEAN Regional Forum and the Organization for Security and Cooperation in Europe (OSCE). The need for consultative and research linkages among think-tanks, universities and institutes of international affairs and strategic studies in the region was stressed.

THE PERTH CONFERENCE

The Perth Conference on the International Forum for the Indian Ocean Region (11-13 June 1995) was a more representative gathering of the Indian Ocean States, in which 122 participants from business, academia and the government from 23 regional countries participated in their personal capacity.[9] The main areas of substantive discussion included trade, investment and economic cooperation, environment, maritime issues, human resource development and options for security dialogue.

The background papers focused on some major imperatives and rationale for cooperation. A history of the Indian Ocean region explored the historical basis of regional commercial and economic interaction through cross-fertilization of cultures and technologies, prior to the arrival of the European powers and after their entrenchment as colonial powers.

The second aspect considered was the nature of current economic characteristics and linkages in the Indian Ocean Region (IOR). The IOR comprises a collection of economically diverse and disparate countries, with significant variations in levels of wealth and economic development, economic and trade interests, dependence on regional trade, and varying levels of political interest in regional cooperation. Any approaches to cooperation in the region must take into consideration the predicaments and possibilities defined by these realities. It was proposed that the IFIOR undertake a descriptive and comparative survey of different types of regional economic arrangements. A possible model, according to this approach, was to consider tripartite groupings such as the Pacific Economic Cooperation Council (PECC), as a loose consultative arrangement.

The next aspect discussed were the global and regional security arrangements in general and the security characteristics of the IOR in particular. Discussions viewed approaches to security considerations through a global survey of regional and sub-regional approaches to security. The most pronounced transformations in security arrangements and networks and non-security cooperation and dialogue have been in Europe and Asia. The proceedings were not clear about the possible future role of IFIOR in intra-regional conflicts, though growing world-wide emphasis on conflict prevention mechanisms was noted.

Non-military security issues, their trans-boundary and international impact and, hence, the need for multinational and regional cooperation drew considerable attention. These were: illicit drugs; diseases; illegal movements of people; piracy within coastal waters and on the high seas; natural disasters; terrorism and border disputes. Over-arching these non-military security issues were the population rise and the ever widening gap between the richest and the poorest countries. Options considered for the management of such issues included the use of existing organizations, establishing new bodies and increasing co-operation between existing bodies.

Finally, the conference examined the existing networks of co-operation and their prospects for further development, through issues and interests which could provide the basis of 'building blocks' for wider IOR cooperation. It was noted that other than the various UN or UN-sponsored bodies, a large number of sub-regional groupings existed representing particular specialist areas and sectors. The absence of networking was attributed to lack of awareness, political commitment, financial support and the reluctance of some countries to be involved in multilateral activities, as well as a lingering sensitivity to the involvement of non-littoral countries. Maritime affairs, particularly maritime safety and marine environmental management as common interests of all countries lent themselves easily to such networking activities. It was argued that costly new structures be avoided and cooperation be expanded through networking among existing organizations.

Much stress was laid on developing the marine resources of the IOR, including fisheries and deep seabed mining and human resource development. Concerning the latter aspect, it was noted that all countries of the region shared the urgent and critical need to increase the skills of their work force 'either in response to the needs of growing populations or to maintain a standard of living in the face of international competition . . . the region contains storehouses of knowledge, skills, and policy approaches and experiences which encourage self-reliance and cooperation'. It was noted that the IOR has been less systematically researched than the Pacific and the Atlantic Oceans.

The Economic Working Group identified two broad issue areas: the first was on business facilitation such as the regulatory environment, visas, taxes, currency convertibility, trade promotion and a regional business directory; the second was on technology transfer, transport and telecommunications, human resource development, educational exchanges, financial services, and research and development.

A range of other areas were recommended for cooperation through interactive information activities on research areas, identifying issues of common concern, and looking at issues of literacy, legal rights, health and economic opportunities for women in the IOR. The conference also recommended consideration of comprehensive security approaches and their applicability to the IOR. Five working groups were established to report on: (a) a Charter for a new business organization; (b) information technology, including telecommunications; (c) customs and trade documentation; (d) non-tariff barriers and impediments to investment; and (e) maritime affairs. An Indian Ocean Research Network was set up open to any interested party in the IOR. The possibility of establishing an Eminent Persons Group to consult widely on IOR issues and recommend options was also considered.

One question that remained open was whether further steps in the IFIOR process would be less exclusive and include at least the twenty-three participating States represented at the IFIOR, and eventually embrace the whole region.

SIGNIFICANT LAPSES

A region-based economic organization for the IOR is a laudable idea and in principle would find support in all countries of the region. Both the Mauritius and Perth initiatives were important steps in this connection, in that they focused attention on the possibilities for the future development of the IOR by participants and non-participants alike. Exploratory as these two initiatives were, the varying objectives of some countries left the conceptual basis for cooperation rather murky. There was thus a wide gap between expectations on the one hand and the realities of the IOR on the other.

A significant lapse in both these initiatives was the total absence of any reference to the status of land-locked countries which fall within the hinterland of the IOR, and their partnership potential therein. There was much talk on the exploitation of the Exclusive Economic Zone, understood to be the 200-mile wide expanse acknowledged and sanctified by UNCLOS III. The International Convention on the Law of the Sea fully safeguards the rights of land-locked and geographically disadvantaged States in Articles 69 and 70. These Articles provide that Land-locked and Geographically Disadvantaged States

> shall have the right to participate, on an equitable basis, in the exploitation of an appropriate part of the surplus of the living resources of the exclusive economic zones of coastal States of the same sub-region or region, taking into account the relevant economic and geographical circumstances of all the States concerned and in conformity with the provisions of articles 61 and 62.[10]

The Convention envisaged the terms and modalities of such participation through bilateral, sub-regional or regional arrangements. The IOR has the largest number of land-locked and geographically disadvantaged States in its region.

The fact remains that the initiative has been taken in a world situation with the UNCLOS III dispensation in place. It provides for the right of land-locked and geographically disadvantaged States in fairly comprehensive provisions: freedom of the high seas and right of navigation therein (Articles 87 and 90); right of access to and from the sea and freedom of transit *vis-à-vis* transit States (Articles of Part X); rights to the benefits arising out of the activities undertaken in any part of the seas for the exploitation of resources 'at or beneath the sea-bed, including poly-metallic nodules' (Articles 133, 140 and 141). Article 148 specifically provides for the effective participation of developing States, 'in particular to the special need of the land-locked and geographically disadvantaged among them to overcome obstacles arising from their disadvantaged location, including remoteness from the Area and difficulty of access from it'. This 'particular consideration' would also be extended to such countries in respect of enabling their participation in the authority set up for the purposes of the development, exploration and exploitation of the sea resources (Articles 152, 153 and 160(2)(k)). In connection with any marine scientific research being carried out in a neighbouring area of the sea, the 'rights of neighbouring land-locked and geographically disadvantaged States' are fully acknowledged and safeguarded by Article 254.[11] The question, of course, remains what would be the attitude of a coastal State in the event of hostilities. Equally pertinent would be whether the land-locked States of a region could participate in an EEZ of their choosing in the region they are considered part of. For instance, could a Central Asian State participate in activities in the EEZ off Australia, an African land-locked State in the EEZ off India, and Afghanistan, for instance, in the EEZ off

South Africa? Such potential issues are best addressed by confronting them and not by evading them.

INDIAN OCEAN 'REGIONALISM' AND REGIONAL STRATEGIC ISSUES

Any formal establishment of an economic organization for the Indian Ocean region would not have durable foundations if existing security issues are ignored. Security threats have widened in scope. The Kashmir issue, for instance, with its recently added undertones of human rights abuses, is now matched in intensity by the economic competition being faced by flourishing economies. At an international seminar on 'Indian Ocean, Security and Stability in the Post Cold War Era' held in Islamabad on 18-20 April 1994, some significant country perspectives were presented. The Chinese Ambassador, Zheng Wanzhen, gave the Chinese perceptions on Indian Ocean security. He observed that the Clinton administration's attempts at a rejuvenation of the US domestic economy was aimed at setting up a new global economic order with US dominance. Russia, he said, continued to insist on its major-power status, and still possesses powerful military might and was going ahead with the modernization of its strategic nuclear force. The US naval presence remained a fact in the Indian Ocean. Since 1991, India has become a key State in the United States' relations with other countries in the region. The first US-India joint naval exercises in the Indian Ocean took place on 27 May 1992 and, according to the Chinese Ambassador, it 'has been reported that in return for the use of naval facilities at Visakhapatnam, the United States would transfer high-tech defence equipment to India'. India too was increasing its leverage as a player in world politics. The Chinese position on the Indian Ocean region remains one of opposing hegemony, supporting peaceful settlement of disputes through consultations and negotiations on an equal footing. China stands for equal opportunities and right of navigation by all States to use the Indian Ocean sealanes and oppose the dumping of toxic materials in the high seas and oceans. The Chinese claim not to seek hegemony is considered suspect by the Western media, according to which China 'has long wanted recognition as a great power in Asia and beyond' and, as another opinion put it, 'by pumping steroids into the PLA's muscles'. China's expansion of its naval programme is shown as an indicator. The fact also remains that as a former PLA general reportedly said, 'We (China) cannot recognize the Indian Ocean as India's Ocean.'[12]

The importance of the Indian Ocean in the global politics of powerful nations will ensure that this area remains in the strategic thinking of non-littoral nations. Efforts to establish a regional forum in the IOR will, therefore, draw much attention globally. A new political context has shaped a new security environment quite specific to the Indian Ocean region, which cannot be ignored. The technologically better endowed countries and blocs would inevitably be the directing forces and attempt also to be the international law makers.

One pertinent viewpoint is that in the emerging post-Cold War configuration of international relations, the East-West conflict will probably shift to a North-South confrontation—the *raison d'être* being that in the emerging world order, the global competition for vital resources will sharpen. Specifically in the context of the Indian Ocean, as one observer argues:

> The Indian Ocean region accommodates more than 40 world countries and is considered to be a huge reservoir of raw materials, some of which are among the rarest in the world. *Not only the US, but its economic rivals are crucially, vitally dependent on the resources of this region for sustaining and developing their industrial economies. Therefore, the Indian Ocean region will be one of the most important hotbeds of North-South confrontation in the emerging world order.* (emphasis added)[13]

This observer argues that the policies and postures which evolved and emerged in the Indian Ocean region, in the days of the Cold War, under the mask of an ideological confrontation were virtually resource-based. The rivalry of the superpowers was 'in essence a struggle for domination and control of the resources of the region . . . it was in pursuance of this objective that they built up military bases, wooed allies, positioned warships, and . . . made their own presence in the region sure and secure'. He argues that in the future too, the resources of the Indian Ocean region would affect the emergent patterns and shaping up of policies—or the regional and international geo-political compulsions.

SAARC AND INDIAN OCEAN: IMPLICATIONS AND PROSPECTS

The Indian Ocean Region mirrors the global scenario in rather an interesting way. In its conglomeration of littoral, hinterland and island States, it reflects the various inequalities on the world scene, arising out of objective factors such as: land expanse and thereby area; demography and its ethnic complexities; levels of economic, social and technological development. The specific characteristics of the IOR are also worth consideration. The conceptualization of an economic forum for the IOR comes in a post-Cold War world, which has removed the guise from the actual security motivations, at the level of nation-states or as collectivities, to reveal that generally speaking, arsenals are growing qualitatively and quantitatively. Whatever be the security concerns of nation-states, the end result is that nations are involved in the financing of the costly, defence and security-related research and development, their production and procurement. This means also that they have to face the competing demands for a share of the national revenues from other sectors, for example, the increasing need for development and growing civic amenities arising out of demographic pressures. Regional organizations will also have to face these dilemmas and be in a position to address them. ASEAN has recognized the need for its own security-related organization. This is pertinent to the IOR which is the most highly populated of all such regions. Similarly, SAARC will not be able to avoid confronting the security concerns facing its member States.

Despite well-known predicaments, with regular infusions of initiatives, SAARC has survived to a point where in the consciousness of its member States, it has found a niche of its own, which is reflected in the manner in which SAARC forms part of their internal national political debates and election agendas. There is a growing demand that SAARC be made more effective as a forum for interaction between the governments and the peoples of its member States. It is also argued that it should gradually serve as a forum to deal with 'bilateral and contentious issues' such as the Kashmir dispute between Pakistan and India or the water sharing problem between India and Bangladesh. Regarding the possibility of tensions arising between economic complementarities and competition, the combined population of SAARC countries is, at one level, big enough to accommodate both these aspects. It is a case of seven look-alike siblings, each having his own stature and identity and, therefore, each having an individual approach and point of view.

The sooner the governments of SAARC member States realize the region's vast market potential, the sooner they would be able to forge a meaningful role for SAARC in the formulation of the IFIOR. The advantages are many, as are the problems. In this context it is useful to examine the comparative experience of the European Union and ASEAN specially in view of the international relations of the region.[14] Notably, the IFIOR has adopted the same principle as SAARC with respect to the inclusion of bilateral and contentious issues. In this context it would be useful to analyse the future status of the UN Ad Hoc Committee, specially in view of the new initiative. Equally important to study is the failure of the Indian Ocean Zone of Peace Proposal, even though it was adopted by the United Nations in 1971, and supported by member States of SAARC such as India, Maldives, Pakistan and Sri Lanka.

One important lesson to be drawn from the experience of IOZP is that incompatibility of the idea with the security concerns of many Indian Ocean countries played the divisive part, which in some cases led to the establishment of linkages with extra-regional powers, in order to help even in the maintenance of internal security. An incremental approach, rather than ambitious agenda might develop confidence among the member States of the region. The existing regional cooperation mechanisms should be considered building blocks and for that to happen a very clear idea was needed of the relationship and the role of these regional groups, such as SAARC, within the broader process of IFIOR. Whether it is SAARC or the Indian Ocean region as a whole, it would make more sense if core economic issues like trade, investment and commerce received top priority, which is the global trend. Specifically in the case of SAARC, for instance, if the SAARC countries were to integrate as a regional market then their policies and markets would become much more attractive for the capital-rich countries from outside the region, which would in turn generate greater intra-regional trade and economic interaction in the IOR.

With respect to membership of IFIOR, it is important for any viable regional cooperation initiative to be as inclusive as possible. Arguably, if due regard is to be given to the provisions of the Law of the Sea Convention, the number of States which might be invited to join the grouping is quite large. But that is the reality to be faced if it has to be an Indian Ocean regionalism. Even if all these countries are unable to participate, provisions should be made for their future participation on an equitable basis, regardless of their level of economic development. The present period of flux in global affairs is a time both of immense opportunities and pitfalls. As 'regionalism' shapes up in the Indian Ocean Region it must take note of all these developments and the realities of regional inequalities which exist within its own region *vis-à-vis* other regions of the world. The need for speed in putting such a regional organization in place should not be confounded with haste, as any haste to exclude any regional country, or existent fora, from the dynamics of deliberations would only end up carving up the IOR into sub-regional zones of influence of sub-regional axis powers.

NOTES

1. This right is further enhanced by the recent discovery in South Africa of the most ancient of ancient man, considered to be the missing link in the history of mankind.
2. Trevor Findlay, 'South East Asia and the New Asia Pacific Security Dialogue' in SIPRI, *SIPRI Yearbook 1994,* Oxford University Press, 1994, pp. 125-47. The author views South-East Asia as a coherent Asia-Pacific sub-region, emerging as 'a locus of efforts to create a broader Asia-Pacific regionalism, in both economic and security fields'.
3. *The Economist*, 20 November 1993, pp. 13-14.
4. Robert D. Hormats, 'Making Regionalism Safe', *Foreign Affairs*, March/April 1994, pp. 97-108.
5. *The Indian Ocean Review* 7(1) (March 1994), see pp. 13, 17.
6. Ibid.
7. See Stephen Martin, 'Australia Could Be Regional Headquarters', *Insight,* 21 September 1992, pp. 8-9.
8. *Insight*, 30 November 1992, pp. 13-14.
9. The participating countries were: Australia, Bahrain, Bangladesh, India, Iran, Kenya, Kuwait, Madagascar, Malaysia, Maldives, Mauritius, Mozambique, Oman, Pakistan, Saudi Arabia, Seychelles, Singapore, South Africa, Sri Lanka, Thailand, United Arab Emirates, Yemen. Coastal, island and archipelagic States were thus represented, as were the varying levels of economies—developing and the more industrialized ones.
10. Articles 61 and 62 provide for the responsibility accruing to coastal States for the conservation of the living resources in their respective EEZ.
11. United Nations, *The Law of the Sea, Official Text of the United Nations Convention on the Law of the Sea*, New York, 1983.
12. *The Economist*, 29 April-5 May 1995, pp. 15-16. See also *Time*, 12 April 1993, pp. 23-7.
13. See for details, S. Sadrodin Mossavi, 'Indian Ocean in the Emerging World Order: The Superpower Factor', *Strategic Analysis* (New Delhi) XVI(10) (January 1994).
14. For many of the propositions presented here I am thankful to the insightful comments made by participants in the seminar on 'Regional Economic Trends and South Asian Security', specially, Ahmed Shaheed.

Regional Economic Trends and South Asian Security: A European Perspective

CHRISTIAN WAGNER

THE COLLAPSE of the Soviet Union has changed the political map of the globe considerably. New States have emerged, especially in Eastern Europe and Central Asia, and the military and ideological confrontation of the superpowers and their regional allies has vanished. Although the future of the international system is still unclear, several trends are already noticeable. A multi-polar world system seems to be emerging, which is dominated by regional groupings and regional powers, replacing the ideological conflict between the superpowers with economic competition.[1] At the same time, a growing interdependence between international values and national policies may be observed. What started in the economic field as the global demand for market-oriented policies was followed in the political field with demands for democratization and protection of human rights. Both developments have far-reaching consequences for national policies. The process of market liberalization will lead to new regional, social and sectoral differentiations and inequalities. This will impel more and more societal groups to demand their appropriate share of the benefits of market liberalization. On the basis of democracy, self-determination and protection of human rights, subnational groups, claiming a different religious, ethnic or linguistic identity are demanding greater autonomy or even a separate State. This will increase the number of internal conflicts and force governments to look for peaceful conflict regulation mechanism.

These developments have also led to a radical change in the notion of security. External military threats have mostly been replaced with internal conflicts, whereas external threats have become much more diffuse, dealing, apart from the military threat by rival States, with the dangers of nuclear proliferation, terrorism, arms and drug trafficking. This growing linkage between the constraints of the political and economic changes in the international system on the one hand and the unfinished process of nation-building on the other, seems to be at the heart of the present crisis of governance in many countries.

For the nation-state, regional cooperation offers one strategy to face these challenges. In a world of growing insecurity and conflict, political stability, not only at the national but also on the regional level, requires reliable bilateral and regional relations. Political stability also becomes a prerequisite to attract foreign investment supporting national economic transformation. This is even more necessary in times when many regions are struggling for the scarce funds of foreign investment and shrinking official development assistance by Western countries. The benefits of closer collaboration between States seem obvious, as more and more countries are entering regional organizations in order to seek political alliances or new economic opportunities.

This paper tries to analyse the problems of economic cooperation and security issues in Europe and South Asia. My argument is that the connection between economic cooperation and security issues has changed considerably in the post-Cold War world. Europe tackled these problems by establishing a network of institutions. But even sophisticated models of regional cooperation, like the European Union (EU), have been unable in many cases to find a common stance on foreign policy matters. What was possible in the field of economic cooperation, decision-making by majority rule, thereby implying the transfer of national sovereignty, was impossible in the field of security and military matters. But other institutions, like NATO and the Conference on Security and Cooperation in Europe (CSCE) were established in order to deal with the military and security issues of Europe.

Regional cooperation in South Asia, however, is caught in a dilemma. Given the local roots of conflict, it will not benefit much from the recent international changes and remain a region of chronic instability. The severe socio-economic problems will force the governments to follow the path of economic liberalization. But, given the bilateral problems and the present structure of production, economic collaboration, used in Europe to achieve closer political collaboration, will probably not be a successful strategy in the short run. SAARC will, nevertheless, have an important function, already regarded as a starting point to establish stable bilateral and regional relations despite bilateral conflicts. At the same time, it has to strengthen the political will for collaboration by making clear that the costs of non-cooperation are higher than the costs of cooperation. Moreover, it should encourage the creation of other regional or subregional institutions.

In the first part of the paper, I shall review the experience of Europe in dealing with the challenges of economic cooperation and the question of security by looking at the development of the European Union (EU) and the CSCE. The development of the EU shows the endeavours of States, sharing many common interests, to act as a single player in political and security issues, and the problems they face in this endeavour. The CSCE serves as an example how a continuous process of negotiations was able to install confidence-building measures between the superpowers. I shall then deal with the different security perspectives in South Asia and the prospects of economic interaction in the region.

ECONOMIC DEVELOPMENT AND THE QUESTION OF SECURITY IN EUROPE

The European Union is usually regarded as a success story of regional integration in terms of its economic cooperation. But it is often overlooked that the history of the European Community was also determined by a close relationship of cooperation in political and security issues. The reconstruction of Europe after World War II was guided by three main principles, namely, economic reconstruction, political reconciliation, and common defence against the Soviet Union. The first steps were taken with the foundation of the Organization for Economic Cooperation and Development (OECD) in 1948 and the North Atlantic Treaty Organization (NATO) in 1949. In 1950, the French Foreign Minister Robert Schuman developed a plan to bring the entire coal and steel production of Germany and France under a common authority. By this, he not only wanted to bring the two European arch enemies, Germany and France, together but also intended to control the production of coal and steel, essential for future warfare. When the treaty of the European Coal and Steel Community (ECSC) was signed in 1951, it marked the beginning of closer economic collaboration. But this implied closer cooperation in political and security matters as well. This became evident in 1952 when the treaty on the European Defence Community (EDC) was signed and plans for a closer political collaboration were discussed intensively. In 1954, the Western European Union (WEU) was founded as a system of collective security for Western Europe. But the WEU remained a weak institution. It relinquished its own military infrastructure to NATO, yet remained useful for integrating West Germany into the Western alliance. Security questions were dealt with mainly in the wider framework of NATO. This was opposed by France which was not inclined to submit its national interests to a common military command headed by the United States. It left NATO in 1966 and became an associate member.

The efforts to reach political and military collaboration failed when the French Parliament resisted the plans for a European Defence Community in 1954. After this, plans for European political cooperation were also given up. But the interest in economic cooperation remained and was slowly extended. Following a functional approach, the intention was to achieve political collaboration by intensified economic interaction. In 1957, the Treaty of Rome laid the foundation for the European Economic Community (EEC) and the European Atomic Energy Community (Euratom). The 1960s saw a rapid development of economic collaboration in Europe. Thus the customs union could be finalized already in 1968, one year earlier than originally planned. In 1967 the three communities, ECSC, EEC and Euratom were merged under a single authority.

The plans for closer political cooperation were fostered at that time mainly by Germany and France. The German Chancellor Adenauer and the French President De Gaulle agreed that close relations between their countries should become the core of future European political cooperation. In 1963 the German-French Friendship Treaty laid the foundation for a permanent rapprochement between them. At the European level, the next attempt to achieve closer political cooperation started with the Davignon Report in 1970 that recommended a harmonization of the divergent foreign policies. Although France opposed this move it was agreed that the foreign ministers of the European Community (EC) should discuss the question of political cooperation twice a year. This established a process of regular exchange and close consultations on political issues among the EC which were always kept officially apart from normal EC meetings as they were not covered by the Treaty of Rome. Political cooperation rested on national interests and national sovereignty so that decisions could be reached by consensus alone. This rule was slowly abandoned in favour of other means of decision-making in the official framework of the EC. It was only after the Single European Act in 1986 that European Political Cooperation (EPC) became a pillar of the European Community. It was institutionalized with a common secretariat in Brussels. The European Commission and the European Parliament were subsequently included in the consultations in order to achieve better coordination and harmonization of foreign policy affairs.

The changes in the international scene beginning in 1989 also affected the EU. The breakdown of the communist system made it necessary to support the process of democratization and economic transformation in Central and Eastern Europe, often accompanied by violent nationalistic movements. The Treaty of Maastricht (1991) aimed again at closer political union to be able to face these challenges. Apart from the endeavours to achieve an Economic and Monetary Union and closer collaboration in legal and internal affairs the Common Foreign and Security Policy (CFSP) was formulated in order to achieve better coordination in foreign policy matters.

It may be seen from this brief review that the EU has always been more successful in the economic than in the political field. When the plans for a European Defence Community failed, the agenda of military collaboration was transferred to NATO so that security concerns were dealt with in the larger framework of the Western community including the United States and Canada. In many policy fields the EC introduced decision-making by simple or qualified majorities, thus handing over national sovereignty in these areas to supra-national institutions. But despite regular exchange and close consultations this was not possible in foreign policy and security matters. In these fields political cooperation was limited by divergent national interests. Political cooperation was a successful instrument for the EU when it dealt with international issues. Important political declarations were passed, for instance, in 1980 when the EC suggested that the Palestine Liberation Organization (PLO) should take part in the peace process in the Middle East. Other successful examples were the trade sanctions imposed on South Africa in protest against the apartheid system and against Iraq after the invasion in Kuwait. In addition, the EC was an important actor in the negotiations in the CSCE and often acted as a single actor in the UN General Assembly.[2] The resentments against a transfer of power in the sensitive field of foreign policy became obvious again in the Treaty of Maastricht. The idea of bringing foreign policy and security matters into the procedures on the Community, which would have implied decision-making by majority rule and therefore a loss of national sovereignty was rejected by Great Britain. A common foreign and security policy of the EU is still to be achieved by intergovernmental collaboration resting on the principle of consensus.

The CSCE can serve as a good example of how a continuing diplomatic process was able to smooth the consequences of East-West confrontation in Europe. Established by the Helsinki Accords in 1975, the CSCE rested on the principle of national sovereignty. It started with thirty-five countries from the Western and Eastern blocs, which agreed on permanent consultations and confidence-building measures (CBMs) in three different fields, namely, military and security issues; economic, scientific and technological cooperation; and human rights affairs. The Helsinki Accords were also the starting point for a series of CSCE follow-up conferences in Belgrade (1977-8), Madrid (1980-3), Vienna (1986-9) and Helsinki (1992), which were accompanied by summits of the Heads of State every two years. Simultaneously, workshops and expert meetings on human rights, disarmament, economic cooperation, people-to-people contacts, and conflict resolution were held in order to intensify collaboration in these fields among the CSCE countries. The Stockholm Conference on Security and Confidence Building Measures (1986) institutionalized military CBMs like exchange on information on military activities, observation of manoeuvres and obligatory on-site inspections. In 1990, the Charter of Paris for a New Europe brought a common commitment of all States to the principles of human rights, protection of minorities, democracy, rule of law, and environmental protection. It was also the starting point for institutionalization of the CSCE in order to deal with the new internal challenges of its member countries, especially in Central and Eastern Europe. The CSCE Council, consisting of the foreign ministers, which met at least once a year, has become the central political authority. The Committee of high-level Bureaucrats supports the Council and coordinates the activities of the CSCE. Other institutions were established like the CSCE Secretariat in Prague, a Centre for Conflict Prevention in Vienna, a Bureau for Free Elections in Warsaw and a High Commissioner for Minorities.

As an institution the CSCE successfully helped overcome the tensions of the Cold War by diplomatic means. Its documents and agreements were no international treaties but acted only as a framework of explicit norms, procedures, and regulations. These agreements were not intended to defeat the other side but were used to improve slowly the relations between both ideological blocs in military matters, economic collaboration and people-to-people contacts.

The rise of nationalistic movements in Eastern Europe and the outbreak of the civil war in former Yugoslavia have raised a debate on the extent to which organizations like the EU or the CSCE have failed. There have been failures, for instance, when the EU was not able to work out a common line towards recognition of the emerging States of former Yugoslavia; it was the German government which moved ahead and recognized Slovenia and Croatia as sovereign States. But the criticism does not take into account the original goals of these organizations. They were founded during the Cold War in order to deal with European security issues in a bipolar world. The proceedings and regulations that were worked out to specific international conflict constellations were evidently not suited to deal with internal conflicts as in former Yugoslavia. The focus of the EU and the CSCE had mainly been on diplomatic activities and negotiations in order to create a system of conflict prevention. For resolution of an existing conflict where military involvement would have become necessary they had no means by which to intervene in order to stop civil war.

Despite all the criticism, the success of European institutions should not be overlooked. Unlike earlier, the different national interests in South-East Europe did not lead to a serious conflict between the great powers. All European actors, including Russia and also the United States, shared a common interest to end military fighting and to find a peaceful solution for the troubles in former Yugoslavia. Without the close diplomatic network of the EU, NATO and the CSCE, this would have been much more difficult to achieve. The institutional networks established essentially as instruments of bipolar confrontation also helped initiate a process of permanent exchange and consultations both between the member countries and between the antagonistic blocs. Thus, the experiences of Western and European organizations established during the Cold War bring into focus the close connection between political, economic and security issues.

REGIONAL COOPERATION AND SECURITY IN SOUTH ASIA

South Asia has been characterized as a region of 'chronic instability'[3] and 'economic disintegration'.[4] Politically, the region is shaped by various conflicts dealing both with territorial disputes on land and resources and demands of various subnational groups for greater autonomy, self-determination or even independence. In socio-economic criteria, South Asia is placed at the bottom of the scale in international statistics. In 1993, the GNP per capita was only \$310.[5] According to the *Human Development Index*, all South Asian countries except Sri Lanka and the Maldives belong to the lowest category; in other words, the majority of their population faces extremely meagre living conditions.[6] Politically, the most serious issue is the Kashmir conflict between India and Pakistan. What was once a territorial conflict with strong ideological undertones has evolved into a movement by Kashmiri Muslims demanding self-determination and independence both from India and Pakistan. A political solution that would allow both countries to keep face seems unlikely. The Kashmir conflict has already caused two wars and has initiated an arms race with both conventional and nuclear dimensions. The Kashmir issue also reflects divergent concepts of national security. India has always regarded itself as a regional or even global power, with South Asia being part of its national security; that the influence of external powers should, therefore, be reduced in the region. The neighbouring States have never accepted these perceptions. They tried to internationalize their conflicts with India and were looking for economic, political and military support from external powers. The conflicts, which arise because of these divergent notions of security, have strained India's relations with its neighbours. The Indian military intervention in Sri Lanka from 1987 to 1990 failed to solve the antagonisms between the Sinhalese and the Tamil minority. Nepal's efforts to obtain better relations with China and its attempts to renegotiate the Friendship Treaty with India, met with China's resistance. Likewise, there are various conflicts between India and Bangladesh, for instance, the distribution of Ganga waters and the immigration of Bangladeshis into India.

There are numerous examples of internal conflicts caused by subnational groups demanding more autonomy from their central government or even a separate State. At present, the Indian government has to face these challenges in the Punjab, Kashmir and the north-east, Pakistan in Sindh, and Sri Lanka in its northern areas. The global trends towards democratization, liberalization and protection of human rights will enhance such internal conflicts in the future when more and more subnational and social groups will articulate their demands on this basis. In many cases, these conflicts have been aggravated by external support from neighbouring States, providing financial and material support as well as training facilities for such movements. The rise of religious fundamentalism constitutes another internal threat to the nation-state by offering an alternative paradigm of development and society. In addition, it can become a new source of bilateral tensions, as became evident by the riots in Pakistan and Bangladesh after the destruction of the mosque in Ayodhya by Hindu nationalists.[7]

In the tense national and bilateral context and the changing international environment, the countries of South Asia face three major challenges. These are: to improve the socio-economic situation of their people, to find ways for internal conflict resolution, and to adapt their concepts of security to changing national and international environment. Evidently, regional cooperation is more than desirable. As noted by the former SAARC Secretary-General, 'regionalism today seems to be the instrument of economic growth and development in the world of ever increasing cut-throat competition'[8]. But the expectations of achieving this goal in the immediate future should remain subdued. Regional collaboration alone will not by miracle solve all problems. The potential to foster economic growth rates and to eradicate poverty by regional cooperation alone is limited. But it is clear from the experiences in other regions that in the long-term perspective the costs of non-cooperation are much higher. Regional cooperation, often accompanied by setbacks, failures and compromises, must be regarded as a long-term process that can establish stable bilateral and intra-regional relations. This must include a network of different organizations, not only on the political level but on the societal level as well.[9]

When SAARC was founded in 1985, it seemed to be an agglomeration of countries with hardly any common interests. It was an assembly of different political regimes including military dictatorships, monarchies and democracies following different economic policies. Moreover, the SAARC countries did not share common foreign policy perspectives or common perceptions of external threats. What seemed to be a nearly impossible undertaking in regard to regional cooperation was nevertheless to some extent successful. Supported by national changes in recent years, the South Asian countries have found more common grounds today. The great majority of the population is living under democratic governments since the beginning of the 1990s and nearly all countries are now pursuing free market and economic liberalization policies. This development is highly valuable for the region as a whole. First, the establishment of democracy will foster common values, making South Asia the biggest democratic region in the world. The strengthening of parliamentary institutions will also have a positive impact on internal conflict situation. Second, pursuing similar economic policies will facilitate economic collaboration, which can be established as a second pillar for the future of SAARC. Third, closer collaboration can help to adapt the divergent security perceptions. Fourth, an increasing political understanding and stability can improve the global importance of South Asia, making it more attractive for foreign investors.

PROSPECTS OF ECONOMIC COOPERATION IN SOUTH ASIA

Intensified intra-regional economic collaboration enjoys the greatest attraction in times of growing liberalization and globalization. The accounts of the EU are most impressive in this respect as nearly 60 to 70 per cent of total trade is conducted between member States. But the benefits of regional integration were often overestimated, specially in regard to developing countries. Comparative studies show that regional integration 'has failed to offer a viable development strategy for the catching-up process'[10]. Although there are high expectations connected with the expansion of intra-regional trade, one should be cautious, because closer economic cooperation cannot be a 'substitute for appropriate domestic economic policies'[11]. The economic progress of the SAARC countries will therefore depend more on the continuation of their national liberalization policy than on the expansion of regional trade.

In 1989, intra-regional trade in South Asia was only 3.4 per cent of total trade, a rate marginal compared to Europe (70 per cent) or even ASEAN (18 per cent). Until today, bilateral tensions have hampered the creation of adequate infrastructure and communication systems in South Asia.[12] Apart from political factors, economic and infrastructural obstacles limit the extension of intra-regional trade. The present structure of production clearly shows that most South Asian economies do not have many complementarities, but compete with their major export goods on the world market.[13] The importance of neighbouring economies as potential trading partners will, therefore, remain limited except for land-locked countries like Nepal and Bhutan. This trend may be verified from the three major regional economies, India, Pakistan and Bangladesh. In 1992, intra-regional imports for India were below 1 per cent of total imports, for Pakistan only 1.5 per cent and 9.7 per cent for Bangladesh. Intra-regional exports were only 3.0 per cent of total exports for India, 4.9 per cent for Pakistan, and 2.2 per cent for Bangladesh. Even for Sri Lanka, which has followed an export-oriented policy since 1977, the countries of the region remain only marginal trading partners. Although the share of intra-regional imports rose from 6.5 per cent in 1980 to 9.5 per cent in 1992, the share of intra-regional exports declined in the same period from 7.1 per cent to 1.9 per cent.[14] The SAARC Preferential Trading Arrangement (SAPTA), recently ratified by all SAARC countries, will certainly intensify intra-regional trade. But this can only be the beginning and the coming years will show to what extent SAPTA can help increase intra-regional trade.

The picture of infrastructure is even worse. How can one talk on extension of intra-regional trade when there is only one border station between the two biggest economies? How can business persons look for new economic opportunities in the neighbouring countries when visa regulations are highly restrictive? In addition, various tariff and non-tariff barriers restrict the exchange of goods and the flow of capital.[15] Given these factors, the intra-regional trade flow will not change considerably in the coming years. The industrialized countries of the West and the East, the newly industrialized countries of South-East Asia and the Middle East will remain the most important trading partners for South Asia.

CONCLUSION

Taking into account the growing linkage between the imperatives of economic globalization and the increase of internal threats in the post-Cold War period, the importance of political stability in order to achieve socio-economic development is quite obvious. The EU had already had a high level of political understanding when it started closer economic interaction in order to achieve the political integration of its member States. Becoming an economic giant, the EU has still not reached political integration. Although this subject remained on the agenda of the Treaty of Maastricht, it will still take a long time to overcome the objections of national interests. But looking not only at the EU, but at the European and Western development in general, it becomes clear that the creation and linkage of various regional institutional networks is important to handle economic, political and security issues.

The countries of South-East Asia seemed to be fully aware of the importance of such networks. Apart from their economic cooperation, the ASEAN countries developed Post Ministerial Conferences (PMC) as a multilateral forum in order to discuss political and economic questions of common interest. Given the international changes, it was only a logical step when the ASEAN Regional Forum (ARF) was established in 1993 which included the most important external powers of the Asia-Pacific region, and which is mainly concerned with security matters of the region.

South Asia is facing a difficult task. For a long time there were neither common political interests nor economic incentives to enter into closer collaboration. Like the EU, members of ASEAN started their cooperation from an already high level of common political understanding and could use economic interaction to further intensify linkages. The SAARC countries have to take another direction. The low level of economic interaction will make it necessary first to strengthen political understanding with confidence-building measures. This will create a favourable climate which will pave the way for closer economic collaboration.

Despite its shortcomings, a general assessment of SAARC should be broadly positive, given the political context and conflicts in the region. Politically, SAARC is already a crucial institution as the only forum where confidence-building measures can take place at the highest political level. Moreover, the regular meetings of foreign ministers, foreign secretaries and high-level bureaucrats offer additional platforms to enhance mutual understanding. Economically, SAPTA is the first economic agreement between all member countries. It will give new momentum to intra-regional trade, thereby intensifying bilateral relations. But SAPTA will be no substitute for world-market integration of the national economies. Especially in regard to the pressing problems of underdevelopment, it will become necessary to attract foreign investment. This has become more difficult as the countries in Eastern Europe and Central Asia also compete for establishing themselves as targets of growing foreign investments. SAARC declarations on democracy and market-oriented economy can certainly strengthen the region's international standing, and hence competitiveness.

SAARC, and for that matter SAPTA, can only be regarded as a starting point. Transnational interaction between societal and professional groups must be expanded and strengthened in order to promote people-to-people contacts. Sub-regional collaboration including three or four member States for specific fields like infrastructure should become another instrument to intensify regional interaction. These efforts should be combined with a 'South Asian Regional Initiative' (SARI), proposed by S.P. Cohen in order to establish what may be called a 'South Asia House'.[16] The various activities initiated by SAARC will help to extend existing networks and to establish a permanent process of exchange, communication, and consultation. In a long-term perspective, only such strategy will reduce hostile perceptions and will create common understanding among the ruling elite in the region that the costs of non-cooperation are always higher than the costs of cooperation. Any critical reflection on South Asian developments during the last forty years will confirm this fact. In the near future, the major challenge for SAARC will be to take regional cooperation from the national bureaucracies and research institutions to the markets and the people of South Asia.

NOTES

1. R. Gilpin, 'The Political Economy of International Relations', Princeton, 1987; B. Buzan, 'New Patterns of Global Security in the Twenty-First Century', *International Affairs* 67(3), 1991, pp. 431-51.
2. R. Owen and M. Dynes, *The Single European Market*, London, 1993, pp. 277-9.
3. S. Gordon, 'Resources and Instability in South Asia', *Survival* 35(2), 1993, p. 66.
4. A.H. Khan and A. Mahmood, *Complementarities, Comparative Advantages, and Benefits and Costs of Regional Cooperation in Land Transport and Communication*, Coordinating Group for Studies on South Asian Perspectives, Islamabad, 1993, p. 91.
5. World Bank, *World Development Report 1995*, Washington, 1995.
6. UNDP, *Human Development Report 1993*, Washington, 1993.
7. For an overview see S. Ganguly, 'Ethno-religious Conflict in South Asia', *Survival* 35(2), 1993, pp. 88-109.
8. I.H. Zaki, 'Recent Developments in SAARC and Prospects for the Future', *South Asian Survey* 1(1), 1994, p. 7.
9. Especially the experiences in Europe and the development of German-French friendship show the importance of special programmes designed to promote people-to-people contacts. See C. Wagner, *Can the European Model Serve as a Model for SAARC?*, Nepal Foundation for Advanced Studies, Kathmandu, 1994, pp. 19-22.
10. R.J. Langhammer and U. Hiemenz, *Regional Integration Among Developing Countries*, Tuebingen, 1990, p. 59.
11. Ibid., p. 73.
12. Khan and Mahmood, pp. 121-33.
13. World Bank.
14. IMF, *Direction of Trade Statistics, Year Book 1993*.
15. V.R. Panchamukhi, N. Kumar, V.L. Rao *et al.*, *Economic Cooperation in the SAARC Region*, Interest Publications, New Delhi, 1990, pp. 234-55.
16. S.P. Cohen, 'SARI: A Peace Process for South Asia', *Swords and Ploughshares*, ACDIS 8(2, 3), 1994, pp. 21-5.

National Security and Regional Cooperation: The Case of South Asia

P. R. CHARI

It is becoming increasingly apparent that South Asia is one of the most insecure, but intractable, regions in the world. A shared colonial history; similar cultural and civilizational values; existing familial, linguistic and religious ties; apart from trade and commercial linkages deriving from the subcontinent's unique geographical character and stretching back into antiquity—have failed to establish an ambience conducive to greater economic and political cooperation within the region. On the other hand, the empirical evidence proves that, in terms of regional comparisons, South Asia has witnessed the largest number of inter-State conflicts since World War II. It also remains resistantly crisis-prone despite the end of the Cold War and the current pre-sentiments of peace unfolding in other tension-ridden regions of the world.

No doubt the confrontation between India and Pakistan, which has continued unabated since their independence, is the major reason for South Asia's inability to reap the post-Cold War peace dividend. It is now believed to have acquired nuclear overtones. Another factor to explain this parlous state of affairs is the intrinsic geo-political structure of the subcontinent. India is the predominant country in South Asia due to the strength and diversification of its economy, greater military strength, access to natural resources, gross domestic product, industrial potential and so on. These indices delineate the traditional appurtenances of power in the international system. Furthermore, India shares common maritime and/or land boundaries with the other South Asian countries. More significantly, no other South Asian country shares common boundaries, except across the oceans, with each other. This ineluctable fact leads to a deep psychological scarring of the South Asian psyche, with India hoping that its natural predominance in the region would be accepted as a given. But this is resisted by its neighbours. Their conviction remains unshakable that India wishes to play the regional hegemon. These basic problems underlie South Asian polity, and predispose the region towards internecine strife rather than inter-State cooperation.

Not unexpectedly, the prevailing situation in South Asia has resulted in horrendous conditions for its citizenry. The statistics speak for themselves. The nations of South Asia lie at the lowest end of the Human Development Index (HDI) calculated by the UNDP. The HDI value for the South Asian region, *c*. 1992, has been computed to be 0.453, whereas this stands at 0.570 for all developing countries and 0.759 for the world. Only sub-Saharan Africa has a lower HDI value (0.389) than South Asia.[1] Proceeding further, the South Asian countries have been assigned a HDI value and HDI ranking as follows amongst the developing countries totalling 174 in 1992: Sri Lanka (0.704, 97); Maldives (0.554, 118); Pakistan (0.483, 128); India (0.439, 134); Bangladesh (0.364, 146); Nepal (0.343, 151); and Bhutan (0.305, 160).[2]

The construction of the HDI value for countries involves several complexities. But it has three essential components, viz., life expectancy at birth; adult literacy/enrolment ratio; and income in terms of purchasing power parity. One could, of course, delve further to discover the contradictions inhering in these rankings. Appendix I would illustrate that public expenditure by China, for instance, on education and health at 2.3 per cent and 2.1 per cent of its GDP is lower than that made by several South Asian countries. However, a marked difference obtains between their efficiencies in utilization of these social sector expenditures. India's adult literacy rate of 49.9 per cent and life expectancy at birth of 60.7 years compares poorly with China's relative figures of 79.3 per cent and 68.5 years, despite the former's larger outlays on education and public health. The reasons for this anomalous situation, particularly if sub-regional variations within South Asia are also considered, are very complex. But it would suffice to emphasize that the commonly voiced belief urging that inadequacy of social sector outlays is responsible for poverty in South Asia is not accurate since the efficiency of utilization of resources is of the essence. Nor is high military expenditure responsible for this situation as is also commonly believed. This becomes apparent from Appendix II that indicates important trends relevant to military expenditure comparisons in South Asia. Worthy of note therein is that the strength of the armed forces and military expenditures as a proportion of the GDP is reducing markedly, except in Sri Lanka which reflects its continuing ethnic conflict. But military expenditure *per se* has not shown any decrease. A discussion of the reasons underlying this phenomenon would distract us, but some comparative aspects of military expenditure related to social sector outlays are revealing. The armed forces/teacher ratio in India, Pakistan and China is 0.3, 1.5 and 0.4 respectively. Military expenditure, as compared to outlays on education and public health, is 65 per cent, 125 per cent and 114 per cent for these three countries, as informed by the *Human Development Report 1995*.

In this milieu the relevant question arises what is the role available to regional cooperation to mitigate the national security concerns in South Asia. How could regional cooperation be enlarged to achieve this objective? Linked to this issue is the question of emplacing confidence-building measures, especially belonging to the non-military genre, in South Asia. Does 'Track-II' diplomacy have significance for these purposes? Does the private sector have a role in fostering confidence-building measures? Can non-governmental agencies ameliorate a regional ambience which the State machinery finds difficult to attain? How will globalization trends in the world economy, and liberalization impulses in the South Asian economies, influence these efforts? These questions would be discussed in this paper before analysing the possibilities and limitations of a regional cooperation approach to alleviate national security concerns in South Asia.

II

In theory, the post-Cold War, post-Soviet and post-military blocs era was expected to erode traditional concepts of national sovereignty and territoriality imperatives. Regionalism and internationalism were expected to be emplaced on a new pedestal in appreciation of a multipolar world emerging. Thereby, the geopolitical divisions between nations would be shaded over by enlarging the web of regional institutions existing. A broad range of cooperative interactions would thereby be created to foster common interests and usher in peace and stability between the countries of South Asia.

However, the glacial progress of the South Asian Association for Regional Cooperation (SAARC) since its establishment in 1985 is reflective of the enormous difficulties in reconciling the prevalence of bilateral tensions and instabilities with the impulse for greater regional cooperation in the region. It is noteworthy that, despite the concept of SAARC being mooted by Bangladesh in 1980, it required seven official level meetings before the SAARC declaration was possible in August 1983. Two further meetings of the foreign ministers were needed before the first South Asian summit could be held in December 1985. It finally endorsed the SAARC Charter that led to its establishment.[3] The Charter, *inter alia*, envisages:

(a) the acceleration of economic growth, social progress and cultural development;
(b) the promotion and strengthening of collective self-reliance;
(c) the promotion and mutual collaboration and assistance in economic, social, cultural, technical and scientific fields; and
(d) cooperation with international and similar regional associations.

The areas envisaged for regional cooperation were extensive. This list has been added to over the years to include security-related activities like the suppression of terrorism, prevention of drug trafficking and food security reserve. Progress in these salubrious areas of regional security cooperation, however, leaves everything to be desired. One single example pertaining to the suppression of terrorism would illustrate this assertion.

A SAARC Regional Convention in this regard was ratified by the South Asian nations in August 1988. Its operating provisions require the State that is appropriately approached to either extradite an identified offender or place the matter before its relevant authority for considering prosecution. This arrangement would apply both to subsisting extradition agreements and such other agreements as might be reached in future. Naturally the success of these salubrious measures is conditioned by the political will obtaining to act in accordance with the Convention, and the reciprocity that develops between the contracting nations. Very disconcertingly, the Delhi Declaration of April 1995, following the eighth SAARC Summit, needed to urge the member States 'which had not yet done so, [Pakistan and Bangladesh], to enact expeditiously the enabling legislation at the national level to implement the (Suppression of Terrorism) convention'. This one example makes clear the difficulties in implementing security-related and political-cooperation-dependent arrangements in South Asia, especially between India and Pakistan/Bangladesh, despite the available aegis of SAARC.

In terms of the SAARC Charter, moreover, consideration of bilateral and contentious issues between South Asian countries is excluded from its deliberations. Furthermore, SAARC's decisions have to be unanimous. These undergirding principles of the SAARC Charter have, no doubt, enabled it to remain in existence for over a decade without disintegrating in spite of internecine conflicts and internal divisions. But adherence to the principle that bilateral and contentious issues would not be discussed has not permitted SAARC to grapple with the security-related and political issues that bedevil South Asia. These differences are the primary reason for the glacial pace of economic and regional cooperation in the region. Such contentions have been reduced to 'core' issues like Kashmir between India and Pakistan, or Farakka between India and Bangladesh. These 'core' issues make progress on other security-related and political issues hostage to these currently irresoluble problems.

The future of regional cooperation in South Asia is inextricably linked, therefore, with the politics of the subcontinent. The extent to which SAARC can succeed will depend on the willingness of the South Asian countries to subordinate their mutual animosities for achieving the larger extra-territorial objective of regional cooperation. Unfortunately these mutual animosities derive from elite perceptions of their national interests. As astutely noted: '. . . it is the interplay between a common supranational interest, separate national interests, and the political will of the governments of South Asia that will determine whether or not SAARC will accomplish what it has set out to do. The last—political will—is decisive. . . .'[4]

Apropos, the relevant statistics pertaining to trade and commerce are dismal. The share of South Asia in global trade is currently less than 1 per cent. Intra-regional trade is only 3 per cent of total trading by the SAARC nations. Conversely, 97 per cent of its trade occurs with countries outside South Asia. This compares unfavourably with the situation obtaining in other regions wherein intra-regional trade averages roughly 50 per cent. Intra-regional trade is around 70 per cent in the European Community.

South Asia's case is exceptional because it constitutes a discrete and well-defined geo-political and geo-economic entity. A certain natural direction has existed for its trade and commerce following communication routes that have existed over the centuries. Politics has disrupted these linkages, leading to the incongruity that South Asian nations are trading at considerable cost and disadvantage with distant countries whereas the goods are either available or could find markets within South Asia.[5]

Nevertheless, there is recognition now that economic cooperation through the instrumentality of SAARC is essential to meet the challenges arising from the rapid changes occurring in the international economy. This has catalysed the establishment of SAARC's Economic Cooperation Committee and its endorsement of the SAARC Preferential Trading Arrangement (SAPTA) at SAARC's Seventh Summit in April 1993. SAPTA's goals only envisage, however, the establishment of reciprocal trade agreements, which involves product-by-product negotiations to ease tariff and non-tariff barriers. This is a less ambitious goal than the customs union achieved by the European Community or the North American Free Trade Area. But a clear recognition exists in the Delhi Declaration of May 1995 that an urgency obtains for 'broadening and deepening cooperation within a specific and rapid time-frame in the core areas of trade and economic relations in the region'.[6] It also noted that the fast changing international economic environment, creation of major trading and economic groupings, and establishment of the World Trade Organization could materially affect this objective.

A case could further be made for enlarging SAPTA's scope to include technical cooperation, foreign direct investment, and extra-regional trade. Admittedly, the creation of expert groups, holding of seminars and conferences, publication of reports and so on have been useful, and do permit interactions between professional groups. But a mere enlargement of these activities would not effect any 'broadening and deepening' of cooperation between the South Asian countries unless the political will is available to take meaningful steps for achieving this purpose. And the realization obtains that a more dynamic free trade regime within the South Asian region would be to the advantage of all the States therein.

Attention might now be drawn to the call given by the President of Sri Lanka urging that South Asia be jointly promoted as a destination for foreign investment. This proposal envisages the abolition of trade barriers within this investment zone and creation of a single market. India could become the prime mover and catalyse this process by the abolition of licensing requirements for imports from its South Asian neighbours, and by either reducing or abolishing tariffs on goods that meet a certain minimum value addition within the proposed single market. India could offer an incentive for the formation of this single market by allowing the South Asian countries joining it to raise capital in the Indian capital market.

The likelihood that Sri Lanka, Bangladesh and Nepal would join this grouping is high, which presents an opportunity and a challenge to India's economic diplomacy. Consequently, '. . . economic integration can be more potent in international relations than the force of arms; it can be more finely calibrated to create bonds strong enough to encapsulate xenophobic politicians. India should work towards a united South Asia which would compare with China in economic weight and performance.'[7] The anxieties in Pakistan that a South Asian single market/free trade zone would result in Indian goods flooding its markets and Indian hegemony getting established needs to be discussed at this stage. Two facts are relevant here.

First, a dichotomy of interests exists between the manufacturing and trading communities in Pakistan. The former want to protect their industries from Indian competition, while the latter wish to profit from the opportunities afforded by more extensive Indo-Pak trade. So, opinion within Pakistan is polarized on this issue. Currently the manufacturing interests are dominant because of their proximity to the ruling elite.

Second, an informed estimate places the total annual trade between India and Pakistan at $950 million, but official trade is only $150 million. Trade via third countries accounts for another $650 million. 'Informal border trade', which is a euphemism for smuggling, accounts for the remaining $150 million.[8] Further, the items traded through non-official channels are considerably more diversified than what occurs in regulated items through official trade. The resulting loss of customs revenue to the public exchequer is one aspect of the matter. More significantly, the opportunities for smugglers and other anti-social elements to enrich themselves have been enhanced in this milieu. They are openly gaining entry into the political process.

Viewed in this perspective, a relaxation of Indo-Pak trade barriers would let market forces transcend political borders and reverse the steady criminalization of politics in India and Pakistan, which is among the root causes of their crisis of governance. These dangers need to be articulated more forcefully by opinion-makers in the region. The appreciation is, however, growing that 'while politicians from both countries could do what they wanted . . . on political issues like Kashmir, businessmen must take upon themselves the responsibility to open up their respective nations'.[9]

Nevertheless, the prospects for an early relaxation of Indo-Pak trade barriers, either through bilateral initiatives or the aegis of SAARC, are not exactly propitious. Nor are the prospects of either country taking unilateral steps to relax these trade barriers especially bright. Note, for example, the denial of MFN status by Pakistan to India, which has continued despite soothing reassurances by the former, these, too, are hedged by several conditionalities. Apropos, bilateral initiatives, the SAARC aegis and unilateralism are unexceptionable propositions. But they ignore the reality of domestic politics, which inhibits the pursuit of these beneficial steps lest the opposition parties denigrate them as a 'sellout'. The statesmanship to accept temporary political disadvantage to secure the commonwealth of the region is conspicuously absent.

This frailty persists despite the reality that a technological revolution has occurred that profoundly alters the intrinsic nature of international economic relations. Knowledge- and information-based technologies deriving from advances in micro-electronics, materials sciences, computer applications and so on are eroding the traditional advantages enjoyed by developed countries. Hence their feverish efforts to cartelize access to these and related high/emerging technologies by developing countries. Common prudence dictates that the potentialities of SAPTA and, more generically, SAARC be exploited to enable the South Asian nations to enlarge their individual and collective bargaining strength and enhance their autonomy. SAPTA and SAARC could thus subserve the broader interests of South-South cooperation, while enhancing their national security.

III

What of confidence-building measures (CBMs)? They could be described as 'arrangements designed to enhance . . . assurance of mind and belief in the trustworthiness of States . . . confidence is the product of much broader patterns of relations than those which relate to military security. In fact, the latter have to be woven into a complex texture of economic, cultural, technical and social relationships'.[10]

CBMs have a special function to perform in mitigating the fears and anxieties that prevail in South Asia. They comprise both military and non-military measures, and 'such cooperation can comprise political consultations including . . . just and equitable economic relations . . . and cooperation in cultural, social, educational and humanitarian fields, including freer movements and contacts among peoples, and education specifically designed for promoting peace and disarmament'.[11]

The focus has shifted almost completely towards military CBMs in the Indo-Pak context in recent years, occasioned by the many crises that occurred in this troubled relationship during the 1980s. These range from anxieties in Pakistan that its nuclear installations would be attacked (1984-6), through the Brasstacks Exercise-related crisis (1986-7), to the Kashmir-related tensions (1990), apart from several other crisis situations in the recent past. Several military CBMs were emplaced between India and Pakistan thereafter, and are functioning satisfactorily. Their utility lies in their capacity to attenuate the risk of inadvertent conflict. Consequently, steps like the establishment of hotlines between the two military establishments can also be categorized as Conflict Avoidance Measures (CAMs) that could hopefully develop into bilateral arms control and disarmament agreements. Some part of this alacrity to negotiate military CBMs could be deriving from an appreciation of the horrendous costs of present-day conventional war. Both countries are further believed to be capable of assembling nuclear weapons at short notice; hence the likelihood of a conventional conflict becoming nuclear could also be salubrious for the military CBM process.

Whatever be the reason for the current focus on military CBMs, the consequence has been the comparative neglect of non-military CBMs. The most vivid example is the lamentable fate of the Indo-Pak Joint Commission established in March 1983, intended to strengthen good-neighbourly relations and promote cooperation in the non-military and non-political areas. Four Sub-Commissions were constituted thereunder to promote cooperation in tourism and consular matters; science and technology; sports; and economics. But no meetings have been held since 1989. This is all the more distressing because the Simla Agreement (1972) recognized that the restoration and normalization of Indo-Pak relations requires that:

(i) Steps shall be taken to resume communications, postal, telegraphic, sea, land including border, posts and air links including overflights;
(ii) Appropriate steps shall be taken to promote travel facilities for the nationals of the other country;
(iii) Trade and cooperation in economic and other agreed fields will be resumed as far as possible; and
(iv) Exchange in the fields of science and culture will be promoted.

Progress in these several directions has either halted or is proceeding at a glacial pace. The value of these non-military CBMs is that they 'are designed to soften the edges of mutual suspicions by enlarging the areas of cooperation between adversarial States. Military CBMs are prophylactic in character. Non-military CBMs hope to generate an atmosphere conducive to stability'.[12] Indeed, the measures envisaged by the Simla Agreement offer a model for non-military CBMs that could be pursued to normalize/restore good relations between the South Asian countries.

There is no dearth of specific proposals for the establishment of non-military CBMs in the subcontinent. They include joint efforts for the exploitation of land and water resources; sharing of expertise in the energy sector; mutual cooperation in the areas of environment, science and technology; disposal of atomic waste; apart from cooperation in the media and educational fields.[13] Appendix III contains a detailed list of non-military CBMs that could be negotiated within the short and long term in South Asia. This list was finalized by consensus following discussions thereon during the fourth South Asia Dialogue. This list could be further extended. But three non-military CBMs are of prime significance to South Asia.

First, the cessation of negative propaganda against each other, which clearly enjoys official support because the electronic and visual media largely remain under State control in South Asia. This negative propaganda becomes especially virulent during crisis situations. For instance the destruction of temples and mosques in Bangladesh, Pakistan and India, following the wanton destruction of the Babri Masjid in December 1992 led to the unleashing of vicious, officially inspired propaganda which exacerbated the communal situation. Playing on religio-communal sentiments for domestic political advantage is obviously the motive for this policy. But its ill-effects in subverting the SAARC process are evident. This emphasizes the urgent need for a code of conduct to be evolved by the South Asian countries to desist from directing such negative, particularly communal, propaganda against each other.

Second, despite an Indo-Pak Agreement committing both countries to refrain from misrepresentations in textbooks, such distortions continue unabated. This is especially disconcerting in history books that have a great influence upon young and impressionable minds. For instance, 'non-Islamic' history is currently ignored in Pakistani textbooks. Indian textbooks tend to eulogize the Mughal Emperor Akbar for his secular beliefs, while denigrating Aurangzeb for his bigotry. Such motivated versions of a common history and civilization have, regrettably, succeeded in establishing an adversarial imagery that has embedded itself in the psyche of ordinary citizens in both countries.[14] An erosion of mistrust and suspicions which is essential to proceed with a CBM process, requires the toning down, if not elimination, of such incendiary passages from history textbooks. A worthwhile SAARC initiative would, therefore, be for historians from the entire region to address its history objectively, and draw up suitable guidelines in this regard.

Third, it hardly needs emphasis that an enlargement of people-to-people contacts offers the most fruitful means to erode the mistrust and suspicion pervading the region. But the ruling elite have chosen, not inadvertently, to make visa requirements as restrictive as possible. Unofficial quotas, involved application procedures, bureaucratic delays and so on, are calculated to discourage all but the most persistent visa applicants, particularly in the Indo-Pak situation. The most humiliating condition imposed upon visitors from India/Pakistan is to report at the nearest police station on arrival and before departure. An anguished commentary on this system holds that: 'We have a relationship of "low tension" between India and Pakistan . . . reinforced by a whole lot of taboos and restrictions. We have a visa system which demands reporting regularly to the police, which can by no means be regarded as congenial for mutual goodwill.'[15]

These restrictions are justified as needed to ensure reciprocity. But they are also calculated to minimize people-to-people contacts which would lead to reduction of mutual tensions. To the well-recognized vested interests that have a stake in the continuance of Indo-Pak tensions and instabilities this is anathema. In this milieu, it would greatly improve the Indo-Pak ambience and mitigate India's 'hegemon' image if it would unilaterally liberalize its visa restrictions, particularly for Pakistani and Bangladesh visitors. Such liberalization could start with travellers visiting India on pilgrimage to religious shrines and professional/business groups. This would not have any great security implications as terrorists and espionage agents are hardly likely to enter India with passports and visas.

A last question concerns us here. Should fundamental disputes like Kashmir and Farakka be first resolved before furthering a CBM process? Or, could the two be pursued autonomously? Wisdom suggests that a two-track policy be pursued to address the core and peripheral issues in contention. Seeking to first resolve the long-enduring and difficult core problems would only ensure that the CBM process is altogether derailed. At the same time, the CBM route to peace and stability in South Asia can be over-emphasized. It cannot supplant more substantive arms control and disarmament agreements. Besides, a certain momentum is required to sustain this process between adversarial States, which is not possible unless the political will obtains to explore the path of reconciliation instead of confrontation. Lethal to generating this political will is the belief system of the decision-making elite that one must plan for the worst while hoping for the best, accord credence to capabilities rather than intentions and so on. Generation of this political will would be greatly assisted if India and Pakistan appreciated the paradox that their diplomatic energy is being largely expended in addressing the United States. But they remain unwilling to engage each other in dialogue and pursue the CBM route to mutual security.

IV

The opportunities for strengthening Track-II diplomacy in South Asia can now be discussed. This form of people-to-people diplomacy has been described as

> a process of unofficial dialogues between disputing polities conducted directly, or with the help of a third party, by influential citizens who normally have access to their governments and/or an ability to influence public opinion. The goal of track-two diplomacy is usually to prevent or resolve conflicts, or build confidence between the parties they represent. Such elite exercises are distinct from well meaning peace efforts made by individuals or grassroots level organizations that do not have an impact on State policy or a wider public audience.[16]

The twin objectives of Track-II diplomacy are conflict resolution and economic cooperation.

Much effort has been expended by India and Pakistan on conflict resolution dialogues. This was occasioned by the realization that an easing of security-related issues was essential if political and economic cooperation was to be proceeded with hopefully; and partly by beliefs that the nuclear standoff between the two countries required to be managed. The results achieved by the prominent security-oriented Track-II efforts like the Nimrana process, South Asian Dialogue, Parlance Initiative and so on, have, however, been modest. They have undoubtedly succeeded in establishing an unofficial channel of communications. The in-depth and frank discussions possible within these intellectual encounters allow bilateral and region-wise contacts being maintained by respected personages, who often have access to the ruling elite in their respective countries.

But these exercises become routinized over time, especially if there are no fresh entrants to these processes. The need is for more purposeful Track-II efforts that would identify action-oriented programmes to operationalize confidence-building and tension-reduction measures in the region. The lack of follow-up measures to coordinate and implement the laudable decisions taken within these initiatives is largely responsible for this dismal state of affairs.

A recent initiative that shows much promise is the meeting between some 200 concerned citizens from India and Pakistan to debate issues in contention between the two countries. An extension of such citizens' groups to others would enlarge the constituency in the two countries with a commitment to subcontinental peace and stability. Thereby, the ruling elite would also be engaged, and their propensity to externalize their internal problems would hopefully be reduced.

It is also ironical that political leaders in opposition become imbued with virtuous wisdom that had escaped them in office. Apropos, an Opposition Leaders' seminar was held in Karachi in September 1992. It issued a declaration emphasizing the need to settle bilateral disputes by peaceful means and seek political solutions to regional problems. Among its several resolves was the necessity to take concrete steps and provide an impetus to economic and political cooperation within SAARC; identify and develop unexplored areas of economic cooperation between SAARC countries; and jointly tackle problems of human rights and environmental pollution by collective endeavours.[17] Regular contacts between opposition leaders in SAARC countries should become an institutionalized form of Track-II diplomacy. Hopefully, their commitment to absolute values in such conferences would temper their opposition to regional cooperation and influence them should they achieve power.

Of equal consequence is a recent initiative to establish a network of young opinion-makers—academics, media persons and NGOs in the region. The modus was the organization of a Summer School to bring together some 25-30 young opinion-makers in India, Pakistan and China to discuss arms control, conflict resolution, verification and related issues with an international teaching faculty. This initiative was informed by the belief that a third post-independence generation is emerging in South Asia, with a greater exposure to international influences through the electronic media, travel and so on. They also have a greater concern with their present and future quality of life rather than remaining preoccupied with the gloomy history of Indo-Pak relations. This third generation also possesses competence and interest in matters of consequence like economic and environmental issues, and could bring a fresh outlook to bear on the intractable problems bequeathed to them by the post-partition first and second generations.[18] The Summer School initiative seeks to address this constituency. The success of three such events in the recent past has kindled great optimism about this Track-II instrumentality.

How could Track-II diplomacy be extended from conflict resolution efforts to economic cooperation? Several initiatives can be envisaged through the Chambers of Commerce as, for example:

(a) Making available and disseminating business and trade information that would be of especial value to small and medium entrepreneurs;
(b) Arranging academic exchanges between business and management schools in South Asian countries; and
(c) Initiating a CEOs' dialogue between young entrepreneurs/businessmen and professional consultants in the region.[19]

A beginning in this direction has been achieved by the launch of a software programme 'SaarcNet', that would link the seven SAARC nations, and contains relevant economic, social and infrastructural data. This would enable businessmen in India and Pakistan, for instance, to interact directly without the stultifying intervention of their governments.[20] They have resolved incidentally to jointly oppose the non-tariff barriers being imposed by the developed countries on Third World nations, despite the emergence of a post-GATT liberalized international economic environment. Ironically, the issue of removing such non-tariff barriers between and within SAARC countries has yet to be addressed. These resolves are a hopeful augury for the future of SAARC and South Asia.

V

A prognostication may now be attempted of the emerging international system of relevance to regional cooperation and national security in South Asia. The end of the Cold War has forced military establishments, weapon laboratories, defence production units, and strategic communities to search desperately for new enemies. These governmental and non-official constituencies were obsessively concerned with the East-West conflict, but are currently dirigible following the disintegration of the Soviet Union. Hence their disproportionate attention to the proliferation of Weapons of Mass Destruction (WMD) in the Third World and the construction of technology denial regimes to constrain them. Witness also the extraordinary interest evoked by Huntington's 'Clash of Civilizations' hypothesis. An extension of its inherent logic, inadvertently perhaps, provides regional conflict with an intellectual mooring. There is little doubt that intra-State disputes, as differentiated from inter-State conflicts, are of greater significance to the emerging international security system. Hence, internal security would gain precedence over external security within the governance priorities. Coincidentally, SIPRI has noted that all the thirty-four armed conflicts recognized in 1993 worldwide were intra-State in character.[21] No doubt these concerns could be exacerbated by external powers, but their roots lie within the polity. Consequently, South Asian nations need to shift the focus of their security-related efforts to internal security concerns. This understanding would, hopefully, encourage the South Asian nations to refrain from arms procurements that are irrelevant to intra-State conflicts; this change might, hopefully again, lead to a reduction in their defence budgets.

Furthermore, a condition of 'non-weaponized deterrence' is deemed to exist between India and Pakistan; hence the need for conventional arms racing is further eroded. In the nuclear ethic the availability of nuclear weapons or the capability to manufacture them at short notice would deter both conventional and nuclear conflicts. Hence, inter-State conflicts being improbable in South Asia, and between India and Pakistan in particular, an ambience is now available for pursuit of regional cooperation to further consolidate national security in the region.

This proposition can be argued from yet another perspective. The end of the Cold War and disintegration of the Soviet Union suggests that a truly multi-polar world has evolved. Ideological factors have lost their significance. A sense of egalitarianism pervades the international system. The democratic idea has gained salience within domestic polities. These developments highlight the need for the ruling elite to address the real needs of their people since it would become progressively more difficult for them to deflect attention by conjuring up external bogeys.

We may also note here the growing contention between the sole existing superpower, the United States, and the competing emerging superpower, China. As the Sino-American rivalry, if not hostility, proceeds, a problem of choice would confront the South Asian countries. They could exercise one of four options:

— Join the United States, that would increasingly be viewed as a distant, retreating superpower;
— Ally with China, since it would posit as the proximate and burgeoning superpower;

— Remain neutral between the United States and China by seeking refuge in the time-tested policy of non-alignment: it might acquire a new relevance in coming years and prove as useful in the future as in the past;
— Strengthen their economies with more purposeful regional cooperation: this would provide South Asian countries with the political/military sinews to exercise any of the other options from a position of strength and not helplessness.

Should the last option suggest itself as the most viable, the need would arise to exercise control over military expenditure and increase allocations to the social and infrastructural sectors while paying greater attention to ensuring efficiency in their utilization. A growth rate of 7 per cent, if not a more ambitious 8 per cent, would bring the South Asian economies into closer alignment with those of South-East Asia/East Asia to rival that of China. A 7 or 8 per cent growth path is fully realizable with more purposeful action. Incidentally the GNP growth rate of China, India and Pakistan during the 1980-92 period was 9.1, 5.2 and 6.1 per cent respectively,[22] which is higher than the GNP growth rate of the G-7 countries during this period. Greater credence might therefore be accorded to the contention that: 'Power today grows less and less out of the barrel of a gun and more and more out of economic, scientific and cultural development.'[23] Regional cooperation is thereby imbued with a new prescience in South Asia.

There are two more reasons for pursuing the goal of national security through the regional cooperation route. First, the globalization of the international economy highlights the growing phenomenon of transnationals who are carving up the world in a race to dominate the new global order. Their operations are untrammelled by ethical concerns. Their influence over governments is immense and is being further augmented by a complex web of inter-corporate alliances. Indeed, governments in the Third World countries have often been coerced to further the ambitions of transnational corporations. Regional cooperation would enable the South Asian countries to meet these pressures from transnational corporations, apart from the pressures of external governments and international financial institutions more effectively.

Second, the opposite case could be argued that non-cooperation within the region carries immense financial/economic and political costs. One significant example would be the enormous hydropower potential of the Ganga and Brahmaputra river system, estimated at 93,700 MW and 54,950 MW respectively, which remains largely unexploited. A run-of-the-river project at the Brahmaputra's eastern bend could generate another 18,000 MW if the river was harnessed by structures in China and a powerhouse built in India.[24] This enormous hydropower potential has remained unexploited due to the inability of India, Bangladesh and Nepal to negotiate the bilateral/trilateral agreements needed to construct the necessary projects, because of purely domestic political compulsions. Further the virulence of intra-regional tensions has definitely inhibited foreign investments being attracted to South Asia.

It may be asserted that India is well situated to catalyse regional cooperation in South Asia if this goal receives priority in its foreign policy calculations. This can happen if its leadership raises its sights from the imperatives of domestic politics. That the former Indian Prime Minister, Narasimha Rao, retained the defence and, for all practical purposes, the external affairs portfolio has been severely criticized as downgrading these ministries. But this criticism fails to notice the consequential upgradation of the Economic Affairs Department in particular, and the Finance Ministry in general. What has also escaped notice is the deliberately low-key foreign policy posture adopted by the Rao government. Its basic premises were founded on seeking a non-confrontationist relationship with the United States and China. Added thereto is a low-profile national security policy founded on not proceeding with India's current nuclear and missile capabilities beyond their obtaining stage of arrested development. This quiescent defence posture has been buttressed by a virtually static defence budget and a conscious shunning of adventurism of any sort.

Despite the constant alarms raised by the nuclear/missile enthusiasts, and the vociferous protests made by the self-reliance/self-sufficiency lobby, the Indian Government has held fast to its economic reforms and globalization policies. Their pace has been guided by the compulsions of internal politics, but the direction has not been compromised. Indeed, the ability shown by the government to continue steadily without being deflected by different provocations reveals its inner resilience. It is capable therefore of displaying the necessary leadership to imbue regional cooperation in South Asia with a new content. Naturally, this would be dependent on the other nations of South Asia displaying a similar commitment to this laudable objective that would assure their economic development and national security.

APPENDIX I. PUBLIC EXPENDITURE ON EDUCATION AND HEALTH IN SOUTH ASIAN COUNTRIES AS PERCENTAGE OF GDP (1990)

Country	*Education*	*Health*
Sri Lanka	2.7	1.8
Maldives	9.2	—
Pakistan	3.4	1.8
India	3.5	1.3
Bangladesh	2.0	1.4
Nepal	—	2.2
Bhutan	3.7	—
China	2.3	2.1

Source: UNDP, *Human Development Report 1995*, Table 12, pp. 178-9.

APPENDIX II. DEFENCE EXPENDITURES OF SOUTH ASIAN COUNTRIES COMPARED (1990-4)

Country/Year	*Defence Expenditure ($ bn)*	*Armed Forces ('000)*	*Defence Expenditure as % of GNP*	*Defence Expenditure as % of Central Govt. Expenditure*	*Armed Forces per 1000 Persons*
Bangladesh					
1990	0.322	102.0	1.5	N.A.	0.90
1994	0.402	115.5	—	N.A.	0.92
India					
1990	8.79	1200.0	2.90	14.69	1.42
1994	7.37	1100.0	2.53	15.15	1.20
Nepal					
1990	0.036	35.0	1.31	N.A.	1.96
1994	0.042	35.0	1.29	N.A.	2.01
Pakistan					
1990	2.95	790.00	7.16	34.63	7.07
1994	3.40	800.00	6.88	34.52	6.55
Sri Lanka					
1990	0.439	88.0	5.48	N.A.	5.10
1994	0.488	126.0	—	7.08	7.08

Source: IDSA, *Asian Strategic Review 1994-95*, Institute for Defence Studies and Analyses, New Delhi, 1995.

APPENDIX III. FEASIBLE NON-MILITARY CBMS IN SOUTH ASIA

Non-Military Issues

IMMEDIATE ACTION

General

(a) Ease visa restrictions at the earliest.
(b) Educate the public on the facts of contested issues, such as the Wular barrage problem. Current versions of adversary governments often differ greatly.
(c) Exercise strict controls over violations of sovereignty such as Indian police intrusions in Nepal.
(d) Exchange experience within South Asia on the progress made in areas of constitutional and legal reforms, local government aspects, criminal laws and electoral reforms.
(e) Exchange scientific data.
(f) Political scientists should educate political leaders on the advantages of improvement of relations between South Asian countries.

Economic

(a) Make progress on water sharing schemes for the Himalayan rivers.
(b) Implement SAPTA measures speedily.
(c) Pakistan should remove restrictions on trade with India. In addition:
    (i) Pakistan should accord India MFN status for trade subject to a negative list.
    (ii) Initiate joint Indo-Pak ventures which promise enormous dividends.
    (iii) Give visas to businessmen on priority.
(d) India should be more generous in its trade policies with neighbours.

Social

(a) Encourage cultural, literary and social exchanges.
(b) Improve communications and enhance the frequency in flights.
(c) Create a core team of columnists within South Asia to create awareness about South Asian issues and to look beyond national positions to address issues relating to the region—such as Sri Lankan journalists writing about Nepal and Bhutan.

LONG TERM

General

(a) In the continued absence of political initiatives NGO groups should take the initiative for regional dialogue.
(b) Finalize non-military CBMs in areas of trade, transit, media and water resources.

(c) Use SAARC as a negotiating forum as far as possible for all regional disputes.
(d) Establish a regional data bank for different types of information relating to the region.
(e) Create a body of expert former civil servants to assist with their experience in the furtherance of CBMs.

Economic

(a) Make progress on oil and gas pipeline from West Asia to the region.
(b) Expand areas of regional business and economic interaction.

Social

(a) A people's forum should be postured to counter political rhetoric.
(b) Expand student exchange programme, apart from exchange of visits by journalists and eminent citizens.

Military Issues

Immediate Action

(a) Resolve the Siachen Glacier dispute with adequate political effort.
(b) Sign no-first-strike accord between India and Pakistan.
(c) Formal ban on use of NBC (nuclear, biological and chemical) weapons.
(d) Further define and implement war avoidance measures, especially between India and Pakistan.
(e) Foster greater nuclear transparency.
(f) Create an exchange forum for military officers by encouraging joint exercises/seminars/courses between all South Asian countries, especially India and Pakistan.
(g) Bring low-intensity conflicts on the CBM agenda.

Long Term

(a) Cut down conventional forces deployment and reduce acquisition of arms.
(b) Form a representative group of military officers with earlier experience of CBM dialogues to assist the CBM process.
(c) Institutionalize the right of the adversary to ask questions and receive specific and accurate replies.

NOTES

1. UNDP, *Human Development Report 1995*, Oxford University Press, New Delhi, 1995, p. 22, Table 1.3.
2. Ibid., p. 20, Table 1.2.
3. Arif A. Waqif, 'Perspectives of South Asian Cooperation: An Overview for Selected Studies', in *Perspectives on South Asian Cooperation*, Friedrich Ebert Stiftung, Islamabad, 1994, p. 1.

4. Ross Masood Husain, 'Promotion of Greater Inter-Governmental, Inter-Institutional and Inter-People Understanding in South Asia', in ibid., p. 25.
5. Shoban Saxena, 'Bad Economics Is Bad Politics', *Times of India* (New Delhi), 10 September 1995.
6. Text of Delhi Declaration and Statements made by the SAARC Heads of State at the Eighth Summit might be seen in *Strategic Digest* XXV(6) (IDSA, New Delhi), June 1995.
7. *Business Standard* (New Delhi), 5 September 1995.
8. *Observer of Business and Politics* (New Delhi), 26 September 1995. These estimates were offered by A.K. Rungta, President of the Federation of the Indian Chambers of Commerce and Industry (FICCI), in Islamabad in an address to an Indo-Pak conference on SAPTA.
9. *Business Standard*, 3 October 1995. These views were expressed by Amit Mitra, Secretary, FICCI, in an interview following the return of India's business delegation to Pakistan.
10. John Jorgen Holst, 'Confidence Building Measures: A Conceptual Framework', *Survival* 25(1) (IISS, London), January-February 1983, pp. 2, 4.
11. UN Centre for Disarmament, *Report of the Secretary General, Study on All the Aspects of Regional Disarmament*, United Nations, New York, 1982, pp. 51-2.
12. P.R. Chari, Navnita Chadha, Maroof Raza, *Confidence-Building Measures in South Asia*, Centre for Policy Research, New Delhi, January 1995, p. 5.
13. Moonis Ahmar, 'The Applicability of the Helsinki Model for the Task of Confidence-Building and Conflict Resolution in the Indo-Pak Subcontinent', *Contemporary South Asia* 3(3) (Oxford), p. 244.
14. For a discussion of this thesis see Samina Yasmin and Aabha Dixit, *Confidence Building in South Asia*, The Henry L. Stimson Centre, Washington, September 1995, Occasional Paper no. 23, pp. 10-12.
15. Nikhil Chakravartty, 'People to People Diplomacy Needed', *The Tribune* (Chandigarh), 6 May 1992, cited in Moonis Ahmar, p. 251.
16. Sandeep Waslekar, *Track-Two Diplomacy in South Asia*, University of Illinois at Urbana-Champaign, March 1994, ACDIS Occasional Paper, p. 1. This study has made a systematic effort to collate and briefly describe selected Track-II conflict resolution and peace-related projects in South Asia.
17. Moonis Ahmar, p. 253.
18. Stephen P. Cohen, 'A Generational Change', *Seminar*, no. 422, October 1974, p. 18.
19. Poonam Barua, 'Towards Indo-Pak Economic CBMs', paper presented at the Third Summer School on Arms Control, Technology and Security at Nimrana, India, 23-30 September 1995.
20. Ibid., n. 9.
21. SIPRI, *SIPRI Yearbook 1994: World Armaments and Disarmament*, Oxford University Press, Oxford, 1994, p. 4.
22. Ashok V. Desai, 'Economics of Security in South Asia', *Business Standard*, 5 September 1995.
23. Jonathan Power, 'What Role for the "New Pessimists"?' *Statesman* (New Delhi), 7 October 1995.
24. Fasihuddin Mahtab, 'Environment and Technology in South Asian Cooperation', in Bhabani Sen Gupta (ed.), *The First South Asian Regional Dialogue: A Report*, Centre for Policy Research, New Delhi, May 1992, p. 43.

Contributors

LOK RAJ BARAL is Professor of Political Science at Tribhuvan University, Kathmandu. He recently served as the Nepalese Ambassador to India. His publications include *Regional Migrations, Ethnicity and Security: The South Asian Case*; *Refugees and Regional Security in South Asia* (co-authored and edited); and *South Asia: Democracy and the Road Ahead.*

P.R. CHARI is Co-Director of the Institute for the Study of Peace and Conflict, New Delhi. His publications include *Indo-Pak Nuclear Standoff: The Role of the United States*; *Brasstacks and Beyond: Perception and Management of Crisis in South Asia* (co-authored); and *Nuclear Non-Proliferation in India and Pakistan: South Asian Perspectives* (co-authored and co-edited).

PERVAIZ IQBAL CHEEMA is Professor of International Relations, Quaid-i-Azam University, Islamabad. He is currently Iqbal Fellow, South Asia Institute, University of Heidelberg. His publications include *Brasstacks and Beyond: Perception and Management of Crisis in South Asia* (co-authored); and *Nuclear Non-Proliferation in India and Pakistan: South Asian Perspectives* (co-authored and co-edited).

DIPAK GYAWALI is an economist and water resources engineer. He is a member of the Royal Nepal Academy of Science and Technology. He works with the Nepal Water Conservation Foundation and Inter-disciplinary Analysts, Kathmandu. His publications include *Water in Nepal: An Interdisciplinary Look at Resource Uncertainties, Evolving Problems and Future Prospects*; 'Ecological and Political Aspects of Himalayan Water Resource Management', 'The Himalaya-Ganga: Contending with Interlinkages in a Complex System'; and 'Understanding the Himalaya-Ganga: Widening the Research Horizon & Deepening Co-operation'.

MOHAMED JALEEL is Manager, Economic Research and Statistics Division, Maldives Monetary Authority. He is also Alternate Governor for International Monctary Fund for Maldives.

PREM SHANKAR JHA is a noted columnist based in New Delhi, contributing regularly to the national and international media.

SHAHNAZ KARIM is Lecturer, Department of International Relations, University of Dhaka. She is also Research Associate of the Centre of Policy Dialogue, Dhaka.

ABDUR ROB KHAN is Research Director, Bangladesh Institute of International and Strategic Studies (BIISS). He is also Executive Director of Bangladesh Study Group in Alternative Thinking. He is the editor of the quarterly *BIISS Journal*. His publications include *Security of Small States;* and *Protracted International Conflicts in South Asia: The Route to Intractability in the Kashmir Conflict 1947-1990* (forthcoming).

AMERA SAEED is Senior Researcher at the Institute of Regional Studies, Islamabad. She specializes on the Indian Ocean region and South Asia. Also works on the Asia-Pacific region and regional organizations. Her publications include: 'An Economic Forum for the Indian Ocean Region: Desires, Concepts, and Realities'; 'Rohingya Refugees in Bangladesh: Their Impact on Regional Stability'; 'BJP's Challenge to India's Secular Traditions'; and 'The Law of the Sea: Its impact on Inter-State Relations in SouthAsia'.

AHMED SHAHEED is Director for Foreign Relations in the SAARC Division of the Ministry of Foreign Affairs, Government of Maldives. He specializes on problems of small States, developmental issues and regional cooperation. He is the editor of the *UNAM Chronicle*, magazine of the United Nations Association of Maldives. He writes regularly in the Maldivian media on international politics and developmental issues.

JAYADEVA UYANGODA is Chairman, Sri Lanka Foundation, Colombo. He teaches in the Department of History and Political Science, University of Colombo. He is Director, Centre for Policy Research and Analysis (CEPRA) and co-editor, *Pravada*. He is also associated with the Human Rights and Peace Community of Sri Lanka. He specializes on ethnicity, the State and human rights issues. He is the author of *Sri Lanka: Unmaking Peace* (forthcoming).

CHRISTIAN WAGNER works with the Institute fur Politikwissennschaft, Johannes-Gutenberg Universitat, Mainz, Germany. He was previously Research Fellow, Centre for Modern Oriental Studies, Berlin. He specializes on regional cooperation in comparative perspective. Other areas of his interest include democratization, nationalism and ethnic conflict.

IFTEKHARUZZAMAN is Executive Director, Regional Centre for Strategic Studies. His recent publications include *Nuclear Non-Proliferation in India and Pakistan: South Asian Perspectives* (co-authored and co-edited); *South Asian Security, Primacy of Internal Dimension* (ed.); and *Bangladesh and SAARC: Issues, Perspectives and Outlook* (co-authored and co-edited).